*Handbook
of
Environmental
Education*

'And be sure you study population control, food supply, weather patterns, ecology . . .'

LePelley in *The Christian Science Monitor*,
©1974 TCSPS

Handbook
of
Environmental
Education

WITH INTERNATIONAL CASE STUDIES

Edited by
ROBERT N. SAVELAND

for
*International Union for Conservation of Nature
and Natural Resources, Morges, Switzerland*

JOHN WILEY & SONS
London · New York · Sydney · Toronto

Library of Congress Catalog Card Number: 76-4659

Saveland, Robert N.
    Environmental Education
England   John Wiley & Sons, Ltd.
1976   10 feb 76

ISBN 0 471 75535 4

Typeset in IBM Century by
Preface Limited, Salisbury, Wilts
and printed in Great Britain by
The Pitman Press, Bath

Contributing Authors

CLEARY, JAMES W.   Sunland, Tallahassee, Florida, U.S.A.

JACKSON, JOHN Y.   Environmental Learning Center
                                Isabella, Minnesota.

MALDAGUE, MICHEL   Faculté Foresterie et de Geodesie
                                Université Laval, Quebec, Canada

SAVELAND, ROBERT N.   Social Science Education,
                                The University of Georgia,
                                College of Education, Athens,
                                Georgia 3062, U.S.A.

WITHRINGTON, DAVID   International Youth Federation for
                                Environmental Studies and Conservation,
                                London, U.K.

Preface

The idea for an international handbook on environmental education gained expression in the resolutions of the first International Working Meeting on Environmental Education in the School Curriculum held at Foresta Institute for Ocean and Mountain Studies in the summer of 1970. The idea gained further impetus when Jan Cerovsky, then Education Executive Officer of the I.U.C.N. (International Union for the Conservation of Nature and Natural Resources), came to the Southeastern Regional Conference on the Social Sciences and Environmental at The University of Georgia in April 1971. An outline for the project was drafted the following week-end on Sapelo Island. In October 1971, U.N.E.S.C.O. granted a contract to I.U.C.N. for the preparation of this handbook. Throughout its early development, the project enjoyed the active support and encouragement of P. C. Bandyopadhyay, then of the Section of Curriculum and Reasearch, U.N.E.S.C.O.

Members of the writing team and others involved in the project met at the International Youth Conference on the Human Environment at McMasters University, Hamilton, Ontario, in August 1971. Further meetings were held at the European Working Conference on Environmental Conservation Education at Rüschlikon, Switzerland, in December 1971 and at the International Workshop on Environmental Studies in Higher Education and Teacher Training at the University of Western Ontario in September, 1972. The first-draft edition of the handbook was published in mimeographed form and mailed to readers around the world in March, 1973.

The members of the original writing team with their chapter responsibilities were as follows:

1—2. Robert N. Saveland, editor

3. Matthew Brennan, Brentree Environmental Center, Milford, Pennsylvania, U.S.A., followed by Robert N. Saveland.

4. John Y. Jackson, then Department of Education, State of South Carolina, U.S.A.

5. David Withrington, International Youth Federation for Environmental Studies and Conservation, London, U.K.

6. Michel Maldague, Université Laval, Quebec, Canada

7. Richard G. Miller, Foresta Institute for Ocean and Mountain Studies, Carson City, Nevada, U.S.A. followed by James Cleary, Sunland, Tallahassee, Florida, U.S.A.

The editor was greatly helped throughout the project by frequent communications from Ian Hore-Lacy, Environmental Scientist, C.R.A., Melbourne, Australia.

Because of the cost of air postage, the first-draft edition had to be sent by surface mail. In several instances, a year elapsed before the book reached its destination. Approximately 150 copies were mailed to environmental education leaders with a request for their comments and contributions towards refining the project. Each of the members of the Commission on Education of the I.U.C.N. received a copy

A partial idea of the number of contributors of this handbook can be gained by reading the listings in Appendix B. Special notice should be taken of certain members of the first international meeting on environmental education at Carson City who followed the project from its inception, particularly S. Doraiswami (India), Sidy Lamine Gueye (Senegal), E. Selai Mohapi (Lesotho), V. Ninan (Nigeria), Rudolph J. H. Schafer (U.S.A.), William M. Taylor (U.S.A.), Yozo Tshukamoto (Japan/U.S.A.), and Harry Wals (The Netherlands).

Members of the I.U.C.N. Commission on Education who fully responded to requests included James L. Aldrich (U.S.A.), W. Erz (Federal Republic of Germany), Ricardo Luti (Argentina), and Vice-Chairman T. Pritchard (U.K.). The Chairman of the Commission is L. K. Shaposhnikov (U.S.S.R.).

Other correspondents who sent materials and editorial comments included S. Beer (Italy), Lore Steubing (German National Committee for M.A.B.), Magda Staudinger (Federal Republic of Germany), Robert Roth and Bob Howe (ERIC Center, Columbus, Ohio), David Kromm (Kansas State University), B. J. VandenHazel (Canada), I. D. Zverev (U.S.S.R.) and Raymond Smyke (W.C.O.T.P., Switzerland).

Thanks are especially due to the I.U.C.N. and its administrative officers, especially Alfred H. Hoffmann, Project Officer, I.U.C.N./W.W.F. Joint Project Operations, and Frank G. Nicholls, Deputy Director General. Statements in this handbook should not be construed as necessarily representing the views of I.U.C.N. or U.N.E.S.C.O.

Finally appreciation is due to my department, the College of Education, and The University of Georgia for providing the essential environment and the research time needed in completing a work of this nature.

The University of Georgia   ROBERT N. SAVELAND
U.S.A.

Contents

I

Perspectives

ROBERT N. SAVELAND

Purpose and Procedures

An art lesson in perspective is the task of drawing a pair of railway tracks extending across a plain away from the viewer. The tracks appear to converge in the distance. Perspective is our way of looking at things. In addition to geometric perspective, there is a time perspective and a space perspective, and an entire book (Manners and Mikesell, 1974) has been written on the subject as it pertains to environment. Various disciplines have their own perspectives, as witnessed by the sometimes divergent views of economists and ecologists. This is not to say that all economists think alike, but there is a general similarity in their approach to the world.

One form of perspective recently referred to in environmental education writings is that of 'tunnel vision'. A person afflicted with this sympton sees only the light at the end of the tunnel (his goal) and he perceives nothing of what is on either side of him at the present. While this handbook will seek to maintain the distant goal in its perspective, it will also give attention to that which is going on in the field around it.

One of the purposes of this handbook it to provide data to help the reader respond to the question, 'Where are we now in environmental education?'. Although an urgent need for such an education has been widely recognized, its inclusion in the curriculum is still fragmentary and incomplete. Yet examples of workable practices abound. It is the task of this handbook to select some of these, organize them into meaningful relationships, and present them in a manner that will permit the international reader to make his own applications and synthesis for his part of the world.

The case study will be the main device used to provide the data mentioned above. For purposes of this handbook, the term *case study* will be interpreted rather broadly to include a variety of documentary materials. The problems of the case study approach are those encountered whenever a selection process is involved. In a field which has had such a rapid expansion and surge of interest as environmental education, it is difficult to keep up with the burgeoning literature. Thus, some practices which would make excellent case studies go unheralded. As explained in the Acknowledgements, the system of preparing a first-draft edition and sending it to readers around the world sought to allay this problem.

Criteria for selecting case studies can be logically and objectively determined. However, the decision for inclusion of a case study inevitably includes some degree of subjective judgement, and this is also recognized as a problem. For this handbook, the major criteria were:

1. Is it innovative? Is it creative?
2. Does it have high transfer value? Is it replicable in other situations?
3. Does it fit a geographical distribution pattern? (An attempt was made to get as wide a distribution as possible, but in this we did not succeed.)
4. Does it have the time quality of either reflecting the current situation or being of continuing value in the future?
5. Is it truly representative of environmental education, as currently defined?

This last item is a 'sticky wicket' because it brings up the whole problem of environmental definitions.

Definitions

New words are continually being added to the vocabulary of the general populace. Note the rise in the use of the term *ecology* in the late 1960s. The frequency in use of certain words can serve as a barometer measuring the climate of opinion, the intellectual interests and the values of a group of people.

There is often a fuzzy quality to new terms, or old terms used in new ways, for it takes time for them to acquire generally accepted meanings that can be codified in a dictionary. Take, for instance, the words *perspective* and *perception* which are appearing frequently in environmental literature (Yi-Fu Tuan, 1974). While both words look alike and are related, they have some important distinctions to which the careful reader and writer will be attuned.

A standard definition equates perception with *awareness* of the elements of the physical environment through the senses.

> Many kinds of perception are utilized: the senses of touch, smell, hearing, sight, gravity, and balance, the visual sensations of color, shape, rhythm, and motion are all biological techniques of orientation to the environment. (Rillo, 1971, p. 40)

Psychologists point to the role of needs, values and emotions in developing an individual's mental image of the world. Of special significance is the fact that what we perceive filters to the mind through a cultural screen. This has particular relevance in an international handbook on environmental education. There are many examples of materials which were considered a natural resource in one culture but of little value in another. (An exception seems to be the almost universal respect which has been accorded to gold.) On the current scene, one can see the people of developing countries adopting quite a different view of the resources within their boundaries from that of the industrialized nations which exploit these resources.

Perception, then, deals with *what* we look at, or choose to notice. 'We see, but we do not observe', is an old axiom. What we see is conditioned by how sensitized our receptors are.

Perspective, as mentioned earlier, is *how* we look at things. It is what happens after impressions are internalized. Perspective places things in the context of time and space and is concerned with interrelationships. Thus it can be said that perception precedes perspective.

Not only do somewhat involved and technical terms like *perception* and *perspective* offer a problem in definition, but comparitively simple and general terms like *environment* and *education* have their problems too. From the standpoint of international communications, there is a real need for common agreement on the meaning of terms. It was with this problem that the delegates struggled during the opening sessions of

Photographs by Elizabeth Kellogg

Children get a head start in the 'Annex' run by Frances Hawkins of the Mountain View Center, Boulder, Colorado

the first International Working Meeting on Environmental Education in
the School Curriculum at Foresta Institute in the summer of 1970. The
definition of environmental education which they agreed upon was
based on an existing statement by B. Ray Horn who undoubtedly drew
upon previous writings of Brennan, Brandywine and others. As
adopted, it reads:

> Environmental education is the process of recognizing values
> and clarifying concepts in order to develop skills and attitudes
> necessary to understand and appreciate the inter-relatedness
> among man, his culture, and his biophysical surroundings.
> Environmental education also entails practice in decision making
> and self-formulation of a code of behavior about issues concerning
> environmental quality. (Cerovsky 1971a, p. 17)

This statement has been widely publicized and accepted, but it is not
simple. It requires thoughtful reading.

Environmental education has been defined by the Congress of the
United States through The Environmental Education Act (Public Law
91—516). In order to accomodate two schools of thought, two working
definitions were stated, one emphasizing process and the other stressing
content. Tanner (1974, pp. 29—33) has a further discussion of these
issues. Excerpts from the law are included in this chapter as Case Study
No. 1—1. In subsequent chapters, some of the projects funded under
this act will be described.

Official actions of governmental organizations give status to movements and causes. Presumably a problem has to be of a sufficient
magnitude before it is perceived by lawmakers. The educational side of
environmental problems was so recognized at the United Nations
Conference on the Human Environment in 1972, otherwise known as
the Stockholm meeting. Resolution 96, outlining a task for international agencies, is set forth in this chapter as Case Study 1—2. This
case study serves to give additional perspective on the concerns to
which this handbook seeks to respond.

A complete set of definitions for environmental terms is a project
unto itself. Fortunately others have made the attempt. A convenient
23-page booklet of *Common Environmental Terms* was compiled by
Gloria J. Studdard and published by the U.S. Environmental Protection
Agency in 1973. A part of this glossary is reproduced as Case Study
1—3. The Appendix of this handbook gives the contact addresses for
additional information on any of the case studies.

The compulsion to define environmental education has, at times,
taken on the appearance of an attempt to establish the boundaries of a
discipline. King and Brownwell (1966) identified the isomorphic
features of disciplines as follows:

A discipline is a community of persons.
A discipline is an expression of human imagination.
A discipline is a domain.
A discipline is a tradition.
A discipline is a syntactical structure — a mode of inquiry.
A discipline is a conceptual structure — a substance.
A discipline is a specialized language or other system of symbols.
A discipline is a heritage of literature and artifacts and a network of communications.
A discipline is a valuative and effective stance.
A discipline is an instructive community. (p. 95)

Although a characteristic of environmental education is that it is supposed to transcend the disciplines, through the definition process, it is assuming several of the characteristics of a discipline. Perhaps this is related to an underlying psychological need for structure and order in our lives?

Concepts and Principles
Perception and perspective are involved in the process of concept formation. Much has been written about concepts (Pritchard, 1971), and still the term is elusive. Like moonbeams, you cannot hold them in your hand. To some, concepts refer to the meanings attached to individual words. Thus, concepts of special interest to environmental education would be linked with words, such as B.O.D. (biochemical oxygen demand), euthrophication, cycle, vanishing species, etc. Others prefer to express concepts as a statement, or generalization. Some consider both modes equally valid, for they equate concepts with ideas.

There has been considerable interest in identifying concepts in environmental education. Not only do they need to be identified, but also arranged in some order, or structure. This step is prerequisite to determining a grade placement in a developmental learning sequence.

One of the more definitive works in establishing a concepts list was that of Robert E. Roth in his Ph.D. dissertation at The University of Wisconsin under the direction of Milton O. Pella and Clay A. Schoenfeld. Drawing from college conservation texts, reference books, conservation curriculum guides and previous studies (notably those of Hanselman, Visher, White and Yambert) he prepared an initial list of 89 concepts which were sent to a University of Wisconsin Panel of 67 scholars representing 40 disciplines. Based on the response of this panel and personal interviews, Roth then drew up an expanded list of 157 concepts. This list was submitted to the Wisconsin Panel and the members were asked to judge the credibility of each item. This resulted in a third list of 128 concepts which was submitted to a National Panel of 699 members representing two universities in each of 12 major vegetation zones of the U.S. and 27 universities selected on the basis of being large universities with extensive graduate programmes and holding summer sessions.

The National Panel was asked to rate each concept as to whether they considered it essential (+5), highly desirable (+4), desirable (+3), satisfactory (+2), or unacceptable (—5). Weighted item mean scores were computed on the basis of the values indicated. The maximum attainable score was 5.0. Usable responses were received from 350 of the National Panel and these represented 24 universities and 40 disciplines. Each concept had to receive a 90% or greater level of acceptable responses to be placed on the final list. The concepts were then classified according to topic and arranged in order of assigned importance. The complete list of 111 final concepts with weighted item mean scores is included in this chapter as Case Study No. 1-4. This taxonomy is intended for use in planning programmes of instruction from kindergarten through college. The grade placement remains to be determined.

The method of procedure used by Roth is rather standard and relies heavily on the judgement of academicians. It would be interesting to get responses from the informed lay public to the same questionnaire, and it would be especially interesting to accumulate data on concepts on an international scale, for some of these concepts represent definite western cultural biases. Strangely enough, Roth found that any indication of a respondent's bias associated with his descipline was tenous at best.

Certain of Roth's concepts, such as 15, 19, 39, 57 and 58, deal with a time frame. The theme of change is recognized as a major strand in the social sciences. However, there is a popular misconception that environmental problems sprang upon the world all at once. Those who have been working in the field long enough have seen evolution of thought from the conservation concept at the turn of the century which largely referred to preservation of natural areas and wildlife in a wilderness stage, to the wise-use of resources philosophy prevalent in the 1930s, to the current environmental movement reflecting altered values on the benefits of industrialism and considering the possibilities of placing some limits to growth. In order to place the recent environmental movement in some perspective on a continuum, the following chart of important events is offered.

IMPORTANT EVENTS IN THE ENVIRONMENTAL MOVEMENT

Readers will wish to add to this list other names and occurrences significant for their countries and cultures.

1813	Imperial Forest Institute established in St. Petersburg
1864	George Perkins Marsh, *Man and Nature*
1872	Establishment of Yellowstone National Park
1873	Louis Agassiz founded Nature Study School near Woods Hole

1875	Jean Baptiste Lamarck and Eduard Suess used term *biosphere*
1908	Theodore Roosevelt formed National Conservation Commission
1913	International Conference for the Protection of Nature, Basle (interrupted by World War I)
1916	North American Migratory Birds Treaty
1922	International Committee for Bird Preservation established in London
1926	Vladimir Vernadsky, *Biosphere*
1927	Term *noosphere* put forth by Edouard LeRoy
1933	Tennessee Valley Authority (TVA)
1934	Commission for International Protection of Nature legally established at Brussels
1935	Paul B. Sears, *Deserts on the March*
1942	Signing of Convention on Nature Protection and Wildlife Preservation in the Western Hemisphere
1946	Founding of International Union for the Protection of Nature (Name changed to International Union for the Conservation of Nature and Natural Resources in 1956)
1949	First World Conference on Natural Resources, Lake Success New York (had commission on pesticides)
1957—8	International Geophysical Year
1959	Antarctic Treaty
1961	Formation of World Wildlife Fund
1966	Rachel Carson, *Silent Spring*
1967	Torrey Canyon wreck calls world attention to oil spill
1968	U.N.E.S.C.O. Biosphere Conference in Paris
1970	European Conservation Year
1972	U.N. Conference on the Human Environment, Stockholm

Even though Alvin Toffler in *Future Shock* (1970) rightly pointed out that schools mainly focus on the past and ban the future from the classroom, it must be observed that the old dictum still maintains, 'The past is prologue'.

Another recent writer, Robert Ardrey (1966), popularized a major concept which has great implications for environmental education, that of territoriality. As Cervosky (1971b) has written:

> I believe that every environmentally conscious citizen must have his 'home environment' in which he feels rooted, which he loves, explores, understands, and improves, and which he is ready to defend against every danger and deterioration. A sound global awareness can only grow out of such a background. People lacking a 'home environment' or deprived of it cannot acquire a proper awareness of environmental issues. (p. 8)

A sense of community is thus linked with the concept of territoriality. Individual mobility in industrial societies has weakened the sense of community in many instances. This has frequently been accompanied by deterioration of the environment. A community is the kind of social involvement as well as a place. Communities exist on various scales from the crew of a ship to 100,000 people in a metropolis. A key factor in the community concept is the perception that some kind of 'glue' holds the community together.

On a national scale, the concepts of territoriality and community can expand to embrace that of 'motherland'. This concept has found greater expression in some nations than others. Sometimes the concept has been subverted into a form of super-patriotism. Sibelius' tone poem, *Finlandia*, gives us a feeling for the true concept of 'motherland'.

Beyond national boundaries, the concept of 'Mother Earth' includes the biosphere as the provider of sustenance and shelter. Implied in this concept is a relationship of love between mother and children. Ultimately, environmental education involves the international dimension. As Strong (1974) has stated:

> In the final analysis, nations will have to recognize that there can be no basic or enduring conflict between their national interests and the interests of the whole human community. The same compelling pressures of broader self-interest that induced man to form ever larger social and political units — first the family, then the tribe, the village, the town, the city, the city-state, and finally the nation state — must inevitably impel mankind toward a planetary society. Loyalty to this planetary society will modify but need not negate an individual's loyalty to his nation, any more than loyalty to the nation negates loyalty to the family, the tribe, or the city. (p. 55)

The foregoing concepts of territoriality, community, motherland, and Mother Earth have served to illustrate the different scales at which environmental education operates. This is a problem, for scale can be a great intellectual hurdle. Both a square metre of ground and the entire biosphere are proper fields of study. The microscope and the telescope are both proper tools for increasing perception. Man can be viewed at the same time as one individual, or as all mankind. How can this great diversity be best approached and assimilated by fresh young minds of limited experience?

Concepts become principles when they have broad implications and assume the characteristics of a universal law. In physics, where gravity is a universal force, it is comparatively easy to enumerate principles, such as Archimedes' Principle. In other sciences, it is also possible to find many commonly accepted principles. These extend into genetics and population dynamics. In the social sciences, various disciplines have established principles, especially in economics. All principles, however, are subject to revision as new insights force abandoning of former truths.

Thus far there have been few attempts to formulate sets of principles for environmental education. Because of its trans-disciplinary nature, it borrows concepts from many fields. Many of the data for environmental problems are based on the natural sciences. Responsive action on these problems is in the domain of the social sciences, especially geography (land-use planning) and political science.

To guide the writing and selection of material for this book, a taxonomy of principles was drawn up. This list of principles is set forth, herewith, to indicate to the reader the basic premises upon which this work is based. These principles are neither sacrosanct, nor all inclusive. This effort should stimulate dialogue leading to further efforts at delineating and refining the principles of environmental education.

Synthesis

To sum up, this handbook seeks to provide information on practices that have presumably 'worked' in various parts of the world. In this, it has an inventory function. Secondly, the handbook should promote synthesis, or 'putting it all together'. However, this is, in part, a reader responsibility. Thirdly, the handbook should extend environmental education through the exchange of information on 'new' methods and materials. For some students, it may serve as a training manual. Hopefully, this handbook will stimulate interaction and discourse by serving as a forum topic at environmental education conferences to come.

The printed work will serve to record the state of the field in the mid 1970s. As such, it will have historical value for future students doing longitudinal studies of the environmental movement, and thus contribute to their perspective.

PRINCIPLES FOR E. E. HANDBOOK

1. Man is a rational animal
   1.1 He has developed tools for modifying his surroundings
   1.2 He can make decisions affecting the environment
   1.3 He must live in partnership with nature and in harmony with natural laws and principles. (The ecological approach)
2. Environmental improvement requires cooperative effort
   2.1 Planning is a means of foreseeing the effects of our actions. (The systems approach)
   2.1.1 Data gathering is necessary to assure optimum environmental decisions.
   2.1.2 The patterns of land use reflect the values of a society
   2.1.3 The growth syndrome has placed a premium on development at the expense of the environment
   2.2 The attainment of environments of quality depends on the communication of ideas — an aim of education
   2.2.1 Environmental education is inter-disciplinary, multi-disciplinary, and trans-disciplinary
   2.2.2 Environmental education operates at the grass-roots level and is concerned with individual behaviour
   2.2.3 Environmental education involves students in activities
   2.2.4 Environmental education necessitates field studies, rural or urban, and experiences beyond the classroom
   2.2.5 Environmental education develops an ethic contributing to the quality of life
   2.2.5.1 It respects individual life styles
   2.2.5.2 It is based on constructive attitudes

3. The sharing of resources is a global concern
   3.1   Materials of the earth become resources through human perception of potential uses
   3.2   Earth resources are unevenly distributed and unequally consumed
   3.3   The consumption of resources may convert them into irretrievable forms or into substances dangerously harmful to living organisms
   3.4   Recycling of industrial production and ecologically balanced agricultural production are means of maintaining sustained yields from resources
   3.5   The people of the world are all astronauts on Spaceship Earth
   3.5.1 The earth is our only home; it contains our life-support systems
   3.5.2 The limits of the human population-carrying-capacity of the earth are currently unknown, but observations indicate the desirability of some forms of population limitation and redistribution

Bibliography

Ardrey, Robert M. *The Territorial Imperative: A personal inquiry into the animal origins of property and nation*, Atheneum, New York, 1966, 390 pp.

(a) Cerovsky, Jan, 'Environment Education: Yes — But How?', *Your Environment*, Vol. II No. 1, Spring 1971, pp. 15—19.

(b) Cerovsky, Jan, 'Comprehensive Programmes of Environmental Education', Conference Document 33-6/KP/2, European Working Conference on Environmental Conservation Education, I.U.C.N., Morges, Switzerland, November 1971.

Hanselman, David L. *Interdepartmental Teaching of Conservation at The Ohio State University*, Doctoral Dissertation, The Ohio State University, Columbus, Ohio, 1963.

King, Arthur R. Jr. and Brownwell, John A., *The Curriculum and the Disciplines of Knowledge*, John Wiley & Sons, New York, London, Sydney, 1966, 221 pp.

Manners, Ian R. and Mikesell, Marvin W., *Perspectives on Environment*, Commission on College Geography, Association of American Geographers, Washington, D.C., 1974, 395 pp.

Pritchard, Tom, 'Concepts of Environmental Education', Conference Document 33-6/KP/1, European Working Conference on Environmental Conservation Education, I.U.C.N., Morges, Switzerland, November 1971.

Rillo, Tom, 'Toward an Urban Ecological Structure', *Environmental Education*, Vol. 2 No. 3, Spring, 1971, pp. 40—43.

Roth, Robert E., Pella, Milton O. and Schoenfeld, Clay A., *Environmental Management Concepts — A List*, Technical Report No. 126, Wisconsin Research and Development Center for Cognitive Learning, The University of Wisconsin, Madison, Wisconsin, April 1970, 72 pp.

Strong, Maurice F., 'A Global Imperative for the Environment', *Natural History*, No. 83, March 1974, pp. 41—56.

Tanner, R. Thomas, *Ecology, Environment, and Education*, Professional Educators Publications, Inc., Lincoln, Nebraska, 1974, 106 pp.

Toffler, Alvin, *Future Shock*, Bantam Books, New York, London, Toronto, 1970, 561 pp.

Tuan, Yi-Fu, *Topophilia: A Study of Environmental Perception, Attitudes, and Values*, Prentice-Hall, Englewood Cliffs, N.J., 1974, 260 pp.

Visher, Halene Hatcher, *A Determination of Conservation Principles and Concepts Desirable for Use in the Secondary Schools*, Doctoral Dissertation, University of Indiana, Evansville, Ind., 1960.

White, Roy C., *A Study Associating Selected Conservation Understandings with Available Community Resources for Grades Four Through Twelve*, Doctoral Dissertation, University of Montana, Missoula, Mot., 1967.

Yambert, Paul Abt, *A Principle and Concept Perspective of Conservation*, Doctoral Dissertation, University of Michigan, Ann Arbor, Mich., 1961.

Additional References

Perception of the Environment: An Introduction to the Literature, Occasional Paper 17, Birmingham, Center for Urban and Regional Studies, 1971.

Willensky, Elliot, 'Environmental Education: euphemism or challenge?' *BEE Bulletin of Environmental Education*, 40/41, August—September 1974, pp. 19—21.

Wohlwill, Joachim F. (comp.), *Environment and the Social Sciences*, American Psychological Association, Washington, D.C., 1972, 300 pp.

Case Study 1.1

Financial Assistance for Environmental Education Projects.
U.S. Department of Health, Education, and Welfare/Office
of Education

Subpart A — Description of Program
§ *183.1 Scope and purpose*
(a) The Environmental Education Act (Public Law 91-516; 20 U.S.C. 1531—1536) authorizes a program of grants and contracts to support research, demonstration, and pilot projects designed to educate the public on the problems of environmental quality and ecological balance. Such projects shall support the development of educational processes dealing with man's relationship with his natural and man-made surroundings, and include the relation of population, pollution, resource allocation and depletion conservation, transportation, technology, and urban and rural planning to the total human environment. These processes would be designed to help the learner both to perceive and understand the concepts of 'environment' and environmental principles and problems and to be able to identify and evaluate alternative solutions to environmental problems. Emphasis shall be placed on the development of skills and insights needed to understand the structure, requirements, and impact within and among various environmental entities, subsystems and systems.

Part 2 — Environmental Education
Sec 2.1 *Background*. Environmental education is a relatively new activity still undergoing important developments in its practical application and theoretical foundations. The interaction of the practical and the theoretical has evolved into two working definitions of environmental education that, taken together, reflect the consensus established among many educators, ecologists, environmentalists, and other citizens concerning the basic aspects of environmental education.

Sec. 2.2 *Working definition: process and theory* — (a) *Multidisciplinary*. (1) Environmental education is the process that fosters greater understanding of society's environmental problems and also the processes of environmental problem-solving and decision-making. This is accomplished by teaching the ecological relationships and principles that underlie these problems and showing the nature of the possible alternative approaches and solutions.

That is, the process of environmental education helps the learner perceive and understand environmental principles and problems, and enables him to identify and evaluate the possible alternative solutions to these problems and assess their benefits and risks. It involves the development of skills and insights needed to understand the structure, requirements, and impact of interactions within and among various environmental entities, subsystems, and systems.

(20 U.S.C. 1531 (b))

2.3 *Working definition: content and purposes.* (1) One of the most important concepts in environmental education is the definition of 'environment.' Clearly environment can no longer be assumed to imply only endangered species and walks in the wilderness; it includes these but is something far more encompassing.

(2) Because the environment itself is so vast and complex, environmental education is much more comprehensive than specialized approaches to environmental subjects, such as traditionally defined approaches to conservation and resource use education, environmental science, nature study, and outdoor education. These approaches normally do not give consideration to mutually reinforcing social, physical, cultural, political, economic, technological, and ethical implications of their areas of focus. It is generally agreed, however, that environmental education projects would undoubtedly draw upon some of the ideas and materials of these traditional subjects and emphases, but would do so in synthesis with ideas and materials from many other areas, such as the social sciences, the applied and theoretical natural sciences, the arts, and other areas of the humanities, all as appropriate and needed for the particular topic of inquiry.

Case Study 1.2

Recommendation 96. Report of the United Nations Conference on the Human Environment

1. *It is recommended* that the Secretary-General, the organizations of the United Nations system, especially the United Nations Educational, Scientific and Cultural Organization and the other international agencies concerned, should, after consultation and agreement, take the necessary steps to establish an international program in environmental education, interdisciplinary in approach, in school and out of school, encompassing all levels of education and directed towards the general public, in particular the ordinary citizen living in rural and urban areas, youth and adult alike, with a view to educating him as to the simple steps he might take, within his means, to manage and control his environment. A program of technical and financial cooperation and assistance will be needed to support this program, taking into account the priorities agreed upon according to the resources available. This program should include, among other things:

(*a*) The preparation of an inventory of existing systems of education which include environmental education;
(*b*) The exchange of information on such systems and, in particular, dissemination of the results of experiments in teaching;
(*c*) The training and retraining of professional workers in various disciplines at various levels (including teacher training);
(*d*) Consideration of the formation of groups of experts in environmental disciplines and activities, including those concerning the economic, sociological, tourist and other sectors, in order to facilitate the exchange of experience between countries which have similar environmental conditions and comparable levels of development;
(*e*) The development of new materials and methods for all types and levels of environmental education.

Case Study 1.3

Common Environmental Terms — A Glossary. Compiled by
Gloria J. Studdard

In sum, we have endeavored in a single listing to compile and define the most common words and terms essential to the study, understanding and solution of environmental problems. Where so many words and terms are concerned, it is sometimes difficult to settle upon definitions acceptable to users who represent a great variety of pursuits and interests. This is particularly true of the newer words generated by science and technology. It may be recalled that Dr. Samuel Johnson once described a compiler of dictionaries as a 'harmless drudge' and observed: 'Dictionaries are like watches; the worst is better than none, and the best cannot be expected to go quite true.'

We do not expect this glossary to be used extensively by technicians and professionals in environmental control. It was not designed for that purpose. Rather, it is our hope that it will stimulate and improve a student's understanding of man's environment and the interrelationship of the forces and elements that comprise it.

air pollution: The presence of contaminants in the air in concentrations that prevent the normal dispersive ability of the air and that interfere directly or indirectly with man's health, safety or comfort or with the full use and enjoyment of his property.

biochemical oxygen demand (BOD): A measure of the amount of oxygen consumed in the biological processes that break down organic matter in water. Large amounts of organic waste use up large amounts of dissolved oxygen, thus the greater the degree of pollution, the greater the BOD.

channelization: The straightening and deepening of streams to permit water to move faster, to reduce flooding or to drain marshy acreage for farming. However, channelization reduces the organic waste assimilation capacity of the stream and may disturb fish breeding and destroy the stream's natural beuaty.

DDT: The first of the modern chlorinated hydrocarbon insecticides whose chemical name is 1,1,1-tricholoro-2,2-bis (p-chlori-phenyl)-ethane. It has a half-life of 15 years, and its residues can become concentrated in the fatty tissues of certain organisms, especially fish. Because of its persistence in the environment and its ability to accumulate and magnify in the food chain, EPA has banned the registration and interstate sale of DDT for nearly all uses in the United States effective December 31, 1972.

environment: The sum of all external conditions and influences affecting the life, development and, ultimately, the survival of an organism.

fecal coliform bacteria: A group of organisms common to the intestinal tracts of man and of animals. The presence of fecal coliform bacteria in water is an indicator of pollution and of potentially dangerous bacterial contamination.

greenhouse effect: The heating effect of the atmosphere upon the earth. Light waves from the sun pass through the air and are absorbed by the earth. The earth then reradiates this energy as heat waves that are absorbed by the air, specifically by carbon dioxide. The air thus behaves like glass in a greenhouse, allowing the passage of light but not of heat. Thus many scientists theorize that an increase in the atmospheric concentration of CO_2 can eventually cause an increase in the earth's surface temperature.

habitat: The sum total of environmental conditions of a specific place that is occupied by an organism, a population or a community.

implementation plan: A document of the steps to be taken to ensure attainment of environmental quality standards within a specified time period. Implementation plans are required by various laws.

limnology: The study of the physical, chemical, meteorological and biological aspects of fresh waters.

monitoring: Periodic or continuous determination of the amount of pollutants or radioactive contamination present in the environment.

natural selection: The natural process by which the organisms best adapted to their environment survive and those less well adapted are eliminated.

opacity: Degree of obscuration of light. For example, a window has zero opacity; a wall is 100 per cent opaque. The Ringelmann system of evaluating smoke density is based on opacity.

pH: A measure of the acidity or alkalinity of a material, liquid or solid. pH is represented on a scale of 0 to 17 with 7 representing a neutral state, 0 representing the most acid and 14, the most alkaline.

riparian rights: Rights of a land owner to the water on or bordering his property, including the right to prevent diversion or misuse of upstream water.

solid waste: Useless, unwanted or discarded material with insufficient liquid content to be free flowing. Also see waste. (1) agricultural — solid waste that results from the raising and slaughtering of animals, and the processing of animal products and orchard and field crops. (2) commercial — waste generated by stores, offices and other activities that do not actually turn out a product. (3) industrial — waste that results from industrial processes and manufacturing. (4) institutional — waste originating from educational, health care and research facilities. (5) municipal — residential and commercial solid waste generated within a community. (6) pesticide — the residue from the manufacturing, handling or use of chemicals intended for killing plant and animal pests. (7) residential — waste that normally originates in a residential environment. Sometimes called domestic solid waste.

tertiary treatment: Waste water treatment beyond the secondary, or biological stage that includes removal of nutrients such as phosphorus and nitrogen, and a high percentage of suspended solids. Tertiary treatment, also known as advanced waste treatment, produces a high quality effluent.

urban runoff: Storm water from city streets and gutters that usually contains a great deal of litter and organic and bacterial wastes.

variance: Sanction granted by a governing body for delay or exception in the application of a given law, ordinance or regulation.

water quality standard: A plan for water quality management containing four major elements: the use (recreation, drinking water, fish and wildlife propagation, industrial or agricultural) to be made of the water; criteria to protect those uses; implementation plans (for needed industrial-municipal waste treatment improvements) and enforcement plans, and an anti-degradation statement to protect existing high quality waters.

zoo plankton: Planktonic animals that supply food for fish.

Case Study 1.4

Taxonomic List of Concepts for Environmental Management Education
(R. Roth)

*Weighted Item
Mean Scores*

1. Living things are interdependent with one another and their environment. — 4.85

ENVIRONMENTAL MANAGEMENT

2. Man has been a factor affecting plant and animal succession and environmental processes. — 4.58
3. The management of natural resources to meet the needs of successive generations demands long-range planning. — 4.42
4. Environmental management involves the application of knowledge from many different disciplines. — 4.27
5. Modern man affects the structure of his environment. — 4.08
6. Esthetic resources and recreational facilities of economic and noneconomic value are becoming increasingly important in leisure-time activities. — 4.08
7. Man has ability to manipulate and change the environment. — 4.01
8. A knowledge of the social, physical, and biological sciences and humanities are important for environmental understanding. — 3.98
9. Social and technological changes alter the interrelationships, importance, and uses for natural resources. — 3.93
10. There are certain risks taken, and limitations experienced, when manipulating the natural environment. — 3.92
11. Resource depletion can be slowed by the development and adoption of alternatives. — 3.84
12. Environmental management has effects on individuals and social institutions. — 3.74
13. Man's need for food, fiber, and minerals increases as populations expand and levels of consumption rise. — 3.67

14. Conflicts emerge between private land use rights and the maintenance of environmental quality for the general public.   3.65

15. A cultural and time lag exists between the development of knowledge in science and technology and application of the knowledge to resource and environmental problems.   3.44

16. Management is the result of technical and scientific knowledge being applied in a rational direction to achieve a particular objective.   2.62

17. The management of natural resources is culture bound.   2.52

MANAGEMENT TECHNIQUES

18. Increased population mobility is changing the nature of the demands upon some resources.   3.61

19. Options available to future generations must not be foreclosed.   3.51

20. A variety of institutional structures are involved in planning and managing the environment.   3.49

21. Hunting regulations are useful in maintaining and restoring populations as well as in distributing the game harvest.   3.43

22. Multiple use is a practice in which a given land area functions in two or more compatible ways.   3.41

23. Management of habitat is considered to be an effective technique of wildlife management when the desire is to increase numbers of particular populations.   3.35

24. Architecture can be one of the positively persuasive influences in developing a congenial environment.   3.27

25. Zoning is a practice in which land uses are prescribed based upon value judgements regarding the needs of society.   3.20

ECONOMICS

26. Ready transportation, growing interest, money surpluses and increased leisure time combine to create heavy pressures on existing recreation facilities and demands for new ones.   3.96

27. Outdoor recreation is an increasingly important part of our culture and our economy.   3.93

28. The economy of a region depends on the utilization of its natural, human, and cultural resources and technologies over time.   3.79

29. Economic efficiency does not always result in conservation of a natural resource.   3.79

30. The distribution or location of resources in relation to population, technological, and economic factors are critical to problems of resource conservation and use.   3.73

31. The political and economic strength of a country is, in part, dependent upon its access to domestic and foreign resources and international relationships.   3.67

32. Conservation policy is determined by the interaction of science and technology; social and political factors; and aesthetic, ethical, and economic considerations.   3.61

33. Conventional benefit-cost analyses do not always result in sound conservation decisions.   3.54

34. A sound natural resource policy is dependent upon a flexible political system, pragmatically appraising and reappraising policies and programmes in terms of their effect upon the public interest and in light of scientific knowledge about the natural resources.   3.53

35. Consumption practices are constantly being expanded by our ability to produce and create wants and market, which affects the rate of resource use.   3.45

36. Individuals tend to select short term economic gains, often at the expense of greater long term environmental benefits.   3.27

37. Increasing population and per capita use of resources have brought changed land-to-man or resource-to-population ratios.   3.21

38. Goods and services are produced by the interaction of labor, capital, natural resources and technology.   3.18

39. Long range planning for the use and allocation

of natural and human resources is continually evolving.   3.17

40. Choices between needs (essentials) and wants or desires (nonessentials) are often in conflict.   3.15

41. Raw materials and energy supplies are generally obtained from those resources and places where they are available at least cost, usually in short economic terms.   2.96

42. Supply and demand, in relation to values held by society, determines what is a resource and its economic values.   2.86

43. The more efficient use of some resources is the result of technical and marketing improvements. 2.76

ENVIRONMENTAL PROBLEMS

44. Safe waste disposal, including the reduction of harmful and cumulative effects of various solids, liquids, gases, radio-active wastes and heat, is important if the well being of man and the environment is to be preserved.   4.65

45. Pollutants and contaminants are produced by natural and man-made processes.   4.09

46. Increasing human populations, rising levels of living, and the resultant demands for greater industrial and agricultural productivity promotes increasing environmental contamination.   4.01

ENVIRONMENTAL ECOLOGY

47. Natural resources are interdependent and the use or misuse of one will effect others.   4.35

48. In any environment, one component like: space, water, air, or food may become a limiting factor.   4.22

49. Most resources are vulnerable to depletion in quantity, quality, or both.   4.17

50. The interaction of environmental and biological factors determines the size and range of species and populations.   3.84

51. Natural resources, water and minerals in particular, are unequally distributed with respect to land areas and political boundaries.   3.75

52. The renewable resource base can be extended by reproduction, growth, and management. 3.75
53. Natural resources affect and are affected by the material welfare of a culture and directly or indirectly by philosophy, religion, government, and the arts. 3.58
54. The natural environment is irreplaceable. 2.96

ADAPTATION AND EVOLUTION

55. An organism is the product of its heredity and environment. 4.14
56. Man is influenced by many of the same hereditary and environmental factors that affect other organisms and their populations. 3.80
57. The rate of change in an environment may exceed the rate of organism adaptation. 3.76
58. Organisms and environments are in constant change. 3.56
59. All living things, including man, are continually evolving. 3.49
60. The form of life present depends upon the coincidence of the life needs and their availability in an environment. 3.25
61. Biological systems are described as dynamic because the materials and energy involved are parts of continuous cycles; inorganic materials and energy become part of organic materials and are subsequently broken down into simple substances and energy as a result of the operation of organic systems. 3.09
62. Animal populations are renewable resources. 3.08
63. Succession is the gradual and continuous replacement of one kind of plant or animal complex by another and is characterized by gradual changes in species composition. 3.03

NATURAL RESOURCES
(Water)

64. Water supplies, both in quantity and quality are important to all levels of living. 4.39
65. The earth and life on it are greatly affected by the atmosphere. 4.29

66. Water is a reusable and transient resource, but the available quantity may be reduced or quality impaired.   4.17

67. As populations increase competition for the use of water increases resulting in a need for establishing water use priorities.   4.13

68. The amount of precipitation that becomes available for use by man varies with topography, land use, and applied management practices.   3.52

(Minerals)

69. Mineral conservation involves the utilization of all known minerals of the earth's crust that will cause them to serve more people for a longer time.   3.27

70. The nonrenewable resource base is considered finite.   3.27

71. Soil is classified as a renewable resource, but, because it may take a few years to thousands of years to be 'renewed,' it is more practically termed a depletable resource.   2.94

72. Minerals are nonrenewable resources.   2.87

(Soil)

73. Maintaining, improving, and in some cases restoring soil productivity is important to the welfare of people.   4.25

74. Geological processes like erosion and deposition modify the landscape.   3.61

75. Soil productivity can be maintained by utilizing known agronomic, mechanical, and chemical processes.   3.51

(Plants)

76. Green plants are the ultimate sources of food, clothing, shelter, and energy in most societies.   3.56

77. Plants are renewable resources.   3.44

78. Energy is supplied to an ecosystem by the activities of green plants.   3.36

(Animals)

79. Wildlife refuges, undisturbed natural areas, and

preserves may be of value in protecting endangered species and perpetuating the gene pool. 3.99
80. Wildlife populations are important economic-
ally, aesthetically, and biologically. 3.69
81. Wildlife is considered to be a public resource. 3.26

THE SOCIO-CULTURAL ENVIRONMENT

82. Man has responsibility to develop an appreciation of and respect for the rights of others. 4.38
83. Individual citizens should be stimulated to
become well informed about resource issues,
problems, management procedures, and ecological principles. 4.29
84. Conservation responsibilities should be shared
by individuals, businesses and industries, special
interest groups, and all levels of government and
education. 4.16
85. Man has moral reponsibility for his environmental decisions. 3.94
86. Knowledge of the social structures, institutions,
and culture of a society must be brought to bear
on environmental considerations. 3.75
87. The relationships between man and the natural
environment are mediated by his culture. 3.65
88. Man is developing the technical and sociological
knowledge needed to control population
growth, modify environments, and alter resource
use patterns. 3.58
89. Social values and mores influence personal conservation behavior. 3.34
90. Public opinion constitutes a control over the use
of conservation practices. 3.11
91. In a democracy, a basic theory is that increasing
restrictions on resource allocation and use are
imposed by the consent or insistence of the
people. 2.92

CULTURE

92. The culture of a group is its learned behavior in
the form of customs, habits, attitudes, institutions, and lifeways that are transmitted to its
progeny. 3.49

93. Man has psychobiological and biosocial needs. 3.27
94. Human resources include the physical and mental abilities with which man is endowed and the knowledge he has generated. 3.26
95. Historically, cultures with high technological development have used more natural resources than those with lower levels of technological development. 2.98

POLITICS

96. Individual citizens should be stimulated to become active in the political process. 3.85
97. We have 'legal' ownership of some resources like real estate and control over others during our lifetime, but ethically we are 'stewards' rather than owners of the resource base. 3.75
98. Policies, including natural resource policies, came about as a result of the interacting social processes: science and technology, government operations, private interests, and public attitudes. 3.51
99. Conservation policies are often the result of group action. 3.51
100. As populations increase and/or as resource supplies decrease, the freedom of the individual to use the resources as he wishes decreases irrespective of the form of government. 3.44

THE FAMILY

101. Family planning and the limiting of family size are important if overpopulation is to be avoided and a reasonable standard of living assured for successive generations. 3.88

THE INDIVIDUAL

102. An individual must develop his ability to perceive if he is to increase awareness and develop environmental perspective. 3.63
103. Individuals perceive different self-roles depending upon their position in the social and environmental context. 2.99

104. Man has the capability of improving society through sociology, psychology, and science. 2.95
105. Man is a high animal form because of his ability to reason. 2.83
106. Man is continually developing an ethical base for making value judgements. 2.65
107. Man performs some tasks at a high physiological cost. 2.62

PSYCHOLOGICAL ASPECTS

108. Opportunities to experience and enjoy nature are psychologically rewarding to many and are important to mental health. 3.60
109. The need of man to turn inward for self renewal can be stimulated by his external esthetic experiences. 2.79
110. Resources have a psychological impact on people. 2.78
111. Emotional reactions can be elicited by exposure to physical objects and geometric forms. 2.54

2
Curriculum Design

ROBERT SAVELAND

Search for a Rationale

This chapter is addressed to those persons who have been given, or who have assumed, some responsibility in formulating a curriculum in environmental education. It recognizes that students can make their own curriculum, since curriculum is here used to denote patterns of learning experiences (Berman, 1968). However, by and large, prescribed curricula exist, and any long-range development in environmental education involves finding a place within the mandated framework.

The starting place for curriculum building is usually the identification of the basic principles upon which the curriculum is constructed. The current stage of identifying principles for environmental education was indicated in the last chapter. The search for a rationale is apparent in several of the case studies in this handbook and in other curriculum writings. When seeking a rationale on an international level, the task is complicated by varying levels of educational development and contrasting, even conflicting, value systems and ideologies. Nevertheless, it may be safely asserted that at least three major goals are common to the educative process wherever encountered. These are:

1. The curriculum should promote entry into the world at work — a vocational goal.
2. The curriculum should provide for the continuing functioning of society — a citizenship goal.
3. The curriculum should help individuals to enjoy many-sided and meaningful lives — a personal goal. (Adapted from Flanagan, 1973.)

It may be noted that these goals apply to learning from elders in aboriginal societies as well as to factory-style instruction in highly integrated state schools of industrial societies.

Data, skills and concepts from environmental education contribute to each of these goals in a major way. Goal 1 involves everyone as consumers and producers in the unending process of resource conversion. Goal 2 relates to the intelligence which can be brought to bear on environmental problems through laws and human behaviour whereby people will act as stewards in partnership with nature rather than as its adversaries. For goal 3, the role of nature as an uplifter of the human spirit may be difficult to document, but it is attested to by hundreds of thousands of persons.

Curriculum builders, in addition to adhering to a set of environmental principles, should follow a set of educational principles. Again the problems of common agreement and wide applicability must be faced. Also, theories of learning are an educational frontier, and the role of memory is largely an unexplored territory. However, four major educational principles will be boldly set forth here, because they are inherent in developing a curriculum design. They include:

1. The curriculum should provide for individual differences.
2. The curriculum should have meaning (relevance) for the student.
3. The curriculum should be developmental (in phase with maturation rates).
4. The curriculum should be balanced.

Principle number 1 has long been given lip service but is frequently violated in large modern school systems. The types of activities often associated with environmental education usually promote individual expression and creativity. It is clear how environmental problems contribute to principle number 2. Principle number 3 gives difficulty because maturation levels and growth stages are still being identified. The latter part of this chapter and Case Study 2-8 will attempt to extend this principle into the field of environmental education. Principle number 4 is an ecological principle that can also be applied to personal lives. A balanced curriculum provides a variety that contributes to motivation as well as to the development of well-rounded personalities mentioned previously.

The achievement of balance is also related to a seldom-mentioned component of unusual importance, that of pacing (Glaser, 1973). Pacing refers to the rate of learning and thus is also linked with principles 1 and 3. The achievement of a balanced, well-paced curriculum is partly an art, partly the result of concentrated, serious study, and partly acquired through the trial-and-error method. Although teachers alter the pace of prescribed curricula, inevitably students pace themselves.

Organization Alternatives

Once a rationale has been set forth, there remain numerous organizational decisions to be made by the curriculum designer. Factors to be taken into consideration include:

1. Past experiences — what are the weak points and strong points of the current curriculum, the attitudes and skills of the teachers, the availability of materials?

2. Economy of time — do the behavioural outcomes have a positive correlation with the energy expended to achieve them?

3. Transferability — the 'carry over' value to future knowledge and technology is difficult to ascertain in advance. Advocates of the process approach claim this advantage.

4. Flexibility — rigor mortis tends to set in once a curriculum is established. Perhaps it is for this reason that much environmental education has been done in an *ad hoc*, informal way.

While not denigrating the value of informal environmental education, it is still necessary to obtain sanction from the managers of the system if change is to be affected in the schools. Case Study 2-1 is a demonstration of official recognition and action in support of environmental education on the part of the Committee of Ministers of the Council of Europe. As such, it should be noted that this is a political document. The Appendix statement, 'It would be presumptuous to make fundamental changes in the educational structures and school curricula in the near future', reflects the cautious attitude required in such proclamations. It will be noted that a multi-disciplinary approach is suggested rather than a trans-disciplinary one. (See pages 8—9.) This topic is further developed in the next case study.

Case Study 2-2 from India sets forth three approaches to incorporating environmental education into the curriculum. The first two approaches, dispersion through the curriculum and utilizing specially designed units, are put forth as preliminary steps in moving to option three which makes a case for the separate, but equal, course in environmental education. A fourth possibility briefly mentioned in this case study, that of total curriculum revision, will receive attention later in this chapter.

Following Case Study 2-2, four case studies are presented in succession. Case Study 2-3 from Yugoslavia details tasks at succeeding grade levels and adheres to developmental principles. Case Study 2-4 gives an Australian example of curriculum development, especially in the middle school (in this case 9th and 10th grade). Case Study 2-5 indicates suggested content and themes for environmental studies in the high schools of Argentina. Note that centres for obtaining information and materials are designated in different parts of the country. Case Study 2-6 is a syllabus from the United Kingdom for an environmental studies course in the sixth form (16—18 years old). This is followed by Case Study 2-7, a California guide for the development of an inter-disciplinary environmental education curriculum from kindergarten through high school. Both the California (U.S.A.) and the Wiltshire (U.K.) case studies reflect the tendency to develop a separate course at the secondary level. Note that the Wiltshire syllabus includes the urban environment which is too frequently left out of environmental education programmes. (See Stranz, 1974, for a further discussion of the Wiltshire as well as the Hertfordshire syllabi.) The *Ekistics* model from California attempts a cognitive-affective schema in its conceptual framework.

The few case studies presented here scarcely scratch the surface of curriculum developments in environmental education on a world-wide basis. They have mainly served to introduce some organization alternatives. Case studies in Chapter 3, Method, and in other parts of this book give further ideas for curriculum design.

Content Focus
In the preceding chapter the Roth study identified some major concepts pertinent to environmental education. This chapter has indicated some goals and principles for environmental curriculum design. Examples of organization alternatives have been put forth. An important part of the process of curriculum revision is the formulation of objectives. Normally this takes place early in the planning process, but it may also be a part of evaluating a new curriculum either in the pilot stage or as a part of a continuing assessment.

A concise display of major areas of objectives is given in Case Study 2-8. The discussion focuses on behavioural objectives. A bias towards science education and biology is admitted, but the author calls for a balanced curriculum with varied activities and experiences providing the breadth and depth for developing individual sensitivity, enjoyment, appreciations, attitudes and values.

Perhaps the most essential part of curriculum design is the making of decisions relative to the content focus. This raises the question of how structured the curriculum should be (Bloom, 1971) but even educators who advocate a non-structured curriculum allow that the students need something to inquire about. Common structural forms are based on spatial, temporal and topical frameworks (Saveland, 1972). The spatial framework reflects expanding environments from the home to the state to the nation to the world. The temporal framework has a time base and usually starts with the distant past and works towards the present. The topical framework takes a variety of forms. It may be discipline-oriented and proceed from addition to subtraction to multiplication and division. It may be problem-oriented and range from inquiry into what is civilization (a humanistic study) to what is the chemical composition of a substance (a scientific study).

The content focus for environmental education drew the attention of the delegates to the first International Working Meeting on Environmental Education in the School Curriculum. The report of Working Group IV from this conference constitutes Case Study 2-9. What is advocated here is a sort of Magna Carta, a broad general framework setting forth the metes and bounds of an environmental curriculum at three stages. It is broad enough to permit a wide range of applications.

By using factors of the physical and social environment, this plan integrates content from many disciplines into a comprehensive core. The three stages, or levels, correspond to primary, middle and upper schools and thus take cognizance of the emerging middle-school movement. The primary stage, generally ages 5—10, concentrates upon observing, identifying and classifying into sets various factors of the environment. For instance, one of the first units of study could be that of ants. Reading research has indicated that in English a vowel and two consonants constitute the easiest words to read. Ant is such a word. Furthermore, ants are ubiquitous, they can be found in rural and urban environments. Children can count ant's legs and the parts of their bodies. They can discover different varieties, and the fact that ants have a means of communication. They can observe their food-gathering habits and their division of labour. They can use alliterative words like pants and plants to make up poems and stories. They may find that some ants, like fire ants, are an environmental problem, but, over all, ants are a significant part of the web of life. From ants, the study could proceed to other insects to meet the performance objectives under Plants and Animals, Stage I, on the chart.

The middle stage (ages 11—14) calls for perceiving patterns of environmental interrelationships at national and world-wide scales. The division of the world into continents, culture areas and biomes can be comprehended in the middle grades. For instance, Latin America can be identified on a map as a part of the world possessing certain characteristics. It can be noted that a rainforest occurs here and elsewhere in equatorial regions, but the rainforest is subject to incursion by population growth and development as roads are cut into the forest. The study of the Amazon rainforest would combine elements from the natural sciences, i.e. meteorology and biology, with elements from the social sciences, i.e. history, geography and economics. Observe how this study would fit the performance objectives under Stage II, especially the people category, in the chart.

At the upper stage (ages 14—17), students are better able to comprehend movements and issues, and thus this stage has an ethical focus. The Renaissance may, at first, appear to be a phenomena of the Western World having little to do with environmental education. However, most parts of the world felt some effect from the Renaissance movement in Europe and all have experienced a cultural reawakening at one time or another. The art and literature of such a movement tell how the environment was perceived and valued.

The performance objectives on the chart are those to be attained at the conclusion of a given stage. The attainment of these objectives seems to imply that the schools have a function in directing social change. It should be indicated here, however, that the curriculum in general (and this plan is no exception) reflects rather than moulds the social milieu.

The problems of the individuals who do not attain these performances are the same as those with any curriculum, except that for an environmental curriculum such individuals assume special importance. Hopefully, the environmental learning process, with its emphasis on involvement and field activity, would minimize the problem of rejection. As schools move toward the quarter system and other methods of greater flexibility in curriculum scheduling, competency-based instruction can come to the fore. The assumption here is that mastery learning is not only possible, but highly desirable (Block, 1972).

Prospects

We have previously noted that much environmental education has been introduced into the curriculum in an informal, unstructured way. Case studies in this chapter and elsewhere in the book are indicative of efforts to incorporate environmental education into authorized curricula. The inscrutable question, 'Where are we going?' remains always with us, but a few impactors can be recognized.

At the outset we must note that environmental problems are a public issue. As such, they receive considerable attention from the press, radio and television. In a sense, the media are doing part of the curriculum for us: more on this in Chapter 4. Therefore, a school function is to

Cartoon by Gene Basset. Winner of Editorial Category Award in the 1974 Population Cartoon Contest. Reproduced from *The New Era*, Vol. 56, No. 1, Jan./Feb., 1975. By permission of Scripps-Howard Newspapers

develop habits of evaluating the media to separate fact from fiction, and to recognize persuasion tactics.

No amount of exhortation will produce curricular change without concomitant development of materials. In fact, the availability of materials is somewhat a barometer of the extent to which a subject has been introduced into the curriculum, although there is a certain time-lag factor. Materials are also further discussed in Chapter 4.

Environmental education changes result from the communication of ideas. Conferences, workshops, courses and teachers' meetings are among the ways of communicating new ideas in education circles. Fortunately there are some conferences which inform the participants, get them involved, and thus generate further transmission of ideas. Suffice to say, teacher education is an important part of curricular change — more of this in Chapter 7.

During the autumn of 1968, the Swedish National Board of Education appointed a special committee on environmental education in the schools, called SMIL. This committee was given the task of revising the curricula and they adopted the following model (Forselius, 1971):

A model for curriculum development in environmental education

Planning
↓
Pilot study
↓
Feedback analysis
↓
Construction
↓
Extensive field trials — evaluation
↓
Production of teaching aids
↓
In-service education of teachers
↓
Established routine

Pilot studies and extensive field trials are unfortunately too frequently omitted in curricular revision. In practice pioneering schools try new methods which, if successful, are imitated by others who may learn of them by one means or another. Inevitably change depends on how receptive individual teachers are to innovation. Once attempted, an innovation will be repeated if the experience has been rewarding or satisfying.

34

Bibliography

Berman, Louise M., *New priorities in the Curriculum*, Charles E. Merrill, Columbus, Ohio, 1968, 241 pp.

Block, James H., 'Student Learning and the Setting of Mastery Performance Standards', *Educational Horizons*, Vol. 50, No. 4, Summer 1972, pp. 183—191.

Bloom, B. S., Hastings, T. M., and Madaus, G. F., *Handbook on formative and summative evaluation of student learning*, McGraw-Hill, New York, 1971.

Flanagan, John C., 'Education: How and For What', *American Psychologist*, Vol. 28, No. 7, July, 1973, pp. 551—556.

Forselius, Sten, *Environmental Education in the School Curriculum*, European Working Conference on Environmental Conservation Education, Paper 33—6, I.U.C.N. Moyes, 1971, p. 5.

Glaser, Robert, 'Educational Psychology and Education', *American Psychologist*, Vol. 28, No. 7, July, 1973, pp. 557—566.

Saveland, Robert N., 'As Universal as Mathematics', *The New Era Journal of World Education Fellowship*, Vol. 53, No. 8, Sept.—Oct. 1972, pp. 6—8.

Stranz, Walter, 'The Environmental Studies Debate', *BEE Bulletin of Environmental Education*, No. 36, April 1974, pp. 5—6.

Additional Reference

Wert, Jonathan M., Developing Environmental Education Curriculum Material, Tennessee Valley Authority, Knoxville, TN 37902, August 1974, 39 pp.

Case Study 2.1

Resolution (71) 14
(Adopted by the Ministers' Deputies on 30 June 1971)

On the Introduction of the Principles of Nature Conservation into Education

The Committee of Ministers,

Noting that man's influence on his natural environment is daily increasing;

Convinced that ecology is the scientific basis of a new attitude toward nature and of a rational management of natural resources;

Conscious of the fundamental importance of education which must provide the citizens of each country with the necessary elements to enable them to shoulder their responsibilities, including those relating to the preservation of their environment, with full knowledge of all the facts;

Having regard to Recommendation No. 65 adopted at the 31st Session of the International Conference on Public Education (Geneva, 1968) and the recommendations of the International Conference on the Scientific Basis for the Rational Use and Conservation of the Resources of the Biosphere (UNESCO, 1968);

Having due regard to the Declaration on the Management of the Natural Environment of Europe adopted by the European Conservation Conference (Strasbourg, 1970),

Decides to recommend that the governments of the member States;

1. introduce the principles of nature conservation and ecology into their educational programmes at all levels and in all appropriate disciplines;

2. take due account, when drawing up or revising their curricula, of the principles in appendix to this resolution relating to the need, in selecting the items for such curricula, to adapt them to the disclipline and educational level.

Appendix
Principles relating to the need, when selecting items for educational programmes, to adapt them to the discipline and educational level concerned

Education must provide each individual with those elements which he needs if he is to accept, with full knowledge of the facts, the responsibilities laid upon him, including those concerning the environment.

This part of his responsibility grows daily, in direct proportion to the ever growing influence of man upon the environment.

Ecology is the scientific basis of a new attitude towards nature and of a rational management of its resources. It is for this reason that ecology, together with its practical applications, grouped under the title 'Nature conservation', must appear in teaching programmes at all levels.

It would be presumptuous to wish to make fundamental changes in the educational structures and the school curricula in the near future, but as from now it is essential to study the means by which notions of nature conservation and of ecology may be inserted into the various traditional disciplines concerned.

These disciplines may be grouped as follows;

  (i) the social sciences;
  (ii) the natural sciences;
  (iii) the applied sciences.

As the child grows, so he must realize that man implants himself in nature (of which in fact he is part), that he transforms and exploits it. The problems which such actions bring forth can only be dealt with in a multidisciplinary context.

It is therefore desirable to tackle these problems by themes, which will be illuminated by the various disciplines under discussion, and adapted to the level of education concerned.

1. Nursery schools (kindergarten)
Respect for all forms of life.
Care for animals (food, drink, shelter, nesting-boxes etc.) and for plants.

2. Primary schools
A. *Study of the environment*
  (i) awaken interest in nature in general;
  (ii) study of surroundings; introduction;
  (*a*) to the interdependence of living creatures by the study of natural communities (forest pond, copse, mountain, beach etc.) and also of artificial communities (park, field, town etc.);
  (*b*) to the influence of man on nature and vice versa;
  (*c*) to the essential natural resources: water — air — soil — plants and animals.

B. *Civics* (ethical and religious instruction)
  (i) respect for life and all living things;
  (ii) the duties of young people, and particularly their behaviour towards nature.

Much time should be devoted to field studies, observation of the natural environment and practical conservation work.

3. Secondary schools

A. *Biology*

(i) basic principles of ecology:

— interdependence of living creatures and the physical environment;

— notions of the biosphere;

— trophic chains;

— energy flows;

— C, O_2, N_2, H_2O cycles (see geography (ii));

— ecological pyramids, population surges, natural selection, over-population,

— natural balances and their dynamics, disturbance of the natural balance, e.g. by the introduction of species;

— sequences, climates, ecosystems;

(ii) man's effect on the distribution of species;

(iii) the importance of protecting genetic assets;

(iv) the significance and importance of nature reserves and other protected areas;

(v) the effects of pesticides and other pollutants on the natural balance.

B. *Geography*

(i) notions of the biosphere (see biology);

(ii) the water cycle (see also physics);

(iii) land formation and evolution;

(iv) man's effect on the countryside: possibilities, limits, dangers, balance-sheet:

— study of some interesting development techniques (irrigation, drainage, afforestation, dry farming, game cropping, sea farming etc.),

— study of phenomena such as the various kinds of erosion, eutrophication, formation of deserts, over-grazing, salination etc.;

(v) distribution of natural resources throughout the world (see also economy):

— requirements and assets;

— renewable and non-renewable resources; their rational management;

(vi) regional planning, the need for it, examples.

C. *Chemistry*

(i) synthesis and decomposition, C, O_2, H_2 cycles (see also biology) but drawing attention to the chemical process of chlorophyl synthesis. The role of CO_2, $-CO_3$, $-HCO_3$ etc.;

(ii) study of pollution and the damage it does:

— air pollution: sprays, smokes, CO, $-SO_2$, $-H_2S$, $-O_3$, $-NO$, $-NO_2$, etc.;

— fresh water: phenols, detergents;

— seawater: oil;

— soil pollution.

D. *Physics*

  (i) the water cycle (see biology, geography and chemistry);

  (ii) air pollution: sprays (see chemistry);

  (iii) fresh water pollution: phenols and detergents (see chemistry);

  (iv) sea pollution; oil (see chemistry);

  (v) effect of radiation; radio-activity and radio-active wastes.

E. *History*

  (i) the main steps of man's history and his increasing mastery of nature — from the prehistoric tool to modern technical methods;

  (ii) disorders and wars following disturbances to the balance between man and his environment, mass human migrations;

  (iii) the decline of civilizations caused by wrongful use of natural resources, examples.

F. *Economy* (if this subject is not taught, the following items might be included in the geography curriculum)

  (i) wise and wrongful management of natural resources;

  (ii) world famine: origin, evolution of the situation, remedies, new sources of proteins etc.;

  (iii) economic effects of disturbances to the natural balance, e.g. by the introduction of unsuitable species.

G. *Man in society:* politics, civics, ethics, morals, religion

  (i) respect for life;

  (ii) respect for the property of one's fellow-man, the fruit of his labours;

  (iii) civic duties and responsibilities towards the environment;

  (iv) obligations of each man to his fellows and to future generations, international co-operation;

  (v) demography and the consequences of a population explosion, individual responsibility;

  (vi) behaviour in the countryside.

Case Study 2.2

Three Approaches to School Environmental Education as Consecutive Stages of Its Implementation (V. M. Galushin - S. Doraiswami)

At present no one doubts the necessity of introducing environmental education into the schools. Its basic principles and ideas are fairly well developed in essence. The urgent question is how to do it practically. For this purpose

(a) a comprehensive school curriculum for environmental education has to be developed;
(b) this curriculum should be suitable and, at the same time, acceptable in terms of space and duration within the over-all school time budget.

Various approaches to the solution of these problems have been proclaimed. They can be roughly grouped into three kinds of suggestions:

(1) Environmental topics may be dispersed through the entire curriculum by certain insertions in the syllabi of various disciplines.
(2) A specially designed nature conservancy unit may be a unit within the framework of one of the existing school subjects.
(3) An integrated course of environmental education(by a number of titles) may be offered as a separate discipline equal with other school subjects.

Each of the above approaches has its advantages and disadvantages; the general conclusion being that the more valuable and attractive proposal is the introduction of the entire environmental concept. However, this seems to be difficult for practical implementation within the school curricula. That is understandable enough in view of the already overstrained school time budget. We shall treat these three approaches as successive stages, rather than as alternatives, in the practical introduction of environmental education into the school curricula.

The first stage, which is the easiest to implement, should be the 'topics' approach. At present, one can hardly find school curricula without any environmental topics in biology, geography, and other syllabi. Therefore, we keep this somewhat out-moded recommendation mostly for the purpose of maintaining the sequence of stages.

In our view, this is the time to concentrate efforts on introducing the second stage, namely the unit approach in biology and geography curricula. Firstly, it is much easier under the existing circumstances to achieve a partial revision of those syllabi than to carry out an all-round reform of school curricula as a whole. Secondly, there are practically no biologists or geographers, including curriculum makers, who object to incorporation of environmental conservation into their subjects. Thirdly, this stage when preceded by the dispersion of environmental topics, provides a good opportunity to sum up this scattered knowledge into a coherent whole.

The most complete 'integrated' approach should be considered the third and final stage of implementing environmental education. We do not think that favourable circumstances for its immediate introduction into the school curriculum exist in many countries for the reasons mentioned above. This does not mean that the working out of an integrated curriculum for environmental education should be given up. On the contrary, such a syllabus should be ready for implementation as soon as circumstances allow.

Our favouring the unit approach reflects our own experience. In the course of developing a new science curriculum for Indian schools it was this approach which was chosen to introduce environmental education concepts. It is a natural follow up and is combined with the environmental topics in the courses of general science (primary school), biology, geography, chemistry, etc. In other words, the latter are crowned by a special chapter, 'Conservation of Nature', within the first part of the biology syllabus for the high secondary school (Class 9, ages 14—15). This chapter covers 16 periods or some 90 per cent of the class 9 biology curriculum. It contains the following main themes: 'vital importance of conservation of nature for the existence of life', 'management of natural resources in a rational way', 'conservation of air, water resources, and soil', 'the global role of the green cover', 'protection of wildlife', and 'national and international efforts for effective environmental conservation'.

Case Study 2.3

Work on and Problems in Education for a Sound Attitude toward Environment in
the Socialist Federal Republic of Yugoslavia
(Dusan B. Colic - Vladimir Djordjevic - Ratko Kevo — Slobodan Stajic)

Elementary School. The tasks relevant to nature conservancy were for the first time pointed out in the federal programme for elementary education made by the Yugoslav Education Council in 1969. Among the tasks here are those intended 'to help the pupil to understand how man came to know nature and how he developed his knowledge up to the contemporary science and technology'. As part of the other subject matter, particularly the natural sciences, the task is 'to develop pupil's love for nature interest in the study of nature, and the formation of habits for nature conservation'. This task has been implemented in the syllabi and curricula of all constituent republics.

Each republic has worked out the details of the syllabi according to its specific conditions. Thus the syllabus of Serbia already deals to some extent with nature conservancy education, as part of the subject teaching the fundamentals of nature and society (grades 1—3). For grade 1 the programme covers: care of the greenery, flowers, grassland, trees, and protection of birds and their nests. In grade 2 the pupils become familiar with wildlife in the local area, while in grade 3 the programme concentrates on the need for afforestation, forest and park management, protection, care, and feeding of animals in free nature.

The programme is fairly practical and well suited to psychophysical abilities of pupils 7—9 years old which can be regarded as sufficient for knowing the fundamentals of nature conservation education.

In grade 4 the subject 'air and water' allows teachers to speak about pollution and indispensable control. In the same grade, when teaching the subject 'man changes nature', the teacher can deal with the alteration of natural environment induced by man, in local or wider areas, and the consequences.

The subject for grade 5, 'man uses natural resources', contains a great many elements of nature conservation education. It is to be regretted, however, that the details of this programme are not worked out as yet, so that it is left to the teacher's skill how successful instruction in this field will be.

The greatest possibilities for nature conservation education in elementary schools are offered by the programme for grade 6 which deals with the living world as a whole. In grade 6 the pupils already know the fundamentals of nature, so that they are able to understand the more complex relationships in nature. The part of the programme which pertains to nature conservation in grade 6 specifies the following points: living environment as changed by man, control over the changes in nature, protection of the rare and endangered species of plants and animals, and protection of living habitats and ecosystems.

All biology teaching programs in Yugoslavia are intended to develop pupil's interest in nature conservation. Instructions for the implementation of these programmes in some republics (i.e., Serbia, Montenegro) suggest that the pupil's responsibility should be developed concerning the care for plant cover in the local area, particularly the protection of greenery, grassland, park trees, rare plants, and rare animals.

In Bosnia-Herzegovina, for example, which does not have nature conservation education as a separate subject, textbook authors on their own initiative dedicated special chapters on nature conservation in their books on the fundamentals of nature. This was highly appreciated by teachers and pupils alike.

Secondary Schools: Gymnasium. As early as 1960 ecology was introduced as a teaching subject in the syllabus for Gymnasiums. It includes a particular chapter on the conservation of nature. In most constituent republics grade 3 of both streams of this school (one teaching the social sciences and languages and the other natural sciences and mathematics) has on its programme a separate and complete course entitled, 'nature conservancy'. It covers these points: man's position in the biosphere, ecological changes in living nature, protection of rare or imperiled plant or animal species, protection of the imperiled sites and living communities, man's ecological control of the changes in nature. The official explanations of the curricula further suggest the following be taken notice of in teaching nature conservancy: the properties of the biosphere, changes induced by man in nature with special reference to the situation in each country, the interpretation of the idea of protecting individual territorial wholes, and the characteristics of the country's national parks and major natural preserves.

Surveys made by the institutions for the conservation of nature and for the training of teachers have shown that students are keenly interested in the subject of nature conservancy and even urge biology teachers to undertake common specific drives to protect nature in the local territory of their schools.

Secondary Schools: Vocational. On the basis of the Resolution on Education in the Socialist Federal Republic of Yugoslavia, and to the end of raising the level of general education, biology teaching as a particular subject was introduced in all types of secondary vocational schools as of the school year 1969—1970. The objectives of teaching this subject include 'acquainting the students with the problems of nature conservancy'.

Case Study 2.4

A 'Backyard' Curriculum Development

(Reproduced by permission of Science Teachers Association of Victoria from *Lab. Talk*, October, 1973)

Background

The freedom given to schools in Victoria, Australia in recent years to organize their own curricula up to 10th Grade has produced its crop of new ideas and materials so that, for example, there are now more general science 'courses' than one can comfortably fit on a large library shelf.

The Geelong College tried two of these (N.S.W. 'High School Science', and 'In Search of Science'), looked at others, and the settled down to do its own thing. This decision was made at the same time as sweeping changes in the middle school (9th and 10th Grade structure, which involved integrating the technical and academic streams at these levels, and co-ordinating all subjects more closely than before so that they were arranged into a core (of about 18 hours per week) and elective subjects (taking up about 6 hours). More 'conventional' subject categories pertain at Vth Form (11th Grade) level in both technical and academic divisions.

Structure and Teaching

The demands of this situation called for a searching consideration of what should be core aims and objectives, and what should be elective and related to the specific aims of each student. A chart showing the outline of this curriculum for 9th and 10th Grades is shown below, the two years being treated as one broad stage.

CORE SUBJECTS	ELECTIVES
Physical Science (4—5 hrs.)	Indonesian
Social Science (4 hrs.)	French
Mathematics (4—5 hrs.)	Latin
Fine Arts (3—4 hrs.)	Business Education
Physical Education (1 hr.)	Art
Guided Reading (1 hr.)	Woodwork
	Instumental Drawing
	Motor Mechanics
18—19 hrs. per week plus 8 hrs. homework	6 hrs. per week plus 2 hrs. homework

Notes

1. All boys, from both technical and academic streams, do the core subjects plus two of the electives. Boys who choose two foreign languages also take a multi-craft course at 9th Grade.

2. Physical Science includes units of Physics, Chemistry, Ecology, Meteorology, Plant and Human Physiology, Geology, Physical Geography, Agricultural Science, Genetics and Motor Engineering.

3. Social Science includes Expression, History, Economics, Sociology, Geography, Social Studies and Theology. The major emphasis is on assignment work.

4. Fine Arts include Art, Music and Literature.

5. Guided Reading: A list of suggestions is devised by the student and his tutor, in collaboration with the librarian. Generally, about twenty books are required to be read in a year, with one hour in class and 2½ hours homework being allocated for this each week.

6. Boys' choice of elective subjects is guided both by previous performance and differential aptitude test (D.A.T.) conducted at the start of the 9th Grade, or earlier.

In this system each of the two main core areas (Physical Science and Social Science) has a team of staff who prepare materials according to their specialized abilities, and many of whom teach these grades in the classroom. Where possible the author of a unit teaches it for at least one year. For Physical Science each grade is divided into four classes of about 25, at random (e.g. alphabetically), and one master takes the class for the whole year, using the prepared materials. In Social Science and Mathematics the grade is divided into tutorial groups of 18 boys, and each student is obliged to complete a set of assignments on various subjects, comprising core and elective materials. There is also provision for slower students temporarily to spend time with a remedial tutor instead of attending normal classes. In Fine Arts the grade is again divided into groups of 18, and each boy spends one term on each section of the curriculum. The emphasis is on practical creative work, and appreciation.

Teaching practice involved in such curriculum development is mostly centered on the enquiry method, where students are fed some information, and are stimulated to research questions further in laboratory, library and field. This can mean that students work at their own pace and gain a good deal more in the long run, after coping with their own inertia, frustrations, and often inadequate resources — all of which is more of a real-life situation than being served with pre-arranged conclusions.

Materials and Resources

For staff preparing the actual teaching materials for this sort of classroom practice there are very real problems, notably that of providing enough for the very able student whilst not causing the slow student to be left behind. A system of core material and electives in each unit has proved to be the best solution here. In addition, teachers' notes are often prepared for Physical Science units, outlining objectives and other useful information. A further development is a materials and resources guide for technical staff.

A unit thus consists of core assignments plus electives, each incorporating references or as much textual material as is necessary. Some Physical Science units are largely self-contained, others use a single paperback 'text' pertinent to that unit, others relate to class sets of texts (especially Mathematics), and others simply depend on library references. The school has had to install a multilith printing machine to cope with the great volume of material put into students' hands, and whilst the cost of this is not insignificant there are large savings on textbooks. Usually a unit will be run in one year, evaluated by the staff teaching it, and then re-written. Electives, if not also the core of a unit, often need updating each year.

In Physical Science a considerable strain has been put on laboratory facilities by the scheme in that for 8 classes in 9th and 10th Grade, 36 hours lab. time per week is required. The main factor determining large class sizes in physical sciences is simply the difficulty of further increasing this to 54 hours if they were split up as in the Social Science and Mathematics, though with the demands made upon the teacher/tutor this is increasingly proving to be necessary.

Assessment and Evaluation

An attempt is made to evaluate every aspect of the educational process, though different departments use different means. For assessment of cognitive skills Social Science has comprehensive report sheets which are filled in progressively through the two years by a student's tutors. Maths have a series of three objective tests and tutors' evaluation of an individual's performance in a similar fashion to Social Science. Physical Science uses objective (often multi-choice) tests for which marks are given, plus the checking of notes and assignment work.

In addition some quantitative measurement of attitudes to Physical Science has been undertaken through questionnaires filled in by 9th Grade students in 1971 and 1972. One thing to emerge from this was that there is no correlation between a teacher's subject specialty and his students favouring units in that discipline. This ties in with data from objective (cognitive) tests which show no correlation between a teacher's subject specialty and his students' performance in that area. Predictably 75—80% of students preferred the new type of course to the more conventional ones they had been accustomed to, and they found it 'completely different'.

Regarding approaches to new situations 60—70% preferred a demonstration of new apparatus followed by their own use of it to 'Reading notes and then using it' or 'Experimenting yourself and trying to get it to work alone'. This was supported by answers to 'If you were being taught about the function of the lungs would you prefer to: "read about them and have the teacher explain (6—8% demonstration and explanation, then dissect (76%), or simply dissect on own (3—4%)" '. This would seem to support a varied and balanced teaching method, rather than all didactic or all 'discovery' method.

Regarding grading or not within a year group, the 1971 group were evenly divided on this question, whereas in 1972 about 70% preferred the ungraded divisions. When the 1971 group were asked the same question at the end of their 10th Grade year (1972) 62% favoured the ungraded system. From some named returns it was evident that most of those preferring a graded arrangement were the faster students.

Staff were becoming sensitive about the quantity of course notes handed out, but about 70% felt that they had 'sufficient', about 15% in 1971 and 9% in 1972 felt there were 'far too many'. Certainly the new system does make considerable demands on a student's reading ability.

Evaluation of materials is also a concern of the new project. In Physical Science a staff member completing a unit is expected to fill in a detailed evaluation form which then provides important ideas towards a re-write. In addition a materials evaluation matrix has been prepared so that units being taught are assessed in relation to their objectives on a day to day basis.

Conclusion

It can be seen that the whole project is proceeding both to implement tried new ideas and to adjust and redesign these as it goes. The process is less perfect than any of its protagonists would like, but there are many signs that the general direction is correct and staff who are concerned with the educational theory and production of materials as well as classroom practice are necessarily limited in what they can achieve in a few years. However, whatever the frustrations all the faculties are agreed that the new project is showing its worth and has not, in fact, been over-ambitious even for a small school.

Case Study 2.5

Declaration of the Seminar on 'The Conservation of Renewable Resources in the
High School curricula' Vaquerias, Valle Hermoso, Cordoba, Oct., 1974

Contents

On the basis of the established objectives the following general themes
are recommended for a programme:

1. The ecosystem: structure, operation and regulation. Man transforms the ecosystem by means of work.

2. Matter and energy in the ecosystem. Speed of exchange and
transference of energy. Power usage and biogeochemical cycles. Usage
of power and elements (water, air, soil, flora and fauna) in agriculture,
forestry, animal production (cattle, fish, etc.) and industry.

3. Evolution and dynamics of renewable natural resources in the
Argentine (Latin America) as related to the unilateral usage of some
ecosystems and to the conditioned maintenance of others in different
types of production.

3.1 Industrial revolution. Internal and external dependency
relations. The Argentine (Latin America), as producer of raw material
and importer of manufactured goods. Present situation and the danger
of contaminating industries, especially those which are foreign to our
autonomous development. Ecological impact of these relationships.
Economical, political and social consequences at a national and regional
level:

(a) Regional inequalities: dual models of under-consumption and
opulence. Nutritional, sanitary, educational, etc. defficiencies.

(b) Internal migrations. Ejection of population and urban margin-
ation.

(c) Contamination and environmental deterioration due to industrialization and depredation.

(d) Ruling legislation. Environmental sanitation and conservation.

(e) Political transformations and processes of liberation and change.

Note:

(a) These subjects should be taught with progressive intensity in cycles
so that the student, on finishing the basic level, has been integrally
trained in renewable natural resources.

(b) They should be correlated with other curricular subjects.

(c) Till this correlation is obtained they could be integrally
developed in all the subjects.

48

The Argentine nation is carrying out an historical process tending towards the attainment of a nation in which justice prevails and sovereignty is predominant.

This process requires a planification based on a rational usage of the natural resources.

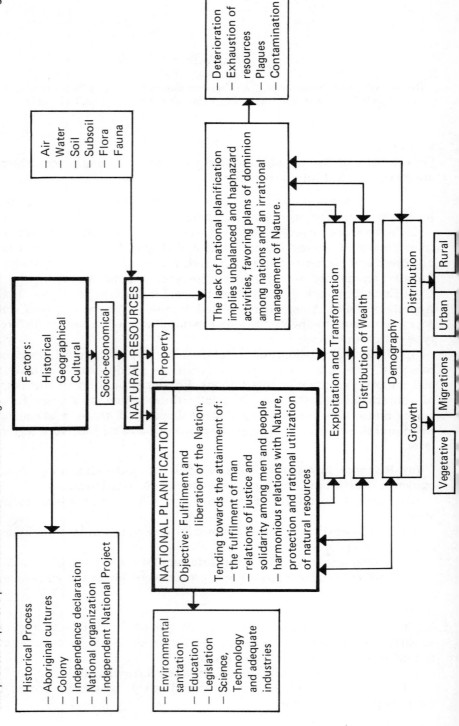

(d) So as to facilitate information or bibliography and material to cover the different items of the subjects the following consultation centres are assigned for the next 12 months: Secretaria de Estado de Recursos Naturales y Ambiente Humano de la Nación (25 de Mayo 459, Buenos Aires), Centro de Ecologia y Recursos Naturales Renovables de la Facultad de Ciencias Exactas, Fisicas y Naturales de la Universidad Nacional de Córdoba (Av. Velez Sarsfield 299, Córdoba); Servicio de Enseñanza Superior, Normal, Media y Técnica de Ministerio de Educación y Cultura de la Provincia de Santa Fé (Urquiza 1166 — 1er. Piso, Rosario, Santa Fé).

Case Study 2.6

Wiltshire County Council — Education Committee
Environmental Studies Syllabus at 'A' Level — Mode 2

(Reproduced by permission of The Associated Examining Board for the General
Certificate of Education)

1. The Aims of the Syllabus

The aim of this syllababus is to provide a quantitative and objective approach to the environment, and an appreciation of man's place within it, and his responsibility in the management of it. The approach is essentially practical and, wherever possible, studies carried out in the environment of the school should be closely integrated with laboratory work. The broad range of topics provides adequate scope for a diversity of interests amongst both teachers and pupils.

The approach throughout is basically ecological; with an emphasis on man's interdependence with other living organisms, and his utilization of energy resources. These two themes should form the basis of the various sections into which the syllabus is divided.

2. The Place of the Syllabus in the Sixth Form Curriculum.

This is a syllabus for a normal two-year 'A' level course which needs, and which we hope may involve team work and co-operation between a number of teachers of sixth form subjects: e.g. teachers of Biology, Geography and Rural Studies.

It is not anticipated that any particular subjects will need to have been studied to Ordinary Level in order to take the course at 'A' level, but certain subjects such as Biology and Geography, will clearly provide a useful basis for the more advanced study.

The overlap of content between this syllabus and already existing 'A' level Biology and Geography syllabuses should not be great enough to exclude Environmental Studies from being taken together with any existing subject.

This syllabus could form:

(a) One non-key 'A' level of the three 'A' levels studied by certain candidates for admission to some arts and science courses at Universities.
(b) An 'A' level to take with two other art or science subjects for non-University entrants. From its science content it could provide a more than usually acceptable science subject for art students and

from its sociological and human content it could be a useful, more liberal type of 'A' level area for science students to work in.

(c) A key 'A' level for students proceeding to study Environmental subjects at University or Training College.

3. The Form of the Examination. Mode 2.

(a) Two three-hour papers each to be marked out of 100. These two papers will each contain one compulsory question which will present various data to the candidates, invite them to study these data and to draw specific conclusions from them, and suggest any other lines of investigation which may lead to the further clarification of the problem involved, using any related knowledge that has been gathered in the course of study.

(b) A field-work study to be carried out and reported by the individual candidate, assessed by the teacher, and moderated by the board. It will be marked out of 50, and must be a specific independent investigation of some aspect of the syllabus approved by the board. Approval must be obtained by January 31st in the year preceding that of the examination.

THE SYLLABUS

Content	Teaching Notes
I The Local and National Environment (a) The physical environment. Outline of the main types of rocks (sedimentary, igneous and metamorphic) and conditions under which they are formed; derivation of present day landscapes — weathering and erosion. Soil structure and composition. Climatology in terms of air, sun and water; temperature, pressure, humidity, precipitation, winds, insolation, local and microclimates.	The emphasis will be on the local geology but against a background of the main features of the geology of the British Isles. Practical work should be carried out on the measurement of microclimates, preferably in connection with the study of the ecosystem in (B).
(b) The biotic environment. The interdependence of organisms. The principles of the ecosystem.	One example to be studied in detail, e.g. a pond, balanced aquarium, area of soil, orchard, lawn, hedgerow or rock garden.
Autotrophic nutrition. An outline of the physiology of the energy conversion process; and the anatomy of higher plants as related to the formation and transport of synthesised organic compounds.	
Heterotrophic nutrition. Adaptations of non-autotrophes to obtain, assimilate, absorb and convert synthesised food.	To include a comparative outline study of digestive systems in the main phyla.

Content	Teaching Notes

Respiration. The process of energy release via aerobic and anaerobic respiration.

Biochemical details not required.

Food chains and webs. Producers, consumers and decomposers. Food pyramids. The concept of biomass. Productivity.

To be studied by personal observation wherever possible. These principles should be extended to cover the specific crop or farm animal studied in Section II.

The balance of nature seen in terms of plant-animal relationships and energetics. Conservation of natural resources and what is involved in achieving it.

Useful brief references could be made to the work of bodies such as the Natural Environment Research Council, National Trust and the County Naturalists Trusts.

(c) The structure of populations judged in terms of size, age and geographical distribution. Methods of population control. The problem in man compared with e.g. control of brood size in birds. Population dynamics. Changes in population density treated experimentally.

Practical work should be carried out with organisms such as yeast, Tribolium or Drosophila. Population curves should be plotted and the effect of limiting environmental influences, including density dependant factors, studied.

The local human population: age distribution, occupations, social organisations, local use of land.

This information should be drawn from the Local Registrar's Abstracts of Statistics. 'Local' to mean the area covered by the appropriate Urban or District Council.

(d) *Energy*. This section is fundamental to the whole syllabus, as it is intended that man's relationship with his environment should be studied basically in terms of energy resources and energy flows. The subject should be considered quantitatively as far as possible.

(i) *Energy resources*. Solar radiation. Nuclear energy. Hydroelectric power. Fossil fuels, coal, oil and gas.

The present uses of these forms of energy. Methods by which they are converted for use by man. The limits of these resources including an appreciation of the limited stocks of non-renewable sources.

(ii) *Transfers*. Energy flow systems as the basis of life in plant and animal communities.

Geomorphological changes, meteorology, hydrology, and the nutrition of living organisms should all be treated as examples.

Content	Teaching Notes

II Man's Management of his Environment
(A) *To produce Crops and Livestock.*
Two examples of production, one from each of the groups listed below, are to be studied in detail.

Group 1
 (i) Fruit tree growing.
 (ii) Soft fruit growing.
 (iii) Glasshouse production.
 (iv) Cereal production.
 (v) Fodder crops.
 (vi) Timber production.

Group 2
 (i) Beef production.
 (ii) Milk production.
 (iii) Sheep production.
 (iv) Pig production.
 (v) Poultry production.

General factors affecting productivity should be considered, such as physical environment, relief, climate, mechanisation, and economic factors. The study of the individual crop must be an ecological approach based on energy flow systems. Thus each crop will have an energy input and output, with wastages along the way due to diseases and parasites. Conversion ratios are important here and each crop should be considered not in isolation, but in relation to the energy and land requirements needed to support it, and to the life systems supported by it.

The following aspects of production should be studied where relevant:

(a) Selection of cultivars or breeds. Genetic history where known.
(b) Methods of propagation or stock breeding.
(c) Controlled environments. Modern housing methods. Advantages and disadvantages.
(d) Feeding: materials used and their production; conversion factors and costing.
(e) Marketing of products; quality controls; subsidies; stages involved before product reaches consumer.
(f) Maintenance of stock health, to include a study of one disease and one pest, their economic importance and control.

Questions on this section will be asked in such a way that they may be answered by reference to any of the examples studied.

(B) *To Produce a Setting to Live In.*
Human ecology must be the underlying theme of this section. Land use is an important secondary theme, bearing in mind the limited and ever-reducing land resources available. The conflict between economics and aesthetics must be emphasised.

(i) Planning. Fields where planning is important; land use; the balancing of demands for land; agriculture, industry, urban development, leisure, communications (new roads, airports, etc.). Town and country planning (1946 and subsequent Acts).

Development and construction of M4 Motorway and its effect on local population and its way of life. Consideration of advantages and disadvantages of the sites suggested for the new London Airport. The main provision of these Acts to be known.

Content	Teaching Notes
Urbanization. Definition of a city; morphology of a city; central business district, suburbs (industrial and residential).	The morphology of a specific city to be studied. The significant experiments which have been carried out on the behaviour of mice and rats under conditions of overcrowding and other stresses should be studied and fully appreciated.
Urban expansion. Causes: effects on the surrounding countryside; effects on communication, especially commuter communications. Means of managing urban expansion; green belt policies, expanded towns, new towns, overspill population. Industrial estates (trading estates). Location of Industry. Factors operating in free economy leading to independent location. Reasons for, means of, and effect of government intervention in independent siting. Development areas. Pros and cons of artificially sustaining economically weak areas.	A specific case of urban expansion to be studied. A general study of industrial estates to be based on a local example. Distinction to be made between innately weak and declining economic areas.
(ii) Communications. Early importance of railways, especially electric railways (suburban train and underground train).	Correlation between rail network and the location of industrial centres.
Impact of internal combustion engine; motor bus, private car, commercial vehicles. Effect of towns, suburbanisation. Relative importance of roads and railways. Effect on industrial location and mobility of people, commuting, recreation.	A traffic census should be carried out as part of the practical work to study local transport patterns. The development of container transport.
(iii) Water. Present sources of supply. Increase in consumption due to: growth of population, changed social habits, increased industrial demands. Necessity for water conservation. Reconciliation with other desirable ends; landscape amenity, freedom from pollution, recreation, effect on community. Future water supplies from barrages and desalination.	Visits should be made to the local waterworks. For example, Water Parks.
Sections (iv) and (v) are concerned with the evaluation and amelioration of the effects of man's activities and of technology upon the environment.	The field investigations under (iv) and (v) should form a core of study in these sections of the syllabus.

Content

Teaching Notes

(iv) Waste disposal. A study of the methods and problems of disposal of waste products from the home, industry, mining, road building and armaments, slag heaps, tips and rubbish disposal, derelict canals, quarries, gravel pits, oil, air pollution, noise and radioactivity.

Practical projects and investigations should be carried out on the recolonisation and reclamation of e.g. a rubbish heap, or oil polluted area of ground.

A study of the dangers arising from various forms of pollution, and the legislation and other steps taken to remedy these.

For example, Clean Air Acts.

(v) Improvement. The reclamation and improvement of the environment. A study of either: The provision of parks and ornamental gardens including (a) problems associated with their establishment and maintenance, (b) their design and the selection of suitable plants for them, (c) provision within parks of recreational facilities for all age-groups.

The selection and management of suitable stocks on genetic and ecological grounds and general study of the technology of amenity plant production (to include chemical treatments).

Visits should be made to parks' departments and horticultural research establishments.

Or: The reclamation of a derelict area for recreational use including (a) the local need for such an area and the potential recreational value of the area to be reclaimed, (b) the methods to be employed in the reclamation, (c) the size of the operation involved. Cost. Relation of cost to ultimate value. Future sources of income from the reclaimed area, (d) the agencies involved in the reclamation: national and local government, voluntary bodies, division of labour and cost, if more than one is involved.

Case Study 2.7

Ekistics: A Guide to the Development of an Interdisciplinary Environmental
Education Curriculum (Rudolph J. H. Shafer, Director and Coordinator)

Education is an art-science concerned with the acquisition of knowledge and with the ability to consolidate knowledge which is yet to be discovered. To increase knowledge and to encompass the understanding and wisdom necessary for the wise conduct of life are both the aim and content of education.

When seen in this broader context, education about the environment takes on new dimensions and complexities, and the traditional terminology used to describe such a study appears inadequate. The authors propose the use of the term *ekistics*, which is defined as that field of study, that area of knowledge, and those concepts and values through which man recognizes his interdependence with the environment as well as his responsibility for maintaining a culture that will sustain a healthy and sanative environment.

The discipline of ekistics, which delineates a host of experiences and a life-style as well, is now of consummate significance in the education of man and his young.

Ekistics is defined in the *World Book Dictionary*, 1970 edition, as the study of the ecology of human beings in settlements or communities. The word is often associated with Constantine Doxiadis, a city planner and president of the Institute for the Study of Ekistics in Athens, Greece, but he does not claim to have originated the term. The Athens Center of Ekistics was established in 1963 to further research and to foster international cooperation in all fields related to the science of human settlements.

Cognitive Frameworks and Instructed Learning

A cognitive framework can be developed to give education an intellectual discipline; that is, a network of inferences or relationships that can give structure to a curriculum. Further, the affective options that determine decisions are inseparable from the cognitive-affective schemes. To learn structure is to understand the relationships of objects and events to each other. The interrelatedness of a community of discourse (such as ekistics) can be demonstrated; that is, knowledge can be disciplined so that the method by which further knowledge is acquired has discipline.

A discipline is acquired through disciplined study. The modes of a discipline, as a study, are never haphazard. The student acquires the disciplines or the constructs of ekistics and skills through probing, investigation, and inquiry. This simply means that the student must expend energy in learning. He should not be robbed of the right to bend his own efforts to uncover the concept nor of the 'pain' or effort necessary to discover the concept. The teacher's art is expended in preparing the learning situation in which the investigating occurs.

Early education in ekistics can be based on a structure which is sound because it is built on concepts and values; that is, the elements of the structure are related and relevant. Those who will conserve need grounding in the full scheme of man's past, not in the parochial specifics of conservation or preservation of land or water as practiced in an earlier, agricultural economy. Ekistics is relevant to modern life and to the problems and successes of the future. Furthermore, the structure of concepts gives meaning to experiences because the constructs pervade the school experience; that is, the curricular structure in which the experiences occur. This meaning is not achieved when unrelated bits and pieces are thrown together in a period of time through a sequence of topics that are unrelated in structure.

All data from investigations in curriculum and instruction and in teaching and learning indicate that a study that affects life and living should pervade life and living. The concepts and values that pervade ekistics also pervade growth. Work in ekistics, therefore, should be a part of the elementary, junior high school, and high school years.

Elementary Years

The conceptual pathways can be laid in the primary or intermediate years. Results of investigations in the science, social sciences, and humanities have indicated that children in these years are able to probe the sinews of major concepts. Although the point at which the concept of total environmental interdependence is developed in the child will vary from individual to individual, it will occur for most during the intermediate years. Without the basic probes, it will probably not occur as early as the primary years.

Intermediate Years

In the intermediate and junior high school years, the curriculum should include out-of-door activities.

In the intermediate years, a concentrated experience in the out-of-doors is recommended. A natural environment should be selected that is dominated by plants and animals growing in a verifiable, ecological relationship that has not been seriously disturbed by man. Analyses and syntheses in the field are thus possible. This might constitute an extended camping experience or field trip.

In the junior high school years, the students might make a concentrated study of a town or city for the purpose of observing relationships in such environments. Analyses and syntheses of problems in this selected field are thus possible.

High School Years

In the senior high school, a full-year course in ekistics should be made available to all students. The study would span many fields including the sciences, social sciences, and humanities. The course might be conducted by one teacher or a team of teachers.

The cognitive-affective constructs (concepts and values) that make

A CONCEPTUAL FRAMEWORK IN EKISTICS FOR KINDERGARTEN THROUGH GRADE SIX

Level 6. Man is the prime agent of change of the natural environment.	Level 6. Man modifies the environment in order to utilize his resources and to increase them.	Level 6. Men recreate their environment.
Level 5. The environment is and has been in constant change.	Level 5. Social aims determine the utilization of resources.	Level 5. Men create objects, events, and behaviors that nurture their images of beauty and order.
Level 4. Life converts matter and energy into characteristic species form.	Level 4. Men interact to utilize the world's available resources.	Level 4. Cultures are characterized by their special ways of reacting to the environment.
Level 3. Life and environment interchange matter and energy.	Level 3. Men utilize the environment to secure their needs.	Level 3. Men, responding to special environments, create objects and events symbolic of their interaction.
Level 2. There are different environments, each with characteristic features and life.	Level 2. Men develop different modes of adaptation to life in different environments.	Level 2. Men seek out objects, events, and behaviors symbolic of beauty.
Level 1. In any environment, living things have similar needs.	Level 1. Men live in different environments.	Level 1. Men interact mentally and emotionally to the objects and events in their environment.
Cognitive-Affective Scheme	**Cognitive-Affective Scheme**	**Cognitive-Affective Scheme**
Man is interdependent with his natural and physical environment.	*Man's social behavior is basic to maintaining, altering, adapting, or destroying the environment.*	*Man utilizes his symbolic and oral traditions to maintain or alter the environment.*
Conceptual Pathway A	**Conceptual Pathway B**	**Conceptual Pathway C**
Interpendence — In Interchange of Matter and Energy	Interdependence — In Social Interaction	Interdependence — In Cultural Components and Forms
SCIENCES	**SOCIAL SCIENCES**	**HUMANITIES**

up the framework of ekistics are presented on these pages. They are plotted as conceptual pathways from experience in the first through sixth levels and in junior and senior high schools.

The term level is not interchangeable with grade. Level indicates a level of maturity, experience, and understanding. In certain schools, children in grade one might be engaged in studies fitting a Level 2 concept; in others, children in grade four might be engaged in experiences fitting study of a Level 2 concept. The segmentation of the concepts is, for the sake of convenience, structured for the curriculum planners who must orchestrate the learning experiences throughout the elementary school years.

A Conceptual Framework in Ekistics for the Junior High School

Each cognitive-affective scheme embraces a unit of work within four areas of the curriculum: (1) sciences; (2) social sciences; (3) humanities; and (4) health. The work involves verbal, mathematical and artistic skills. The appropriate placement of each unit depends, of course, on the curricular planning of the school.

Cognitive-Affective Scheme I. Societies perceive environmental issues of their time on the basis of past experience.

Cognitive-Affective Scheme II. The interaction of the culture with available technology determines the nature of the environment, which is planned and developed.

Cognitive-Affective Scheme III. Social issues and decisions alter the environment.

Cognitive-Affective Scheme IV. Social issues and decisions determine the utilization of all resources.

A Conceptual Framework in Ekistics for the High School

Cognitive-Affective Scheme I. In any given environment, organisms are linked within an ecosystem.

Cognitive-Affective Scheme II. Issues and decisions affecting the world ecosystem reflect the pressure of population upon resources.

Cognitive-Affective Scheme III. Wise utilization of the environment is dependent on the organization of shortage.

Cognitive-Affective Scheme IV. The concepts and values man accepts as guides to his future behavior determine the quality of his life, if not his survival.

Case Study 2.8

Environmental Education in the K-12 Span (Balzer)

(From *Environmental Education: A Sourcebook* edited by Cornelius J. Troost & Harold Altman, Wiley, 1972, pp. 242—249. Originally from *The American Biology Teacher*, April, 1971. Reproduced by permission of the National Association of Biology Teachers)

The Need for Objectives
If environmental education is to become effective in changing behavior, objectives with behavioral foci will have to be developed. Curriculum development must then proceed in a manner compatible with these objectives, incorporating instructional strategies which develop behavioral changes. It appears, then, that environmental education must be an attempt to alter the behaviors of modern man by persuasion. There may be differences of opinion regarding the form this persuasion should take. Perhaps one individual will be persuaded on the basis of individual inquiry; perhaps another is persuaded on the basis of appreciations developed in contrasting environments. In any case, the individual is to be persuaded to behave in a manner less detrimental to and more in harmony with, the environment than the past behaviors of modern man have been. We might expect these behaviors to be expressed in at least two forms: (i) behaviors implying concern about the effects of personal environmental destruction; and (ii) behaviors implying concern about the environmental destruction caused by others. Thus environmental education must be that which facilitates the achievement of such behaviors. As a science educator, I would say that such education should also be scientifically legitimate.

As those who have been involved in curriculum development can recognize, the specific behavioral objectives of environmental education will be very numerous. Behavior that is in harmony with the environment has many facets. Some of the areas of concern and behaviors are discussed in the next section.

Areas of Objectives
In Figure 1 are shown some of the major areas of interest to the biology educator, in which behavioral objectives might be specified in environmental education. The activities and experiences of environmental education would constitute the volume of the grid and a given experience (visualized as being *within* the box) would normally have components in each of the three dimensions. In some cases, attitudes might be more heavily emphasized and in other cases one of the other

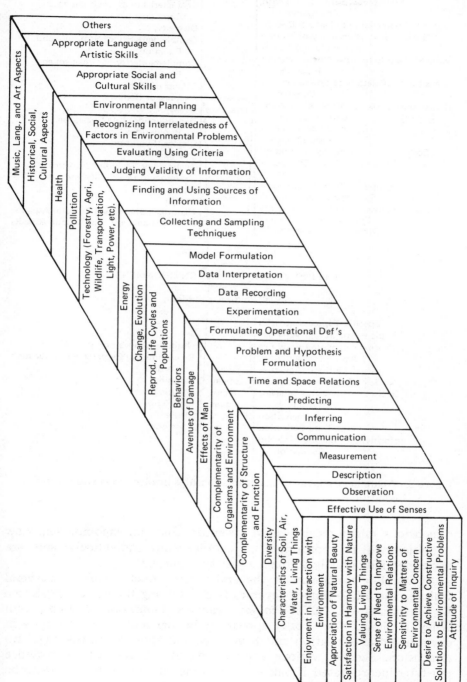

Figure 1. Grid suggesting some major areas of objectives in environmental education

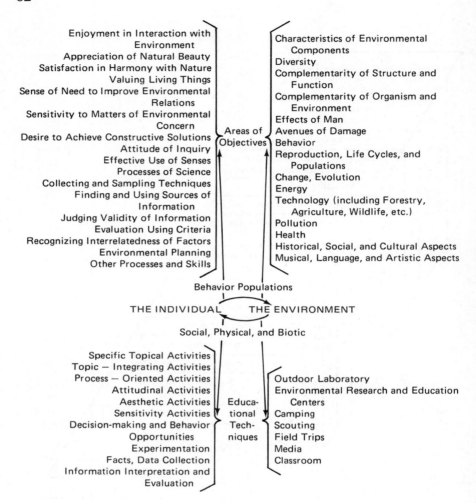

Figure 2. Preliminary scheme of major relationships involved in environmental education

dimensions might receive more attention. Such an encompassing view of objectives is appropriate if people learn individually and are persuaded individually through a variety of means.

A complete discussion of the grid is not possible here, but several features should be noted. Several of the unifying themes of BSCS (see E. Klinckman, ed., 1970: *Biology Teachers' Handbook*, 2nd ed., John Wiley & Sons, New York) appear to be particularly appropriate in environmental education and have been incorporated in the cognitive dimension. Second, various applications of our scientific knowledge must be incorporated if values concerning the environment are to be addressed, so technology is included in the cognitive dimension. Third, if we have the kind of faith in scientific inquiry that we usually claim to have, inquiry should be a major method used. Thus, various processes of science have been incorporated, including those of the process approach (see A. Livermore, 1964: 'The process approach of the AAAS Commission on Science Education', *Journal of Research in Science Teaching* 11: 271—282).

Certainly the grid of Figure 1 should not be seen as complete or final. The major emphasis here is on science, with various other curriculum areas only mentioned. As our understanding of environmental education develops, additions, deletions, or other modifications will be necessary. The point is that if the major behavioral outcomes described in the previous section are to be realized, decisions will need to be made regarding emphasis upon at least these three dimensions in the educational experience. Furthermore, activities considered should be analyzed to ascertain their strengths in these dimensions and to avoid a curriculum heavily imbalanced with respect to the dimensions.

Figure 2 is an attempt to illustrate some of the major relationships of environmental education. At the center of the scheme are the individual and the environment, which interact as indicated. Associated with the individual are numerous areas of objectives within which behavioral examples can be specified. Also associated with the individual are the various types of activities in which he will be participating, thus gaining experience in the performance of the types of behaviors being specified. Associated with the environment are various areas of information with which the student will have experiences and in which cognitive behavioral objectives may be specified. Also associated with the environment are examples of educational techniques in terms of environmental setting. Specific behavioral objectives may also require behaviors integrating these two groups of objectives. The experiences themselves occur in an integrated manner.

Case Study 2.9

Report of Working Group IV International Working Meeting on Environmental Education in the School Curriculum (S.Doraiswami - M. Baibas - R. Saveland - H. Wals)

A. Purpose: To formulate content objectives in environmental education for the total curriculum.

B. Scope: For purposes of organization, the curriculum was divided into three stages:

Stage I   Primary   approximately ages 5—10
Stage II   Middle   approximately ages 11—14
Stage III   Secondary   approximately ages 14—17

The committee recognized that these stages will not conform to practices in many localities, but adaptations can be readily made. This particular plan reflects emerging interest in the middle school, and takes into account the research in educational psychology by Piaget, Bruner, Gagne, and others.

The pre-primary stage was recognized as especially important in the educational pattern. The discussion revealed that this stage is not existing in many localities. In view of this and the fact that time was limited, this stage was omitted from the deliberations.

At each stage it is significant to keep in mind the sequential development of concepts whereby understandings of one stage are built upon previous experiences. In addition to the vertical integration of the curriculum, it is important to plan horizontal integration in order to achieve a trans-disciplinary approach.

C. Major Focus of Each Stage:

Recognizing the developmental process in learning, a major focus was selected for each stage reflecting the over-all objectives of the program at the three levels as follows:

Stage I
Building basic vocabularies and skills leading to an appreciation and awareness of the varieties and similarities in the environment.

Stage II
Emerging patterns and interrelationships of environmental features on local, national and world scales, concentrating on conservation and use. During this stage, particular attention is to be given to case studies illustrating representative man—environment problems.

Stage III

Increasing perception of changes through time with particular reference to in-depth studies of environmental and social problems; in short, developing an environmental ethic.

D. Content

In order to give an indication of the content and objectives of an environmentally oriented curriculum, a chart was prepared. It was agreed that while serving somewhat as a model for a trans-disciplinary, developmental program in environmental education, the chart could be adapted to different national and local situations in a variety of ways.*

The vertical component of the chart is the three curricular stages indicated previously. The horizontal component consists of the various major factors of the natural and cultural environment, rather than traditional subject headings.

The statements given under the headings at each level not only give an indication of content to be interwoven into instruction, but also suggests aims and objectives in furthering environmental education throughout the curriculum. The statements constitute performance objectives to be attained by students who have completed a stage in environmental education.

*The chart has been the subject for further discussion and elaboration by different national groups. The version which follows is from the Dutch journal, *Mens en natuur*, 22e jaargang no. 1 — maart 1971, pp. 12—13. An expanded list of objectives based on the chart is contained in the 'Recommendations regarding secondary school curriculum', pp. 14—23, *Final Report*, European Working Conference on Environmental Conservation Education — Rüschlikon, I.U.C.N., 1972.

stage I	stage II	stage III
area and location		
Experiences basic orientation within the local and national environments. Perceives the earth as the home of man. Observes how man uses and influences the environment.	Perceives the earth as of great magnitude but shrinking in terms of time, distance, and limits of resources. Knows the continuous interaction of man and biosphere.	Supports planning and research on wise land use and landscape management while opposing indiscriminate encroachment on open space.
atmosphere and cosmos		
Can describe and measure climatic factors in the local environment. Recognizes the role of the atmosphere in the life of plants and animals (special storms, evaporation and precipitation and fire).	Can identify and explain the major climate patterns of the world and relate these to vegetative patterns of the earth and economic activities of man. Observes the man-induced climate variations in a local area, noting air pollution and its effects.	Analyses and contributes to decisions affecting the quality of the atmosphere.
landforms, soils and minerals		
Knows that soil is dynamic: (a) it forms (b) it contains living things and supports plant growth (c) it erodes Can identify different kinds of landforms. Sees the interaction between landforms and living things.	Can point out on a map the general arrangement of landforms in his country and the world. Can identify various mineral and energy resources and demonstrate the uneven distribution.	Knows how man accelerates processes of degradation and takes steps to ameliorate these conditions (strip mining, earth moving and sedimentation).
plants and animals		
Knows from firsthand experiences various kinds of plants and animals in their own environment. Recognized interdependence among soil, atmosphere, plants (producers), animals and man (consumers).	Can identify and explain a biological community in relation with its environment. Has a notion of the food chain and ecological balance. Recognizes the main types of biological communities and the impact of man on them, is aware of endangered species, their importance and measures for their conservation.	Acts to create and preserve conditions under which ecologically balanced ecosystems can evolve.
water		
Knows the necessity of water for life and its importance as a natural resource.	Knows the water cycle and the various stages in the evolution of streams, is familar with the distribution of water on the earth and the general circulation pattern of ocean currents. Has an idea of the influence of water in the distribution of biological communities and how the distribution can be disturbed by pollution.	Analyses and contributes to the decisions affecting the availability and quality of water.

stage I	stage II	stage III

people

Recognizes the varieties and similarities among people. Knows how people live in and use different environments. Learns the interrelationships between beliefs and rituals and environment.	Sees population movements and settlement patterns as means by which cultural groups choose their environments. Discovers how people have used the same land in different ways at different times.	Uses data to interpret trends in population growth and distribution in relation to quality of life.

social organization

Recognizes ways in which people organize themselves. Learns individual and group responsibility concerning environment.	Observes the relationships between political and natural boundaries. Sees the state as an agency for working on environmental problems. Recognizes international co-operation as a means of solving environmental problems.	Acts to alleviate environmental problems through laws, public policy, and action programs.

economics

Relates food, clothing and shelter needs to available resources. Finds that specialization of labor increases efficiency.	Observes patterns in organizing resources with an emphasis on their rational use. (Agriculture and grazing, forestry and fishing, mining and manufacturing, transportation and communication).	Works toward domestic and international solutions of environmental problems related to nutrition, poverty, transportation, waste disposal, source and distribution of energy resources.

aesthetics, ethics, language

Builds a basic vocabulary of environmental terms. Names and classifies plants, animals, water features, soils, minerals. Acquires basic skills in using visual arts and music to express feeling for the environment in an elementary way.	Uses visual art, music and dance, drama, language and photography to describe and interpret various environments. Appreciates how great artists and writers have perceived their environments.	Has personal attitudes and habits reflecting a caretaker responsibility toward environment and communicates this feeling to others.

3
Method

ROBERT SAVELAND

Customary Procedures

The methods used in environmental education are also those used in other types of instruction. That is to say, there are no mysteries about methods in environmental education. However, some methods require special adaptation when applied to environmental education, and certain strategies, such as the field-study trip and community studies, are considered essential in environmental teaching. This chapter will seek to demonstrate some of these essential adaptations.

Traditionally, the field of geography has had an environmental concern, or focus. Therefore, it could be anticipated that some of the methods of geography would have a carry-over value into environmental education. Morgan (1971) and others have indicated that geography has not always lived up to its expectations in this regard. An example of the alteration of existing courses to accomodate environmental content and methods is given in Case Study 3.1. In this German experience, the inter-disciplinary primary programme indicates more student involvement than does the reorganized high school geography course. However, at the high school level, students could be expected to deal with higher levels of abstractions.

One of the dilemmas faced by teachers in environmental education is the great emphasis on learning by doing while much time is actually spent in classroom teaching situations. Real-life situations are motivating factors, but abstractions must also be considered. In the German experience in Case Study 3.1, note the reference to the primary activity of photographing factory chimneys polluting the air. This teaching strategy is one of those adopted as a result of environment emphases. At the secondary level, a comparison of smog problems in Los Angeles, London and the Ruhr illustrates the different scales at which environmental education operates. Presumably this comparison would lead to abstracting some general ideas as to what can be done about these conditions by means of government and technology. The point is made by Morgan (1973);

> The realities of environmental conflicts are all around us, the
> ability to deal with these conceptually is of vital importance. It

involves a training in the ability to sort the wheat from the chaff. This surely is the work of the classroom.

Mathematics is also a subject which deals with reality and abstractions. The implications of this subject for environmental education have not been so widely recognized. For this reason, examples from mathematics were used in illustrating the 'strand approach' in Case Study 3.2. The five strands are 'constants' representing a logical sequence of learning from the inventory stage (variety and similarity) through the action stage (interrelation and interdependence) to the stage requiring continuous adjustments and modification (adaptation and evolution). The strands can be applied to a variety of subjects in whatever combination suits the particular situation. As presented in Case Study 3.2, the method used is principally that of open-ended questions leading to student discussions. Although the questions often require further extensive and intensive investigations, i.e. 'What percentage of your city has been adopted for use by the automobile?' (Note that this is a geography as well as a mathematics question.)

An International Meeting of Experts on the U.N.E.S.C.O. Associated Schools Project in Quebec, Canada, raised the following questions about methods in environmental education (U.N.E.S.C.O., 1973a):

> Assuming that any attempt to isolate environmental education as a single subject would tend to limit its content and effect, what are examples of interdisciplinary or team teaching approaches? What are the problems in adopting these methods? Are there other methods which have proved motivating for students? (p. 5)

Case Study 3.3 sets out to give an example of such a team approach. Note that this case study also illustrates the process of moving from inventory (observations) to action activities involving analysis. This case study further reinforces the idea of the different scales at which the environment can be perceived. In this case, the spatial scale levels are correlated with pupils' comprehension and age levels. It is interesting to note how this method apportions responsibility for certain topics among the teachers of the various subject areas. As such, it is a structured approach which the author maintains is necessary to avoid 'a rag-bag of fragments which never add up to anything in the child's mind'.

The textbook gives evidence that there is a high correlation between method and materials. In fact, in education one frequently speaks of the 'textbook method'. In recent years the textbook has been frequently maligned as being dull, out-of-date, not meeting individual needs, etc. It has not generally been recognized that a textbook can be (i) an organizing core, (ii) a data base, (iii) a simulation device and (iv) a mode of inquiry (Saveland, 1971).

In order to demonstrate new techniques of environmental education with old forms of instruction, namely the textbook and Socratic dialogue, Case Study 3.4 is included. The section chosen is a part of an Instructor's Guide to a paperback for student use. The book reproduces an article from *Newsweek* magazine telling about a law in the state of Delaware that would prohibit the further establishment of industry along the state's shoreline on Delaware Bay and the Atlantic Ocean.

The Socratic dialogue which is suggested becomes rather emotionally charged as the teacher challenges the student by advocating a counter position. Not all students, even at the secondary level, are prepared to handle such situations and, as the guide suggests, the teacher switches to another student when one has 'had enough'. Of course, the fact that the teacher is the power figure in the scene can lead to a certain dominance and imposition of views. Presumably in many cases it would be the ringing of the classroom bell which would signal that the boxing round was over.

Particularly note in Case Study 3.4 the emphasis on value issues. The questions are framed so that contrasting values are placed in juxta-position. Students can see that the resolution of environmental issues will require certain trade-offs, which in the strand approach of Case Study 3.2 is called 'adaptation'.

Beyond the Classroom

Some teachers take their classes on field trips on a regular basis. Others have never taken a class outside and might find such a prospect threatening. In tropical countries the distinction of being indoors or outdoors is lessened, and it might be better to speak of being 'under roof'. In any event, outdoor educations is not new. In fact, it is an organized movement of some standing in education.

The research team of the International Meeting of Experts on the U.N.E.S.C.O. Associated Schools Project stated the policy implications for this educational alternative as follows: (U.N.E.S.C.O., 1973b)

> To foster comprehension of complex wholes and of specific in total content, the effective environment must be extended outside the traditional classroom to include the entire life space of the student — the out-of-doors, the inner city, the mass media, etc. In addition, the attitudinal climate needs to be one that frees the student emotionally to struggle with problems for which there are not easy and specific solutions, to adjust to or cope with un-certainties, and to anticipate contingencies. (p. 5)

As in other methods, the activity of moving outside the classroom depends on its objectives. In addition to contributing to a more open and free emotional climate, an obvious purpose is that of data gather-ing. In this regard, Emery, Davey and Milne (1974) make a significant distinction between field teaching and field work:

> ... field teaching, alone, is insufficient if students are to be affected by the environment in which they have been placed. If students are given the opportunity to 'feel' their environment by observing, recording, measuring, interviewing, and generally obtaining an understanding of it 'through the soles of their feet and the palms of their hand,' and if the teacher has contrived purposeful tasks for them, then the flow of questions should be reversed from that of many teaching situations, where the questions are almost solely raised by the teacher, to one where most of the inquiry comes from the students. (p. 15)

Case Study 3.5 tells about an experiment involving students in data collection at the Vikram A. Sarabhai Community Science Centre in Ahmedabad, India. A prototype working programme was set up on Saturdays with groups of participants including high school and college students, elementary and high school teachers. It was presumed that those who participated would carry over the method to their own classrooms. Note the use of the inquiry method at the outset which resulted in 'a number of starts in various directions'. The data collecting activities of each of the groups could be applied to many environments, but space has permitted giving the details for just two of the groups. The drop-off in attendance after one month, especially among teachers, leads one to surmise that those teachers who left the programme placed more value on other activities for their Saturdays. Why?

Another programme involving student collection of data from their community environment is that of INSPECT from Australia. A summary of this programme is given in Case Study 3.6. This programme is unique in its culminating seminar and the way in which it involves parents and seeks to educate adults. A statement from the U.N.E.S.C.O. Associated Schools Project on *Some Pedagogical Approaches to Environmental Education* reinforces this point as follows:

> ... to develop educational environments for facilitating a reexamination of basic premises, values, attitudes, and perception. These environments are characterized by the need of the individual to feel safe in considering the possibility of change. As an example, one of the most important aspects which contributes more to the success of education for the poor and disfranchised group is the repeated success in the experience of gathering, using, organizing, augmenting and ultimately disseminating a knowledge base (about their own community, for example) which they perceive as relevant and useful and over which they have continuing control. (U.N.E.S.C.O. 1973b, p. 5)

Observe how the activities of the 'Me and Water' Group in Case Study 3.5 as well as the INSPECT students fit the above statement. It may also be noted that the 'change' strand from Case Study 3.2 is reinforced here.

As a concluding case study for this section, Case Study 3.7 from Florida gives an example of a planned sequence of field trips in a programme for grades 1 to 10. Planning for field trips has usually been limited to planning an individual field trip, or, at the most, planning a sequence of trips for a course. The planning of a systematic programme of trips for an entire range of grade levels is comparatively rare. However, such planning is needed in order to eliminate duplicated efforts and to give focus to the objectives for individual trips. Also, such planning involves a team effort on the part of the staff, resulting in an inter-disciplinary approach which is so vital to environmental education. Furthermore, a system-wide programme of field trips necessitates administrative decisions to facilitate the participation of individual teachers in the programme.

Since Case Study 3.7 is from a community in a coastal environment, the trips reflect that environment. However, the same conceptual foci can be applied to mountain environments. Of particular interest in this case study is the concluding evaluating form. The feedback from these evaluations can bring about changes and refinements in the programme.

This section has mainly been concerned with the methods for moving beyond the classroom. Facilities for environmental study areas will be taken up in the next chapter.

Extraordinary Methods

So long as there are creative teachers and students there will be innovative methods of environmental education. However, creativity can be encouraged. One of the means of doing this is through competition. Case Study 3.8 reports on the use of Competitions in Czechoslovakia. Science Fairs have been held in the U.S.A. and elsewhere on a local and regional basis for many years. In recent years many of the studies undertaken by the students for these fairs have been directed toward environmental problems. This is demonstrated in the representative topics given in this case study.

From a fair, it is a short step to a carnival. While the need for carnival in our lives is being recognized, its application to environmental education is somewhat surprising. In any event, Colin Ward makes a case for the carnival in Case Study 3.9. In addition to telling how to organize one, he suggests some witty ideas, such as having children dress as parts of the environment, or having them display models and pictures of buildings they would prefer to have built in their community. The idea of returning the streets to the people is also a good one.

Carnival involves role playing, but role playing can be done in the classroom without the benefit of a carnival. Role playing is often a part of simulation games and these have been proliferating in environmental education (Pierfy, 1971). Since the game is a facility, or media, it will be given more attention in the following chapter. Role playing is especially useful when showing contrasting viewpoints toward an environmental problem.

Because environmental education is wrapped up in attitudes, feelings, and values, it uses art forms, poetry and literature to communicate these emotions (Fuller, 1970). The Japanese Haiku is especially adaptable to this purpose. Using three lines of five syllables, seven

Why does a cloud go floating by? I Wonder Why.

It Wants to! So do I.

Lauren D. Young, 7
Seattle, Wash.

HAIKUS

I
The cumulus cloud
Is a fluffy cottonball
In the autumn sky.

II
Rain taps on the roof
Like a small drum — boom, boom, boom.
It sounds very good.

III
Robin twits a tune —
He is singing to his wife,
Entertaining her.

Karl Jogis, 11
Palo Alto, Calif.

'Haikus' by Karl Jogis, with drawing by Lauren D. Young. Reproduced from *The Christian Science Monitor*, © 1974, TCSPS syllables and five syllables, in that order, Haiku seeks to convey a mood in nature. An example of Haiku is:

> Grasses nod and sway
> Bent low by passing wings 'til
> Crushed 'neath passing feet.
>
> (Written by a high school student in a STEP (Students Toward Environmental Participation) programme, Reading, California, July 19, 1973. Courtesy of Pat Stanek, National Park Service, U.S.A.)

The other end of the teaching spectrum from humanistic, creative art and poetry is computer-based programmed instruction. Such instruction limits the range of choices and leads the students in a step-by-step method towards the achievement of pre-set objectives. This is an extraordinary method for environmental education in that it is not commonly used. Part of the reason for this is that few programmed materials have been developed. Again, it is difficult to separate methods from materials (the subject of the next chapter). The State of New Jersey Department of Education has developed and published several computer-based resource-units for environmental education. Information on these units is contained in Case Study 3.10. The systematic procedures imposed in programmed instruction emphasize cognitive development (Saveland, 1973). Even ardent behaviouralists would admit that all environmental education cannot be in the affective domain. There would seem to be room for transmitting essential data and basic concepts via computer programming, yet this remains a frontier area in educational thinking.

Any chapter on teaching methods is necessarily incomplete. This chapter and the one which follows can only hint at the possibilities in presenting environmental education. We can only sum up with the following quote:

> . . . any teaching strategy used efficiently and effectively to impart understandings, skills, and attitudes is a successful method. (Emery, Davey, Milne 1974, p. 15)

Bibliography

Emery, J. S., Davey, C. and Milne, A. K., 'Environmental Education: The Geography Teacher's Contribution', *The Journal of Geography*, Vol. 73 No. 4, April 1974, pp. 8—18. (This paper is a slightly modified version of a working paper presented to the IGU/UNESCO Regional Workshop on the Teaching of Geography in S.E. Asia and the S.W. Pacific held in Sydney in September 1973.)

Fuller, Buckminster, *I Seem to Be a Verb*, Bantom Books, New York, 1970.

Morgan, Les, *Conservation and Environmental Education*, European Working Conference on Environmental Conservation Education, Conference Document 33-6/BP/10, I.U.C.N., Switzerland, 1971, p. 4.

Morgan, Les, District Studies, Peak National Park Study Centre, personal communication, 31, May 1973.

Pierfy, David, 'Simulation Games', *The Southeastern Regional Conference on the Social Sciences and Environmental Education*, The University of Georgia, 1971. *See also* Miller, James R., Pappas, George and Churchill, Eton, 'Eco-Acres: A Land-use Simulation Game; *The Journal of Geography*, Vol 74, No. 3, March 1975, pp. 134—143.

Saveland, Robert N. 'From Relative to Accountable; Textbooks are Progressive', *Publisher's Weekly*, Dec. 6, 1971.

Saveland, Robert N., 'Performance Contracting and Environmental Education', *The Journal of Environmental Education*, Vol. 4 No. 4, Summer 1973, pp. 41—43.

(a) UNESCO, International Meeting of Experts on the UNESCO Associated Schools Project, *Suggestions on Subject Themes for Associated Schools Projects: Environment*, ED. 73/.619/5, Paris, 27 August 1973. Original: English.

(b) UNESCO, International Meeting of Experts on the UNESCO Associated Schools Project, *Some Pedagogical Approaches to Environmental Education*, ED 73/CONF.619/8, Paris, 24 Sept. 1973. Original: English.

Additonal References

Cummings, Stankey J., 'A Methodology for Environmental Education', *The Journal of Environmental Education*, Vol. 6, No. 2, Winter 1974, pp. 16—20.

Howell, Jerry T. Jr., 'Environmental Awareness Determination; A Model', *The Journal of Environmental Education*, Vol. 6, No. 2, Winter 1974, pp. 57—63.

Case Study 3.1

Environmental Studies in German Schools, Anthony Blackbourn.

(Reproduced by permission of the National Council for Geographic Education from *The Journal of Geography*, October 1972, pp. 389—390.)

The environment and its problems are becoming a major part of the curriculum in German schools. Course outlines have recently appeared in a public affairs journal published by the German government (W. W. Puls, 'Umwelt-Gefahren und Schutz,' *Informationen zur politischen Bildung* No. 146, 1971, pp. 1—28). The biology curriculum will be changed slightly to give more emphasis to pollution problems but the real change is in the geography curriculum where a full year course on the environment has been developed. Geographic approaches are stressed in the two interdisciplinary programs developed, and the new approaches to the environment in such technical programs as city and regional planning using geographic methods.

The environment studies program in the geography curriculum is given in the senior years of high school and covers the following topics:

1. Water supply for major German cities
2. Sewage and drinking water supply problems in the Ruhr
3. Deforestation and erosion in hill areas
4. The problems of cleaning up an international river (the Rhine)
5. Airport location problems
6. Wind direction and the pollution of residential areas
7. Air pollution from blast furnaces and power stations
8. Smog problems in the Ruhr, London, New York, and Los Angeles
9. Damage from nineteenth century industrialization, the English Midlands
10. Dangers for men and landscapes, the African Copper belt, gold-mining in Johannesburg, and deforestation in the Mediterranean
11. Environmental problems in U.S.A., Donora and the Tennessee valley, Lake Erie, the Hudson River and Houston Bay
12. National parks in Germany, the U.S.A., Canada, Argentina and East Africa.

This curriculum is impressively comprehensive and progresses from the basic problems affecting the urban German, such as water supply, to the more general problems of preserving unspoiled wilderness areas by the creation of national parks. It starts with local area studies of German cities but gradually draws on foreign examples. English and

American air pollution problems provide additional information to place the Ruhr's problems in persective, but the later studies of African mining are introduced for their intrinsic interest.

The primary school program includes an interdisciplinary course based on the local environment. The course starts with the students collecting all the trash from the school yard and from their homes. This is sorted, classified into different types, and the quantity of each type measured. The students then take a trip to the city sanitation department and learn how they dispose of garbage.

The next topic is water. Students calculate total and per capita water use in their homes and at school before moving on to the study of sewage. In this section of their course, they observe polluted streams and lakes. The water section of the course ends with a visit to the local waterworks and sewage treatment plant.

Air pollution is studied by photographing factory chimneys polluting the air, observing the pollution of cars at traffic lights and of trucks on expressways. Chemical pollution is studied by examining the spraying of fruit trees and weed killing followed by the construction of the compost heap.

This program stresses local problems and shows the child both how he can help fight pollution and how a city tries to protect the environment. Practical work, measurement of amounts of pollution, and visits to local pollution control centers are valuable features of this course.

The interdisciplinary course in the middle school years is also practically oriented with much emphasis on group work to produce research reports. Suggested topics for groups include a cost-benefit study of pollution control, political problems in pollution control, and conflicts between the growth of the city and the protection of the environment.

Both the interdisciplinary courses and the geography course seem valuable additions to a school curriculum. A sequence of all three courses should produce a student who is not only concerned about the environment but also well informed on methods of preserving it for future generations.

Case Study 3.2

Man and His Environment — An Introduction to Using Environmental Study Areas

(Reproduced by permission of the American Alliance for Health, Physical Education and Recreation)

The Strand Approach to Environmental Education

There are many productive ways in which to make use of the environment as an educational vehicle. One approach is strictly taxonomical: everything has a name and a specific way of interacting with the universe. Scientists describing unique objects use the taxonomical method as a principal operational procedure in their investigations. This method, however, has a drawback for the teacher with a limited scientific background, who may not know the multitude of specific names and conditions with which to describe the environment scientifically.

Another way of approaching environmental study is through an investigative, completely open-ended method. The teacher guides the student in his attempts to discover what is present in his surroundings and to place his discoveries into some kind of perspective. The advantage of this method is that it provides the kind of study that activates sensory awareness and enables the student to develop creative problem-solving techniques. The difficulty rests with the development of research skills. Research skills are another tool of the scientific investigator, and although they would provide a good background in problem solving for the student, it takes time to develop them.

The strand approach draws upon the advantages of both of these methods while eliminating the disadvantages. It incorporates both the specific and the investigative approaches into a third approach with which both student and teacher can feel more comfortable. It requires identification and classification, but on a modified basis. It also requires open-ended investigation leading to problem solving. Yet all of its requirements can be taught by a teacher and fulfilled by a student who has little of the rigorous scientific training demanded by the other approaches.

The strand approach makes necessary a reorganization of thinking into unfamiliar patterns, which may at first be difficult. The valuable, unifying characteristic of the strand approach, however, makes whatever initial effort may be necessary unquestionably worthwhile.

The Strands

The strand approach uses five broad, universal concepts as a way of drawing the environment under a total, integrated 'umbrella.' These

80

concepts or strands are five:

 Variety and Similarities

 Patterns

 Interaction and Interdependence

 Continuity and Change

 Evolution and Adaptation.

Mathematics
Lesson Suggestions
Objects in the environment are many and diverse. Mathematics from the simple elementary school level to the sophisticated college level was created largely to keep count of the various objects in the universe — to measure them and describe them in the language of numbers.

A lesson or several lessons that teach students to recognize what, how many of what, and the size of the whats can result in a challenging and realistic relationship with the environment. For example, a lesson that asks the student to count the different kinds of plant life he sees and to arrange them into sets of similarities not only will sharpen the student's appreciation of plant life, but will also clarify for him a basic and highly useful math skill.

Eventually, objects perceived in number language will help the student relate what he counts to the total environment, to all the interactions of his surroundings.

Questions for Student Discussion
How many different things can be counted at this site?
  How many are there in each set?
  How many sets interset (have similar parts)?
  How many equivalent sets are there?
  How many equal sets are there?
  How many disjoint sets are there?
  Can methods of counting environmental objects change the count?
  Why is it critical to count things in the environment?
  How can you make population counts?

Patterns
Lesson Suggestions
Statistics are actually numbers arranged in patterns. Lessons in number arrangements can help the student describe his world in terms of averages, medians, and stanines. Such lessons can show him how to group objects into certain number relationships that show trends (what is happening to his environment, for example) or reveal what objects should or should not be present in his surroundings and in what quantities.

In a pre- or post-site lesson, the student can describe what he learns about the environment from statistical reports in newspapers or from data and counts of student characteristics made right in the classroom. Either way he can get firsthand knowledge about his own surroundings by treating numbers of things in patterns as they relate to the total environment.

Questions for Student Discussion
From a plant and animal count at the site, can you clarify how different topographies in the same area affect plant and animal population groupings?

What kind of statistical expressions can show survival patterns of plants or animals?

Is the number of rocks essential to the toal environmental pattern?

How can statistical evidence clarify the effects of overpopulation on air, water, and earth?

Interaction and Interpendence
Lesson Suggestions
A mathematical notation — ratios, for example — can highlight environmental interactions with amazing clarity. Environmental ratios that deal

with the number of people as compared with the number of productive land acres or the number of tons of available food can measure the balance between animal (including human) and plant life.

The students can calculate relevant findings about the amount of land to the amount of water at a given site or the acres of grassland to the acres of woodland using fractions, percent computations, and more complicated algebraic treatment. Whatever the choice of numerical subject matter, the environment will prove to be a most meaningful source of numbers in relation to the student's life.

Questions for Student Discussion

How many animals and what kinds of animals can interact with an environment for a given time without decimating that environment?

What considerations do planners give to ratios of people to air, water, and earth in establishing or renewing urban areas?

What percentage of air must be composed of foreign materials before it is considered polluted?

What percentage of water must have foreign elements in it before it is considered polluted?

How can you measure environmental interactions?

Continuity and Change

Lesson Suggestions

Because it is often difficult to see spectacular changes on the site, students may wonder if things simply exist from day to day, continuing to be just as they are. Graphing, even by very young students, is a technique that can show change relationships. Measuring and plotting, for example, the height of plants over a span of time will produce a clear illustration of a growth curve.

Other graphing lessons can deal with urban growth and the relationships of populations to housing. Many human environments, such as the classroom itself, will provide evidence of change as one plots and graphs the various characteristics of the changing student population.

In higher mathematics, the use of proportions can show how changing one element of the environment changes the numerical relationships of other environmental factors as well. The lessons suggested here can start with on-site measures and counts, which will whet the students' interest in the outcome of their calculations.

Questions for Student Discussion

What changes do you see when you plot growth curves of plants? population? urban centers?

Calculate how many people can be accomodated in your community, considering requirements of air, earth, and water. What changes would be made by an increase in population? How can such changes be measured?

Remove one environmental factor at a time (some large, some small). Consider the magnitude of changes in the total environment that results from removing each factor.

Evolution and Adaptation
Lesson Suggestions

Perhaps no other method of communications has changed the environment to such a degree as mathematics. Man's advanced technology, resulting in the automation and computerization of industry and providing man with the ability to find out what is happening to the environment in split seconds, has changed and evolved the social, political, and economic structure of the earth.

Man continually needs to adapt to his own inventions and changes. The evolution of his technology will become more and more pronounced. Students at all maturity levels can learn to fit more easily into their world if they are aware of this process. Lesson objectives should lead to basic understandings of how today's computers rapidly calculate numerical relationships and how these calculations affect the environment and help people live more comfortable lives.

Predicting weather, keeping records, and operating such complicated experiments as putting satellites into orbit are examples of computer use which can be translated into functional math lessons. The computer mathematics that describes today's environment and the students' future environment provides material for pragmatic lessons.

Questions for Student Discussion

What percentage of your city has been adapted for use by the automobile?

Has automation changed the on-site environment?

Has the invention of new technologies played a role in the evolution of the environment? For example, in what ways has the wheel changed man's environment?

Could you adapt to a world without numbers?

What role does statistics — the mathematics of chance and probability — play in understanding biological evolution?

84

Case Study 3.3

**Towards a Co-ordinating Framework for Environmental Education —
A Planners View**

(Reproduced by permission of Jean Forbes, from *BEE* 35, March, 1974.)

The 'years' in the diagram below, are simply time blocks which may
last more or less than a calendar year.

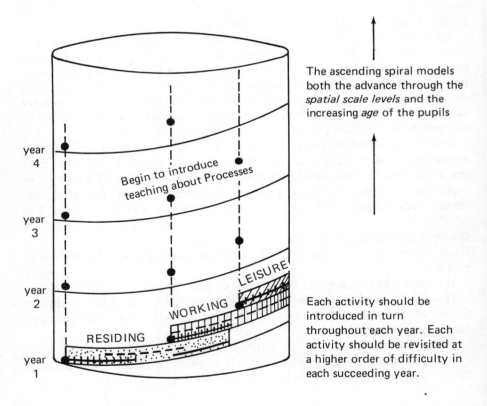

The ascending spiral models
both the advance through the
spatial scale levels and the
increasing *age* of the pupils

Each activity should be
introduced in turn
throughout each year. Each
activity should be revisited at
a higher order of difficulty in
each succeeding year.

Figure 6. A model of the proposed co-ordinating framework to guide the teaching
about activities and space use, and the processes which manage their inter-relation-
ship

Two example disciplines are shown, contributing to the teaching about each activity
(disciplines may follow each other or may overlap in time as the subject matter may
dictate).

The spiral track opened out:

Year 1	Year 2	Year 3
Scale: house — — — — →	Scale: neighbourhood — — →	Scale: district

enlarge this section

Year 1 — → Year 2 — — — →

```
                                    Moving
                             Health
                      Information
              Goods
         Leisure
     Working
Residing
```

A Detailed Look at the Subject Matter in One Year

I would like to focus on just one year and try to be more specific about the kinds of things which might be treated in school at that year — sketching in the rough headings for a scheme of work, so to speak.

I have structured these ideas around the two words 'Assessment' and 'Evaluation'. *Fig 7* is a matrix of headings about the job of Assessment, observing various aspects of the man-environment relationship. (*Fig 8* supplements *Fig 7*). *Fig 9* is a matrix of Evaluation tasks, which seeks to structure the pupil's judgements on the adequacy or effectiveness of what he has observed.

To consider *Fig 7* in detail. Let us imagine that it is one page taken from a group of similar matrix diagrams, each one of them dealing with

Topics Activities	What does the environment look like?		What is its function?	

This section is about OBSERVATIONS

This section is about ANALYSIS

Topics / Activities	What does the environment look like?				What is its function?			
	'Natural' features	Staff	Man-made things	Staff	Location	Staff	Design and jobs	Staff
	(MOSTLY DRAWINGS AND NOTES)				*(MAPS)*		*(DISCUSSIONS)*	
RESIDING	Natural features surrounding the houses	A B	Styles of houses building materials sizes	A M	Location of houses and incidental open spaces	G B	House design and layout, landscaping visual amenity	A B
WORKING	Farm landscapes Quarries	A B	Styles of buildings Sizes	A M	Location of workplaces by kind of work done	G MS	Factory design. Relation to kind of work done	G H S MS
TAKING LEISURE	Open land, rivers, trees, animal life	A B	Man-made features: (i) outdoor (ii) indoor	A B M	Location by kind	G B	Design of outdoor and indoor facilities Organization of sport.	A B G
OBTAINING GOODS AND SERVICES			Styles of shop, grouping, kinds, sizes	A M	Location by kind	G	Shop design relation to retail organization	A G M
EXCHANGING INFORMATION			Styles of schools, post offices and libraries. Sizes.	A M	Location by kind	G	Design of units relation to jobs they do. Org. of telecommunications.	A G H S MS
MAINTAINING HEALTH	(overlap with residing and leisure above)		Styles of clinics, surgeries. Sizes.	A M	Location by kind	G	Design and equipment. Jobs.	A S B
MOVING ABOUT			Types of buildings related to transport, bridges, stations.	A M	Geometry and capacity of networks.	G M	Kinds of traffic flow, volumes, linkage to other areas.	G M

KEY TO STAFF COLUMN: G = Geography, H = History, A = Art, S = Science, B = Biology, M = Maths, MS = Modern Studies.

Scales	Topics / Activities	What does the environment look like?				What is its function?			
		'Natural' features	Staff	Man-made things	Staff	Location	Staff	Design and jobs	Staff
DISTRICT	WORKING	Fishing, mining, farming areas (primary industry)	A B MS	Factories and offices singly and in groups.	A MS H	Location	G	Factory design in relation to terrain. Mfg. processes.	G A MS H
CITY	WORKING	Primary industry areas	A B MS	Industrial estates, major integrated plants, office clusters, city centre.	A MS H	Location of major employment areas, work zones in city.	G H	Design of ind. estates, automation, govt. grants, land values.	G H MS
REGION	WORKING	Primary industry areas; landscapes with features relevant to industry	A MS	Large constructions connected with ind. and power supply and shipping.	A MS	Location of ind. growth centres.	G H MS	Analysis of land supply, economic planning, innovation regional strategy.	G H MS S
NATION	WORKING	Major resources and environmental effects (e.g. oil)	A MS	Major areas of constructions for resource exploitation	A MS	National distribution of resources and people.	G H MS	Economic planning govt. control of industry, regional policies	G H MS

Figure 8. Assessment card showing the activity 'working' at several scales

Evaluation jobs / Activities	Breakdown signals		Unwelcome residents				Absentees			
	(1) Functional	(2) Visual	(3) Natural	(4) Man-made	(5) What to do?		(6) Natural	(7) Man-made	(8) What to do?
RESIDING	Overcrowding	Structural decay	Swamp too near houses	House painted bright pink			No trees or shrubs	No phone box	
WORKING	Men laid off	Factory becoming derelict	Land subsidence	Chemical works fumes				Lack of open space about buildings	
TAKING LEISURE	Football played on roads	Litter gathering in park	Gardens invaded by deer	Noise of building beside music school	DISCUSS THE PUBLIC AGENCIES WHOSE DUTY THESE MATTERS ARE		No flat ground for football pitch	Lack of children's swing park	DISCUSS THE PUBLIC AGENCIES
OBTAINING GOODS	Long queues in shops	Shops run down		Fish and chip shop noisy at night				No food shop in area	
EXCHANGING INFORMATION	Inadequate postal service. Broken telephones	Structural decay of school		Itinerant preacher with loud-speakers			Poor signal on BBC 2	No place for local meetings	
MAINTAINING HEALTH	Closure of local clinic	Visible pollution of stream	Thistles	Effluent from local pig farm on roads			No trees, shrubs or open space	Absence of dentist	
MOVING ABOUT	Traffic jams	Roads badly designed		Heavy lorries parking overnight			No safe walkways	No bus stops	

STAFF APPROPRIATE: Matters in Column 1 = G and MS, Column 2 = A and B, Column 3 = B, Column 4 = G and B, Column 5 = A and B, Column 6 = B and G, Column 7 = G, Columns 5 and 8 are about institutional process, Staff = MS and H.

one spatial scale level. The page in *Fig 7* is all about the scale level Neighborhood. The matrix is divided into two broad areas each sub-divided into two further areas. The Activities list, being the subject matter ordering device, is given at the left. Each major box in the matrix therefore deals with matters which should be treated for a particular Activity under a particular Job heading.

The four small columns labelled 'staff' indicate in a very tentative way, the school disciplines which might appropriately contribute to the Jobs in the adjacent major box.

Take the Activity Working as an example.

Under the major heading 'What does the Environment look like?', we could envisage the pupils recording first those parts of the natural landscape in their neighbourhood which are used by people working. This would apply more likely in a country area and would take in an examination of farmland or quarries for example. The most appropriate teaching might come from the Art and Biology specialists. The pupils would then look at more obviously man-made work environments, such as a factory group or a railway yard, attempting to make a record of the types of buildings, their dimensions and the materials of which they are built. The Art teacher might, in this case, be complemented by the Maths teacher, teaching about survey and measurement.

Moving on to the next major heading 'What is the function of the recorded objects?' one takes the pupils from the stage of *recording* to the stage of *analysis*. First, with the Geography teacher taking the lead, the pupils should establish the locational inter-relationships of the various elements recorded, by mapping them. This will introduce them to the whole field of mapping and to the question of map scales. Then the Biology and Art teachers might join the Geographer in leading discussions about how the various environmental spaces are shaped by the jobs which people do in them. Discussion of a factory, for example, would start from the observed shape and size of the buildings and lead on to a discussion of the production process and mechanized goods handling. The same kind of progression from recording to analysis could take place, in a structured way for each Activity, as shown by the notes in the matrix boxes in *Fig 7*. It is evident that, even at one scale and under that, even at one scale and under one heading, the potential contribution from the disciplines will vary depending on the nature of the Activity.

Fig 8 is a supplement to *Fig 7*. It focusses on the matrix row dealing with Activity Working. The one described above was Working at the Neighbourhood scale.

Fig 8 gives examples of how the matrix rows for Working might look on the successive other matrices dealing with the next scale levels above. The examples given demonstrate how the ascending scale level brings in greater degrees of abstraction and also the institutional processes, as one progresses to national level. It also shows that as the subject matter becomes more complex so a greater variety of disciplines have potential contributions to make.

In *Fig 9* we move into the more difficult world of evaluation. I have tried to structure this on a matrix system which is basically a three part critical analysis of what the pupils have seen and discussed in class, under each Activity heading.

The 'Breakdown Signals'	The 'Unwelcome Residents'	The 'Absentees'
subdivide into: functional/visual	subdivide into: Natural/Man-made	subdivide into: Natural/Man-made

I have also inserted two columns headed 'What to Do'.

The three major groupings deal with the observations of things which appear to the pupils to be wrong, or offensive, or (if absent) needed. This will involve the pupil's judgement together with that of the teachers in Geography, Biology and Art, principally.

The columns dealing with measures which might be taken, seem to me to be in the field of Modern Studies and History specialists, because this matter inevitably introduces the Institutional Processes and the whole field of societal control and regulatory proceedures, together with their historical development.

As with matrices of different scales outlined in *Fig 8*, one can imagine that the Evaluation matrices will increase in the complexity of their subject matter as one moves up the scale levels.

Conclusion

I have propounded here an outline model, in an effort to structure the subject matter of the Man-Environment relationship. I have used the Spatial scales as a surrogate for pupils' comprehension level, and have ordered the subject matter at each scale under the Activities headings. The Activities list, imparts a vertical ordering to the topics, bringing them in successively for renewed study at each turn of the scale spiral.

Whether or not my particular model is the best one, is not the major issue. I would however contend that *some* model must be made before any systematic teaching of the Activity/Environment relationship and the management processes can be done. Without a Co-ordination Framework the subject can never be anything else but a rag-bag of fragments which never add up to anything in the child's mind.

Case Study 3·4

Progress and the Environment: Water and Air Pollution — Instructor's Guide (James P. Shaver & A. Guy Larkin)

(© 1973 Houghton Mifflin Company)

In order to deal adequately with poltical-ethical issues, other kinds of issues must be faced. Some are *factual*, such as: Who pollutes: What is the present level of air or water pollution in different parts of our country? or, How much impurity can industries keep out of the air and water with our present level of technology? These questions require current information and call for critical assessment of those who make 'expert' claims.

A second type of issue revolves around *word usage and definitions*: What is meant by *clean* air or *clean* water? or, How does emotively loaded language effect your attitudes toward pollution?

But of special importance from our point of view are the *value issues* — the conflicts between values, such as economic progress and environmental quality — that should be faced and dealt with in trying to arrive at reasonable policies. Throughout the booklet, *Progress and the Environment*, the student is confronted with conflicts between values related to the quality of life and values related to economic progress.

Assumptions About Learning

This booklet is based on a recognition that factual information is important and that reading is a good source of such information. It is also assumed that reading is going to be of interest to students and facts are more likely to be remembered if the quest for information is related to important issues about which the student is being challenged to think. An important part of the challenge is the confrontation with the need to define and weigh values in making decisions about political-ethical issues. Basically, then, it is assumed that learning will take place when, and as, the students are involved in thinking about issues. . . .

A Socratic Discussion of the Delaware Case

The case from *Newsweek*, 'Delaware: Nature over Industry,' poses a public policy question about banning new industry along the ocean coastline. It was included as the basis for a socratic discussion of the basic value dilemma — economic progress versus the quality of life. . . . It can be used as a model for planning other discussions. . . .

A. Read aloud the introduction to the case and then the case (or have one or more students do so). Then ask questions about the background to the Delaware law to be sure the case is understood and to get a discussion going.

For example:

What was the law that Governor Peterson was to sign?
Why was the law proposed?
How did the businesses to be affected by the law react?
What arguments are mentioned for and against the law? (These might be listed on the blackboard.)

B. Have several students take a stand on the issue posed by the case by asking them, one at a time: Should Delaware have passed a law banning new coastline industry?

C. After several students have taken a stand, challenge one student to defend his position.

1. First state a general value supporting the student's position, such as: 'You believe that it is very important to protect the *quality of the environment*' or 'You believe that *economic growth* is important.'

2. Then state a value conflict, such as 'You think, then, that the *quality of the environment* is more important than the *economic welfare* of a whole region?' or 'You think, then, that we should sacrifice *environmental quality* in order to have *jobs and oil (economic welfare)*?'

3. If, as is likely, the student maintains his position, challenge it with analogies or counter-arguments, such as the following, loaded against his position.

If the student is in favor of the law banning new coastline industry:

a. If a law as drastic as Delaware's is called for, perhaps the federal government should ban new industry everywhere. After all, the quality of the environment in Florida, or Ohio, or Nevada ought to be as important as it is in Delaware.

b. If states like Delaware and Maine ban dockside refineries, there might be a serious oil shortage in the eastern United States in a few years. Do you mean to say that the relatively few people who live in Delaware and Maine ought to have the right to cause serious incovenience, if not suffering, to the millions of people in other states who will be affected by this law? In cases like this, should a state pass a law that will hurt the majority of Americans?

c. If Delaware has the right to stop the increased flow of oil that the rest of the country will need, then maybe Pennsylvania and New Jersey ought to have the right to block the highways and railroads and stop the flow of trucks and trains carrying things to and from Delaware. The trucks and trains help clog the highways and damage the quality of the environment in Pennsylvania and New Jersey.

If the student is opposed to the law banning new coastline industry

a. The article said that Maine and Delaware are the only Atlantic Coast states with deep water potential to service huge dockside refineries, but there might be other ways to supply the needed oil to eastern states. Perhaps the oil companies could build a larger number of smaller refineries, or even place the refineries inland and pipe crude oil to them. This may increase the cost of refined oil, but that doesn't mean that the need for oil can't be met. Should Delaware have to allow huge refineries just so people in other states can have cheaper oil?

b. People claim that oil pollution can be seen in the Delaware Bay, and that the entire northeast section of the Atlantic seacoast — with the exception of a few northern-most areas — suffers from industrial air pollution. Now, the people of Delaware have had enough of this foul air and foul water. They're simply tired of living with it. Don't they have the right to finally say, 'No! We've had enough! No more heavy industry! No additional pollution!'

c. If Delaware doesn't have the right to fight pollution by stopping industrial expansion, then who does? Should we only strive to environmental quality in those states which are unattractive to industry? When it really comes down to the nitty gritty, should we always place industrial growth above environmental quality?

D. When you sense that the student has 'had enough' (he is unable to handle the dilemma, is showing signs of tension, or is able to state a reasoned, acceptable position), shift to other students, one at a time, and go through the same questioning process.

E. Toward the end of the discussion period, ask the students what they think the point of the discussion has been. Ask questions or make statements to point out that the purpose has been to emphasize: Issues such as posed by the Delaware ban on coastline industries cause heated arguments involving important value conflicts; also involved are factual assumptions and disagreements and emotively loaded language; important implications for other situations should be taken into account (the analogous cases); and, questions about how much pollution to tolerate and about the responsibilities for causing and contolling pollution are important and controversial.

Case Study 3.5

Students and the Environment: A feasibility study of student involvement in Environmental Data Collection prepared by Axel Horn, Vikram A. Sarabhai Community Science Center, Ahmedabad, India, 1972.

... for the first working group session, the staff had planned and provided several simple procedures for moving the groups into an inquiry. The aquarium pit was set up as an exhibit gallery with three large tables on which were placed a great number of objects and pictures that acted realistically and symbolically as descriptors of the Ahmedabad environment.

The groups were to do three things in any order they wished:

1. They would take a walk in the meadow behind the Centre. This meadow was a natural outdoor science laboratory with a great number of birds, trees, plants and insects and a variety of contours and characteristics.

2. They would browse about the exhibit tables.

3. They would sit down to a discussion in the meeting room assigned to each group.

The discussion could follow the standard 'Core Program' pattern of descriptions by each group member of his personal, social, and physical background. It could also be built around the effort of the participants to agree on what is a 'beneficial' environment, in order to look at their own and construct some value judgements of it.

From the combination of the three activities during several sessions, it was anticipated that a decision would eventually be arrived at within each group as to what, in their own local environment, might engage their interest, and around which they could orgainize a research inquiry.

After a number of starts in various directions and taking varying times to consolidate into a working inquiry, five stable groups evolved from the original eight. These included:

The Sabarmati River Group
The Water Tap Group
The Animal Habitat Group
The Termite Group
The 'Me and Water' Group

The Water Tap Group decided to ask questions about the water taps in their own homes. Questions included were:

Where does water come from?
Who is responsible for its quality?
Who is responsible to get it into the house?
What is its content?
How is it used and stored?
How many glasses does each family member drink a day?
Is any wasted?
Where does it go after use?

A considerable amount of time was spent in designing and revising a questionnaire that would accumulate useful information and standardize responses. After testing out the efficacy of the questionnaire in their own homes, the group distributed about three hundred to schoolmates and friends.

The group made several field trips to a testing laboratory and a plumbing supply centre and planned to go to the city water purification centre.

In planning the questionnaire they discovered that the large map of Ahmedabad used by the Centre for setting up coordinates was dated 1965 and had practically no information on Navrangpura roads and key buildings. (This is a commentary on the rapidity and suddenness with which this area developed.)

The group members proceeded to do some surveying, using compasses and bicycles with a cloth tied to the wheel as a measuring device. Counting the number of revolutions between intersections, they are in the process of plotting the position of key roads and buildings to up-date the map.

The Termite Group collected termites from various sections of the city. They attempted to study the physical and chemical impact of termites on clay and wood. They also tried to set up colonies of termites in the laboratory to study conditions that inhibit or encourage termite growth. Members of this group developed a questionnaire and visited pest control companies for information on termite control. They developed a set of statistics from the questionnaire. These they translated into a series of charts and graphs. They photographed the effects of termites in wood. They also researched whatever written material on termites was available and produced a compilation of this information. A film on the life of a termite colony was procured and shown to a varied audience.

... a number of interesting structural differences from the traditional school experience became apparent as these five demonstration projects developed:

1. The students were placed in a position where they were continually making decisions, including the definitions of their own inquiries and the sequence of efforts.

2. There was minimum dependence on instrumentation — maximum on direct visual observation. Determinations were less quantitative and relied more on identification of the presence or absence of a number of factors.

3. The inquiries kept opening up new problems that had to be solved in order for the study to proceed to its next phase. There was a continuous process of solving unpredicted problems as they arose.

4. The recognition and utilization of serendipitous happenings become more important as part of the program. Such serendipitous events will be formalized into the second phase of the program.

5. The program was open-ended with different rates of progress in 3½ months by different groups and different individuals within a group. . . .

6. The staff was to be as supportive as possible. The objective was to recognize the 'teachable moment' and to move in to be of help at the time when an individual seemed to be in need of help . . .

7. The Centre was considered a total resource . . . The City and its content were considered a resource.

About one month through the program, participant attendance dropped off noticeably. The teacher participants as a group demonstrated the least ability to relate to and stay with the program. College students were next, especially in the Gujarati medium. The staff felt that the large time gaps between sessions during the initial planning phase contributed to loss of sustained interest, especially since the format of the program was new and strange to the participants.

To test out this assumption it was decided to add one more group to the program which would meet formally three times a week instead of one. By arrangement with St. Xavier's High School, a group of 8th Std. students was added on this basis. The interest and energy of this group seemed to prove the above assumption, as well as to suggest that the younger the students, the better they relate to the program style. Older students seemed more fixed into the traditional school structure.

Case Study 3.6

The Inspect Idea — About Inspect

(Peter Ellyard)

(Reprinted with permission from *Bad Luck, Dead Duck*, The Report of Inspect 1970 by Roger M. Gifford and Peter Ellyard for Society for Social Responsibility in Science (A.C.T.) Dalton Publishing Co., Canberra City, 1971, 70 pp.)

INSPECT is an acronym for Inquiry into the State of Pollution and Environmental Conservation by Thoughtful people. It is a programme in which a public symposium or 'teach-in' is held as a culmination of many weeks research work by High School students. The aim of INSPECT is educational, in that it is designed to stimulate awareness of environmental problems, to encourage thoughtful inquiry into those problems, and to explore courses of action where necessary. The first INSPECT was held in Canberra during 1970.

INSPECT involves High School students for several reasons. Many students are already concerned and interested in such issues. They have the time and energy to carry out the work necessary and will also talk about their efforts with their parents. In this way INSPECT can find its way to the breakfast tables of Australia.

INSPECT begins with talks in the school by visiting speakers, teachers and fellow students. Following these talks, student select problems and commence research. Guidance is provided by a number of scientists, teachers, planners, etc. who have some prior knowledge of the subjects involved. The research may use questionnaires to survey public opinion and practices related to environmental issues or may be based on experimental research and literature surveys. Where possible information should be gathered in a form that could be useful to agencies responsible for correction of the problems.

As a result, the students come to the symposium informed on the problems to the point that they can make original contributions and enter into a worth-while dialogue with 'experts'. Thus the discussions will not only be authoritative but also take a form in which the members of the general public at the symposium will be able to understand and contribute. Possible methods of corrective action should be part of the dialogue. An ideal is to have available at the discussion results of questionnaires which measure the attitudes of the public to projected recommendations.

In this way 'non-experts' can collectively inform themselves to the point where they may press for action. 'Non-experts' may then realize that they can make a significant contribution to the understanding of environmental problems. They may decide that it is necessary for industries, governments or citizens to modify some of their priorities, habits and even values so that all men may achieve and maintain a high standard of living on this 'Spaceship Earth'.

Case Study 3.7

Suggested Field Trips by Grade Level: Lee County Environmental Education Program (Bill Hammond)

I. These field sites and activities were chosen so that:

1. The selected concepts for each grade level would be presented in a field situation.

2. The student population would be exposed to a variety of field sites throughout their time in the public school system.

3. The student would not be exposed to the same field site two years in a row.

4. Classroom studies and activities could be expanded upon, and enhanced by, a field situation.

5. Students would be able to develop an awareness of nature and aesthetic values relating to the environment.

6. Students could gain more understanding of the complex nature of ecosystems.

7. Students could become aware of man's effects on the environment.

II. The field trips are arranged by grade level and also by the order in which they should be taken by the grade.

All trips have pre- and post-trip activities that can be used to develop concepts, knowledge and aesthetics.

Grade One:

Trip 1. Environmental Awareness

Students go to the animal touch farm and see common farm animals. Such things as fur texture, animal color and size, like begets like, and food are brought out. The students also participate in a short nature walk stressing some plant adaptations, uses of plants, and poison plants. Time is given for playground activities.

Trip 2. Community Service Trip — Police station, fire station, post office etc.

This field trip should be used to emphasize the interdependence of people within the community.

Grade Two

Trip 1. Environmental Awareness

Environmental Awareness exercises dealing with similarity and differences in the environment and man's effect on the environment are used. Time is given for shell collecting.

Trip 2 Environmental Awareness

Environmental Awareness exercises dealing with change in the environment, imaginative creativity, and simple classification are used.

Grade Three:

Trip 1. Adaptation and Heredity

Environmental Awareness exercises dealing with plant adaptations to light, seed dispersal and dependency of one plant on another are used.

Trip 2. Producers — Consumers — Decomposers

The dependency of consumers on producer organisms is developed as well as the role of the decomposers in an ecosystem. A partial food web for a mud flat is developed by the students. A booklet is used to help the students in their study of this ecosystem.

Grade Four:

Trip 1. Fresh water Systems

This trip emphasizes the fresh water ecosystem. The role of plants and animals is discussed. Aquarium collections are made by the students so that long term studies can be made in the classroom.

Trip 2. Water and Sewage Treatment

Student guide and question booklets are used to help the students understand the processes and equipment used in water and sewage treatment.

Grade Five:

Trip 1. Attitude Development toward Aesthetics.

Exercises dealing with imaginative creativity, the beauty of nature and imaginative role playing are used to develop attitudes dealing with aesthetics and an empathy for nature.

Trip 2. Forestry and the Forester.

A student semi-programmed booklet is used to develop concepts dealing with tree plantations and the pine tree. Students visit the Forestry Station where they watch a film dealing with forest fires; they climb to fire tower; use a tree bingo game to familiarize themselves with leaf structures; and they see fire fighting equipment.

Grade Six:

Trip 1. Interrelationships

A semi-programmed booklet, *Shady Oaks Ecology Treasure Hunt*, is used by the students. This allows the student to work at his own speed. The field study deals with interrelationships among plants, animals, and the physical environment. The major concept of the study is that the physical environment determines what plants and animals will be found in that area.

Trip 2. Food webs and Interrelationships

This trip uses a semi-programmed student booklet, *Who's Who On*

The Beach?, dealing with interrelationships of marine plants and animals. It stresses food webs and the roles of producers and consumers. The major types of beach intertidal organisms are studied.

Grade Seven:
Trip 1. Plant Zonation and Beach Formation

This trip uses two semi-programmed booklets that allow students to work at their own speed. The booklet, *Why Is A Beach A Beach?*, is used at Point Ybel and concentrates on plant zonation and the reasons for zonation on a beach. The other booklet, *Beaches Have Their Ups and Downs*, is used at Sanibel Nature Center Site. This booklet deals with old berm zonation and beach formation.

Trip 2. Bird Adaptation for Feeding

A semi-programmed booklet, *How to Make It In A Bird's World*, is used by the student. It deals with adaptations of birds for feeding. Most of the common wading birds and ducks are discussed but, in all cases, names of the organisms are not stressed. Instead, the structures and functions of these structures for survival in the environment are examined in the booklet.

Grade Eight:
Trip 1. The Mangrove Ecosystem.

The trip will use a semi-programmed booklet dealing with the major types of mangroves and their effects on the estuary environment. The effects of dredge and fill will also be discussed.

Trip 2. Community Exploration.

A semi-programmed booklet dealing with types of housing, zoning, urban sprawl, and high density strip development will be used by the students. Prospects for future development and city planning will also be included.

Trip 3. Electrical Power.

A semi-programmed guide booklet will be used on this trip. The booklet will deal with electrical power and its uses as well as environmental considerations concerning electrical production.

Grade Nine:
Trip 1. High and Low Energy Beaches.

This trip uses a semi-programmed booklet, *Beaches in Motion*, dealing with differences in high and low energy beaches. The effects of beach erosion are also discussed in the booklet.

Grade Ten:
Trip 1. Succession.

This trip is for 10th Grade Biology classes. The semi-programmed booklet, *Succession — Beauty in Change*, is used by the students to discover the major terrestrial successional changes in Southwest Florida as well as fire ecology and plant adaptation.

FIELD TRIP EVALUATION FORM

Environment Education Center
Lee County Environmental Education Program
2266 Second Street
Fort Myers, Florida

Field trips have become an integral part of the school curriculum. The Environmental Education Program relies heavily upon teacher responses to field trips sponsored and those not sponsored by the Environmental Education Center. In order that your students may have a good field trip experience, the Environmental Education Center is asking all teachers who have field trips to fill out, and send this form to the Center. These forms will be used to evaluate our field program.

Thank you for your cooperation.

School _____

Grade _____

Teacher _____

Number of Students_____

Date of Trip_____

Field Trip Site Visited_____

Brief Description of Activities During Trip:

_____
_____
_____

Recommendations for Future Trips to This Site:

_____
_____
_____

Did this trip fit in with your grade level studies?_____

Why?_____

What changes have you noticed in your classroom and/or students since taking this trip?

_____
_____
_____

Additional Comments:

_____
_____
_ _

Case Study 3.8

Competitions in Czechoslovakia

The 'Golden Leaf' competition for Young Pioneer groups was instituted in autumn 1972. The object of the campaign is to involve Young Pioneers in environmental issues. It is organised by the Central Council of Young Pioneers within the Socialist Union of Youth in co-operation with the Julius Fucik Central House of Young Pioneers and Youth with the support of the Czech Ministry of Education.

The competition consisted of practical activities undertaken by young people both in conservation management and in nature and environmental studies. The sort of tasks undertaken have been cleaning of litter from the countryside, feeding game and birds in the winter, planting of trees and shrubs, promoting and executing biological control of pests, conservation and management of small nature reserves, etc. Each competition was judged on this practical activity and tested on a real nature trail where the competitor's knowledge and experience was tested. The district and regional competitions led to a national final in two age categories — up to 12 years, and up to 15 years. This took place at Chomutov in North-West Bohemia from 21 to 24 June, 1973. The final took the form of a camp where the best groups competed for prizes and benefited from an instructive programme of discussions, film-shows and excursions.

Another activity in the field of environmental education also involving the Prague House of Young Pioneers and Youth is the organisation in 1973—74 of environmental conservation workshops for Prague school-children. The State Institute for Protection of Relics and Conservation of Nature is compiling a series of five 60-minute workshops on different themes in environmental conservation. Within each workshop there is a slide or film presentation, an opportunity for each participant to solve a puzzle linked to the environmental subject matter, and lastly a small competition between teams of participants. For instance, one theme is 'Plants and Animals as Natural Resources' which commences with slides on the conservation of protected species, then the youngsters are asked to connect several living things with the correct lines to get the proper scheme of a food-chain, and finally there is a nature trail competition. These workshops are conducted up to three times a day over a period of two months. Participants are usually groups of school-children between 12 and 15 years of age. (Information supplied by the State Institute for Protection of Relics and Conservation of Nature, Praha, 1974.)

Case Study 3.9

Why a Carnival?

(Reproduced with permission from Colin Ward, *BEE* 38, June 1974.)

The best reason for having a carnival is because it's fun.

Most carnivals are organised to raise money for charity, but there is something to be said for doing it for its own sake. Pat Kitto told me of the shock people got when, assuming that her carnival at Conisbrough had some worthy object, they asked her what it was in aid of. The answer 'just for fun' made them reflect on the last art of *enjoying* the street.

The carnival may also, as in Granby, Liverpool, be just one item in a community festival: a very important item because the procession through the streets tells everyone in the neighbourhood that something is going on.

The festival itself may have been set up to provide stimulus and activity for children during the long summer holiday, or as part of an effort to reinforce a sense of community identity.

Thus Valerie Jenkins wrote last year:

'You can hardly ride around London at week-ends these days without getting tangled up in the bunting somewhere. Every Saturday some neighbourhood or other is suddenly out on the street, with folk in clown's garb and woad on their faces handing out leaflets, and large arrows along the walls directing you to the party . . .

'Because as Londoners are increasingly demonstrating, the best geographical unit is still the village. The mediaeval serfs knew it and so did the wicked squires. London's burgeoning *Festschrifts* are a logical progression from the desperate urge to preserve the human-scale buildings and the trees and the open spaces.

'It is not enough to protect your environment. Today you have also to celebrate it. A day of carnival is really claiming: 'Look at us, we're a real neighbourhood, see what fun we're having.' And, more and more it's saying' 'This land is ours. Leave us alone.'

(*Evening Standard* 20.7.73)

A very important function of the carnival is this re-assertion of the right to use the street. Look at Wandsworth High Street (part of the South Circular route in South London). Here, before the First World War it was taken for granted that the street could be taken over by something as apparently unimportant as a Sunday school procession.

Anyone under about eighty years of age has spent most of his life in a physical setting in which the highest priority in the town has been getting the traffic through. The Highways Engineer has staked his professional reputation on this, and the motorised public has acquiesced. City after city in Britain has been disembowelled in an ultimately vain attempt to achieve this end. Market stalls, ancient trees, enticing alleys and, of course, acres of bricks and mortar were lost in the process. And so was the right of the prople to *use* the street: a deprivation which has affected children and the old most of all.

Gradually, during the last decade, there has been a perceptible revulsion against the automatic priority given to the motor vehicle. Urban motorway projects are being shelved, and even the chairman of the RAC admitted in May that 'the anti-motoring lobby is stronger that it has been at any time since the days when vehicles had to be preceded by a red flag'. It isn't really a matter of being anti-motor car, but of asserting that other people have a right to the street too. And almost every city in Britain is experimenting with the pedestrianisation of inner-city streets.

Rediscovering the Streets

Parallel with this rediscovery of the street is a conscious effort to revive what our grandparents knew and our parents warned us against: the *life* of the street. Not dancing bears, barrel-organs, and muffin men (yet) but street theatre and street festivals. For teachers, particularly in the primary school, concerned with the use of the street and its inhabitants as resources for learning, this street revival provides innumerable opportunities.

The first is in what you might call the re-creation of street characters. Having driven the local homespun philosopher off the street by destroying the venerable tree in whose shade he sat, all in the name of road-widening, we have brought him back as, for example, the unattached youth worker, paid to chat up the boys on the corner.

Town Fools and Others

During the late 1960s, Vancouver had a Town Fool (paid by the Canada Council) who sat on the court house steps dispensing his folly and wisdom. London has at least one street story-teller, who took up his particular branch of local government enterprise after seeing itinerant story-tellers plying their trade in North African cities. Liverpool has a story-cart trundling round the by-ways of Toxteth, with its load of books, music, and things to do on the pavement. It is a project of the Liverpool Community Relations Council. Apart from these 'official' street prople of course, a school which sets about using the resources of the locality will develop its network of contacts who can be called on in journeys of exploration of 'street seminars' as Dick Kitto calls them. In every locality there are many old and retired prople who would be absolutely delighted to be interviewed by groups of children building up the *autobiography of a place* through the experiences of its inhabitants. They are human resources, just waiting to be drawn upon.

Pat and Dick Kitto are the wardens of The Terrace, Conisbrough (a centre funded jointly by the Dartington Trustees and the local education authority) and for them the street seminar and the street carnival are two aspects of the same venture in community education. Children drop in at the centre in the evenings to make and do things, and Pat got them making masks, costumes and musical instruments in preparation for a perambulation of the streets of the town, which grew into a carnival. Several primary schools joined in with projects of their own, like giant caterpillars of chicken-wire and papier mache, propelled by two dozen juvenile legs.

Aileen Boatman, an infant teacher involved in the North Islington Special Project, told me about the environment activity which at its inception involved sixteen schools in the borough. In the event, so difficult is it to co-ordinate the work of several schools, the number involved reduced itself to eight schools, and finally just one pushed the project through to its conclusion. After a session with Alan Strutt, a GLC architect, the children went out to the neighbourhood to look at buildings and analyse what they liked, what they hated, and what they would prefer to see built. Their own pictures, drawings, models and written work were assembled into an exhibition in an old double-decker bus which toured to other schools (whose teachers now regretted they had not taken part themselves).

Finally they had a procession through the streets of the borough, with children dressed up as bits of the environment: houses, trees, vehicles, zebra crossings etc. They had a decorated lorry, a multi-racial street band, and their parade through the streets caused great excitement — a man with his face covered in lather leapt out of the barber's chair to see them pass. The whole affair ended with a torchlight dance and barbecue in the school playground, which was attended by all and sundry, including those parents who had never before made contact with the teachers. From the school's point of view the carnival can serve a variety of social and environmental purposes. For one thing, the experience of walking down the middle of a traffic free road, enables children to *see* the streets for a change. It would be marvellous if we could establish the convention that primary schools paraded through the streets annually, and certainly it would be a good idea to invent an ancient local tradition of Beating the Bounds of the Catchment Area.

It isn't only schools of course who might take the initiative in organising a carnival. The idea might spring from all kinds of youth groups, from tenants' and residents' associations, community action groups, from student rag days, technical or further education colleges, or the local community relations council.

Organising a Carnival

Everything starts with someone. And if the idea starts with you, the first questions to ask are:

1. Is there an existing initiative in the area? Is someone or some body already busy planning a local festival week, a fair, or a Summer Festival that your activity should be dove-tailed into? Is there an actual local tradition — like the Nottingham Goose Fair in which your carnival could find a place? Is there some moribund local festival or ceremony that could be revived? It may be that a carnival is planned for the summer holiday anyway, but this does not preclude running a school-based one in the spring.

2. Who will help? What individuals, organisations, firms and institutions in the district can be drawn upon? If you are in a primary or secondary school, who else in the school can be drawn in and how can you make contacts with other local schools? In fact this is one of the hardest things of all to achieve. Sometimes even the heads of the locality have very little contact with each other. Sometimes there are part-time teachers or for example 'peripatetic' music teachers who can be link-men in such ventures.

3. How far ahead should you plan? The answer is as far as you possibly can. If the carnival is the focus for craft work in making things (as at Conisbrough) then you must allow enough time for everyone to make a goodly collection of carnival gear, and enough time for musicians and singers to work up a first-rate performance. Some participating schools may work faster than others, and you must allow enough time for different finds of institution to get into gear. Ideally secondary schools should be working with and visiting primary schools, and colleges of education should be working with both, in which case it is important to bear in mind examination dates when fixing the date.

Planning the Route

Obviously your carnival should go where it can be seen and where there are things worth seeing. Its finishing point should be somewhere with space for relaxation and enjoyment — food, sports, music, entertainment. You will have to take the police into your confidence as far in advance as possible so that arrangements can be made for the diversion of traffic and the closing of the streets. (The police have had the right for over a century to regulate the route of processions, and many cities have local Acts of Parliament requiring notice to be given to the police.) For the legal position consult the Penguin/NCCL *Handbook of Citizens' Rights*. Often you may find the chief officer willing to undertake traffic diversions just for your little carnival. In one town both the organizers and the inspector were scratching their heads for a formula which would satisfy both parties and found a clause recommending street closure if a 'throng' was anticipated. Since they anticipated a throng, the street was closed to allow the procession to occupy the street.

Finding the Cash

With resources so tight, expecially in school, organizers will probably have to look around for money to pay for materials, publicity, music etc. Enthusiasm can make up part of the deficit, and you should certainly lobby the local brass band or any school which has one. But extra cash must be found from somewhere. The journal *Community Action* No 13, April-May 1974, obtainable for 15p from Community Action, 7a Frederick Mews, Kinnerton Street, London SW1, includes an article 'How to Make Money' with a host of suggestions on sources of money for community festivals. If your carnival is part of a larger festival you should certainly think about their suggestions. They mention such organizations as the local Council of Social Service, Local Authorities, the local Community Relations Officer, Rotary and Round Table Clubs (best approached by nobbling a member). There are also national charities and trusts (see *The Directory of Grant-Making Trusts* and the *Charities Digest* in the local reference library). There are also various obscure local charities which you might find out about, again in the reference library, or from a clergyman or solicitor in the area. The Granby Summer Festival (1A Beaconsfield Street, Liverpool 8) have published a report on last year's festival (10p) and an information pamphlet (send them a large s.a.e.) with a lot of valuable information on their experience.

Contacts and Publicity

'If only I had been told . . .' is the usual comment made when the carnival is over. People are very often so bogged down in the donkey-work of organizing that they don't have time to make contact. Not only does this mean that people miss the carnival, but that people who might be drawn in to help don't get the chance either. Use the local papers, including the 'do-it-yourself' community press. Tell them what you are hoping to do, give them an address so that people can contact you, and write letter in their columns asking specifically for the help you want. Tell the local radio stations and the TV networks too.

If yours is a school-based carnival, send letters home to parents in good time, again being specific about the help you need. Leaflet the shops on the route. Produce posters and get them displayed. Give them a chance to get in on the act.

Yet More on Carnivals and Festivals

If you are thinking seriously about the possibilities of the ideas emerging from this issue of BEE, you ought to get yet another packet of advice in the form of the *Community Festivals Handbook* published by Youth Volunteer Force Foundation, 7 Leonard Street, London EC2 at 30p. inc. postage.

Written by John Hoyland and co-ordinated by Aland Turkie, it declares that a community festival 'can give local people confidence and flair in their organizational ability. It can teach them a lot of practical and organizational skills. It can develop the strength and credibility of community organizations, tenants' associations and other grass-roots groups, and it can build up links between them. It can focus attention on issues of local concern, and increase mobilization round issues. It can be a take-off point for a lot of other activity and work. In fact it can be an important point in a continuing process of grass-roots organization — a useful point around which to organize, an assertion of local people's identity and power.'

All this, and entertainment too!

Case Study 3.10

Computer Based Resource Units:
An Approach to Environmental Education for all Grades

What is a CBRU?
A unique system of information storage and rapid retrieval designed to assist teachers in curriculum planning and to direct class and individual student focus upon specific learner objectives. The teacher receives a Computer Based Resource *Guide* (a portion of a CBRU) containing the objectives selected for the class and individual students, subject matter content, instructional activities, suggested supplemental references and materials, and suggested measuring devices for evaluation.

Who Developed the Idea of CBRU's
CBRU's were conceived and developed by Dr. Robert Haarnock at the State University of New York in the early 1960s.

What Examples of Successful Use are there?
The Research and Development Complex, State University College at Buffalo, N.Y., has promoted the use of CBRU's nationally, and in New Jersey it has been used successfully through Project APPLE, under a ESEA Title VI-G grant providing instructional materials and programs for neurologically and perceptually impaired children.

What Environmental Education Units are Available?
The Council sought the advice of numerous environmental interest groups around the country and embarked on the development of 13 units which should provide a basis for interesting and lively classroom content and activities for youngsters in the New Jersey schools. A listing of the units which are available to teachers follows:

Environment and the Quality of life: Population
Environment and the Quality of Life: Natural Resources
Environment and the Quality of Life: Industrial-Economic Impact
Environment and the Quality of Life: Pollution
Environment and the Quality of Life: Land Use
Environment and the Quality of Life: River Basin (Case Study)
Environment and the Quality of Life: A Pine Barren (Case Study)
Environment and the Quality of Life: Wetlands (Case Study)
Environment and the Quality of Life: Energy-Technology
Environment and the Quality of Life: Energy-Society

Environment and the Quality of Life: Energy-Transportation
Environment and the Quality of Life: Primary Ecology
Environment and the Quality of Life: Environmental Law

How do you find out more and Start Ordering and Using CBRU's?
A training program designed to acquaint New Jersey teachers with the history and use of CBRU's and the procedure for ordering them has been developed. In the meantime, feel free to contact the Council if you have any questions.

Dr. Ed Ambey
New Jersey State Council for Environmental Education
at Montclair State College
Upper Montclair, New Jersey 07043
Phone: (201) 744-0362

4
Materials, Facilities and Media

JOHN Y. JACKSON

Accessibility

Environmental education can undoubtedly be carried on with fewer 'tools' than traditional subjects require. In fact, there are persons who feel that a textbook is inimical to environmental education. Environmental education, with its focus on inquiry and outdoor activities, would appear as a boon to those schools for whom an adequate supply of materials has been a chronic problem.

Nevertheless, materials and equipment can facilitate and improve the quality of environmental studies. Any environmental problem investigated in detail soon requires more data than can be supplied by direct observation. Ideally, a school would have a materials resource centre, a library and a film room which would contain information useful to the student. In addition, each classroom would contain readily accessible materials. In practice, however, materials remain in short supply for hundreds and thousands of students and teachers in the world's schools.

One of the problems associated with educational materials is that of dissemination. How are teachers to know that certain materials exist? In a centralized system of education this problem is met by edict in that certain materials are provided for the teacher. There are always other materials, however, which are outside the scope of officially provided materials, yet which may be available and useful for the teacher or curriculum planner. This is especially true for environmental education.

The specialist must, of course, attempt to keep abreast of the development of materials within a field. The proliferation of materials and the scope of environmental education has made difficult this job of keeping current. In recognition of this need, a system of Educational Resource Information Centers (ERIC's) were established in the United States. The Centers, located in various parts of the country, each focus on a particular discipline, or area of interest. The ERIC for environmental education is located at Columbus, Ohio. Case Study 4.1 gives further details on this ERIC's services.

Other countries have long-established centres for information related to environmental education, such as the Commonwealth Institute in

London and the Central Laboratory for Nature Conservation in Moscow. There has been a recognized need for an international information centre. In 1974 the Center for International Environmental Information began as a part of the United Nations Environment Program (U.N.E.P.). Although its interests are on world environmental problems, its services should be useful to environmental educators. The Center, located at 345 East 46th St., New York, NY 10017, publishes *World Environment News.*

A cataloguing of available materials is not within the scope of this chapter. One needs to maintain a card file, or looseleaf notebook, for this purpose. However, references will be made to sources of such information. For instance, Appendix A is a bibliography of bibliographies in environmental education.

Printed Materials

Traditionally, textbooks for environmental education have been directed toward the established curriculum. The Biological Sciences Curriculum Study (BSCS) is an example of a major effort to improve instruction and materials in science education. The resulting books have received worldwide attention and have a considerable environmental emphasis. Pages from *Biological Science: Patterns and Processes* are reproduced as Case Study 4.3. From this it is possible to see the focus on laboratory activity, and the use of directed questions leading to independent thought.

Case Study 4.3 includes two pages from the textbook, *World Resources*, concerning 'Fishing and Forestry South of the Sahara'. From these pages it is possible to observe the textbook's function of organizing and presenting information. Later, the question is raised, 'What problems do governments have in trying to achieve greater fishing production in tropical Africa?' While this is an environment-related question, this section is mainly concerned with resource development. If the material were being written in the mid-1970's, there would be greater emphasis on the possible effects of development on fish populations. The material in this selection would be difficult for students to research on their own with their usual sources of information, but it represents a step towards understanding environmental and social factors in the world's food problem.

Elementary environmental education materials were developed in the late 1960s and early 1970s. Most of this material has been in the form of lesson units, packets, or modules, to be used for a period of a few days, or weeks, and is not tied directly to any one textbook or course of study. This material has the advantage of being flexible in terms of scheduling during the term. However, such material is often looked upon as an added attraction, something to be engaged in if time permits.

Environmental awareness and issues are being worked in to more and more textbooks at both the elementary and secondary levels. This raises the question of whether or not a textbook that has a short section on air pollution falls into the category of environmental education material, or must it have an environmental theme running throughout? Perhaps the best way to judge this is to examine the objectives of the book. Is it stated or implied that the student should gain a better understanding of his environment and the interacting factors within that environment? Is there content to support this? If so, the book could be considered environmental education material.

Beyond the textbook, there is a wide range of books that come under the heading of supplementary material. Trade book publishers put out many of these each year and Case Study 4.4 is a list of selected ecology books for children. In addition to the trade publishers, organizations such as the Sierra Club, Audubon Society and Friends of the Earth have produced beautiful and useful books. The impact of a single book on the thinking of the people of a nation and the world is exemplified in Rachel Carson's *Silent Spring*. This book is joined by *A Sand County Almanac, Walden, The Population Bomb* and *The Limits to Growth* in the Environmental Books Hall of Fame (Beckman, 1974).

In an effort to assist teachers in relating environmental education to the existing curriculum, various guides have been developed. An example of this is the South Carolina Conservation Curriculum Improvement Project which began in 1966 and culminated in the publication of a series of books entitled *People and Their Environment* (Brennan, 1969). The project utilized writing teams of teachers working within a conceptual framework developed with the help of specialists and consultants. The guides follow the format of having a collection of lessons that relate to specific topics or concepts, i.e. 'The characteristics of groups stem from interaction between individuals and groups' (*People and Their Environment* Social Studies Guide 7-8-9, p. 89), or 'Matter can neither be created or destroyed, simply transformed' (*People and Their Environment* Science Guide 7-8-9, p. 89).

Some less formal teaching guides which almost take on the characteristics of trade books are represented by Mark Terry's *Teaching for Survival** and Ward and Fyson's *Streetwork; The Exploding School*. In the Preface, Ward and Fyson explain what they attempt to do in their book:

It is mainly concerned with the environmental education of the non-academic urban child — in other words with the vast majority of the population. It is a polemical book not a source book — though copious reference is made to the resources available to the teacher.

*Reviewed by Robert N. Saveland in *The Journal of Geography*, Vol. 71, No. 3, March 1972, pp. 188—189.

Nor is it just about techniques, though ample reference is made to methods teachers have found successful. It is a book about *ideas*: ideas of the environment as *the* educational resource, ideas of the enquiring school, the school without walls, the school as a vehicle of citizen participation in environmental decision, ideas above all about a 'problem-oriented' approach to environmental education.

The last chapter of *Streetwork* is on sources and resources and, as such, complements the work of this chapter. Here the authors point out that: 'The streetwork teacher's textbook is the town, but his principal teaching resource is himself' (p. 122). Samples from pages of this chapter are reproduced as Case Study 4.5.

Perhaps the category 'printed materials' is stretched somewhat to include games and simulations, but these devices usually include printed instructions, data sheets, or background information. Generally some reading skill is required for the student to participate. Games have a motivational factor linked to the simulation of reality and to the competitive spirit. One wonders if rivalry is an innate characteristic of children, or is it largely culturally determined? A disadvantage of games is the amount of class time they consume. The same concepts can usually be presented by other means in less time, albeit with perhaps less effectiveness. As with other methods, the main point of the game may sometimes be lost by the participants.

To assist persons with responsibility for the production and use of environmental education materials, the Western Regional Environmental Education Council (WREEC) has published a set of guidelines and recommendations entitled *Resource Guide*. This booklet stresses the importance of first assessing needs and then of identifying and analysing the target audience. Ways of developing activity-oriented classroom materials are also indicated.

A six-volume series of environmental education activities written by teachers has been collected and edited by William B. Stapp and Dorothy Cox. The first book sets forth the philosophy and model, and the remaining books are suggested activities by grade levels from lower elementary to senior high school.

Environmental Study Areas
The most effective method of environmental education includes a direct interrelationship of students with their extended environment. The involvement can be a few minutes of the school day, or it can be a resident programme of weeks' duration. This first-hand experience outside the classroom can be in a forest, outdoor laboratory, school garden, or a pavement, busy intersection or garbage dump. Environmental study areas include those that are operated by schools for their own use and those that are operated by other agencies (such as a

museum, nature centre, or park service) for use by more than one school district. They can be classified still further into two types, formal and informal. The formal outdoor laboratory usually has a well-defined nature trail and information markers that can be used by teachers, students and the general public. In contrast to this, an informal centre may simply be a woodlot or field that the school leaves undisturbed where students can carry on long- and short-term plant and animal studies. The formal outdoor laboratory usually has well-marked boundaries, yet the informal one, by its very nature, has no boundaries. Many teachers find that they use both types of outdoor laboratory during the school year.

The establishment of an environmental study area takes time. One method, used in Australia, is explained in Case Study 4.6. Note particularly in this case study that credit for action is attributed mainly to a relatively small group of persons with vision. Also, it appears that some form of government or private foundation support is needed in order to acquire land for nature study (Schimpff, 1973).

A programme that has been in existence for many years in an urbanized area is that of school gardens in The Netherlands. As a formal programme, it has transfer value to other urbanized parts of the world. For this reason, Case Study 4.7 presents information on this programme in some detail.

There is relatively abundant literature on means of developing and using environmental study areas. Selected references are given at the end of this chapter. Some considerations in planning which may otherwise be overlooked are given herewith:

1. If possible, include flowing water as well as a still body of water. A walkway permits observations and sample collection without endangering student or environment.

2. Protect physical features unique to the site. The cover over artifacts can be removed to give students an understanding of how they were formed. Students may remove from sites a limited quantity of material, such as fossils, if it relates directly to their studies and does not impair, or threaten, the existing feature.

3. Cultural remnants may also be preserved. Thus students can speculate about previous land use from a former house foundation, rusting ploughshare, or an exotic plant or a mill race.

4. An area planted in one tree species can be used for plant growth measurements and other experiments in succeeding years. Another area left in its natural state can be used for studying plant succession. Devise a means of keeping long-term records for such comparisons.

5. Set aside an area for agricultural use. This can be used for studies of energy transformation as well as for investigating the sources of food and fibres and other products.

6. Demonstrate that the area is part of the biosphere which is a part

of the universe by using an upright post as a shadow stick. By noting the length and movement of the shadow as the sun crosses the meridian, students can determine true North and come to understand the movement of rotation. By measuring the shadow at the same time for several days, they will observe that its length changes. The inclination of the axis and the revolution of the earth about the sun are basic factors in establishing the pattern of ecosystems around the world.

7. Provide an outdoor meeting place so that discussions can take place without returning to the classroom. (An area free of biting insects and with some protection from rain.)

8. Consider summertime and after-school use. This may involve the construction of restroom facilities.

9. Examples of some useful equipment:

> Plant press
> Vasculum (for carrying plant specimens)
> Tree, Bird and Wildflower identification keys
> Magnetic compasses (Silva type is best)
> Magnifying glasses
> Topographic maps
> Plane tables
> Alidads
> Butterfly nets
> Dip nets
> Plankton nets
> Seine net
> Geology hammers
> Sight levels
> Sextant
> Increment bore
> Soil auger
> Soil bore
> Soil test kits — can be done in chemistry lab without kit
> Water test kits — can be done in chemistry lab without kit
> Air quality monitoring equipment
> Recording thermometer (max.-min. could be substituted if necessary)
> Recording barometer
> Wet and dry bulb thermometer
> Sling psychrometers
> Soil thermometers
> Air thermometers
> Water thermometers (can usually use air ones)
> Precipitation gauge
> Anemometer

Weather vane
Binoculars
50-foot tape
100-foot tape

Schools which are too small to finance the purchase of a range of equipment such as indicated above can be served by a mobile environmental education laboratory. Case Study 4.8 illustrates such a laboratory developed by the school district of Kingsport, Tennessee. A mini-van was equipped with microscopes, insect-collecting equipment, water study equipment, plant specimen holders, soil-testing kits, etc. The van allowed the equipment to be easily and safely transported from one site to another. The students meet at the study site and use the equipment. This method of having a driver/environmental education specialist who takes the van from one place to another would appear to be very useful in a large geographical area with several small, scattered schools. The van would then serve a function similar to a bookmobile, or travelling library, except that most of the equipment would stay with the van rather than being checked out until the next visit.

Resident field study centres provide facilities for students and teachers to participate in programmes lasting more than a day. These centres are sometimes called 'live-in' centres as contrasted with 'day-use' centres. Generally live-in centres serve more than one school district and may have sleeping space for a hundred or more students. Sleeping accommodation can range from tent sites to modern cabins with plumbing facilities. Such centres often provide students with an opportunity to experience at close range an ecosystem different from their home community, as when urban students are taken to the mountains or the coast.

The resident programme allows the students to conduct investigations that take more than a day, or need some time in the evening. The students may also run studies similar to those they have made in their own community, such as soil testing and water testing, and compare the results from the two regions.

The resident centre also provides opportunities for new forms of social interaction. Students share responsibilities for serving food, cleaning their cabins, and other tasks not usually carried out in the classroom. Resident centres may also provide the opportunity for student teachers or college interns to assist with the programme, thereby introducing them to environmental education methods and materials. The heart of the resident centre is its programme and the people who manage it.

When a new school is being constructed, consideration should be given to incorporating an environmental study area into the plans. The easiest way to do this is to ensure that the school site includes enough land to set aside a portion for such purposes. With the acquisition of sufficient land for the school and the environmental study area, there is no future problem concerning transporting students to the outdoor laboratory. Some interesting ideas in site planning are presented in Case Study 4.9. This represents a rather structured setting, but it reflects what is likely to be encountered when working with architects and landscapers in a developed situation.

Public Information

In all parts of the world, a part of the job of public education is being done by mass media. The press and other news media, whether government or privately managed, generally recognize an obligation to inform the public. In most cases, this obligation takes on some form of indoctrination. Where entertainment is also a function of the media, the information phase may have a secondary order of priority.

The influence of the press is dependent upon the literacy of a population. For this and other reasons the small transistor radio is probably the most universal means of transmitting information and ideas. The programming itself may have little relationship to environmental problems although this means of communication has been used to encourage family planning, the recycling of resources, and other remedial measures for such problems.

Besides radio, television is a major factor in public education in those parts of the world where people have access to this media. This has included the use of television as a major part of the instructional programme in Pago Pago for the island schools of American Samoa. Television producers are aware of the environmental problems that confront all of us. Accordingly, TV brings the more serious environmental problems into the living room with the news several nights a week. In addition, national television systems produce documentary programmes dealing with environmental problems on a global level. These programmes may then be transferred to 16 mm film and released for sale to educational institutions.

In addition to documentary films that have been produced by the television networks, almost all producers of classroom films have marketed environmentally-oriented films. Some of these films are directed specifically to science classes. Others are aimed more at a general audience and are more inter-disciplinary in nature. Originally the focus was an awareness of environmental problems. More recently, films are emphasizing individual and community involvement for the alleviation of these problems.

Filmstrips, slides and tape recordings are comparatively inexpensive and have great flexibility in classroom use. Pictures can be projected for as long as desired so that details and clues may be searched out. Many environmental filmstrips have been produced and, like the movies, they have tended to concentrate on environmental awareness. The still camera and the movie camera have been used as effective tools in the hands of students. (See *Improve Your Enviroment: Fight Pollution with Pictures*, Kodak Customer Service Pamphlet AC-26 $1.00, Rochester, NY 14650.) At a somewhat more sophisticated level, hand-held video-tape equipment and inexpensive sound movie cameras increase the possibility of local productions which will contribute new ideas for improving the quality of the environment in a neighbourhood, community or region.

Newspapers are another way for people to learn about environmental problems facing their community, and what is being done about them. Most responsible newspapers keep the public informed as to what the governmental structure is doing towards enacting or enforcing environmental laws. Large circulation papers may have a special reporter with a primary responsibility for 'environmental news'. Newspapers and news magazines may run an environment section as a regular feature. Case Study 4.10 is an excerpt from such a page in *The Christian Science Monitor*. Sometimes it is difficult to distinguish between environmental news and regular news.

The name *Taraxucum* was chosen to symbolize dandelion seeds blowing around the earth and spreading the message of environmental conservation

There are several special-audience magazines aimed at readers with environmental concerns. These may deal with wildlife, organic gardening, forestry, recreation, education, etc. *BEE Bulletin of Environmental Education* and *The Journal of Environmental Education* are two of the most useful special-audience magazines in the field of environmental education. *Taraxucum* is the journal of the International Youth Federation for Environmental Studies and Conservation. Case Study 5.6 has further information on the IYF. Reference to other periodicals will be found in some of the bibliographies in Appendix A. In addition to the magazines at an adult level, there are some publications directed specifically to the classroom audience. The availability of these varies from country to country. Just as national magazines have shown an increased interest in environmental affairs, so have these school-directed publications. It is probably through these publications, and the discussions of the articles in them, that many school children get an introduction to environmental education.

Finally, the newsletter is a means of communication which has greatly proliferated with the spread of xerography and other inexpensive duplicating devices. It appears that all environmental organizations put out their own newsletter. Some of these are published by national organizations and keep people posted on national issues. There are also numerous newsletters on the local level. All serve a communications function among people with a commonality of interests.

Bibliography

BEE Bulletin of Environmental Education, Town and County Planning Association, 17 Carlton House Terrace, London SW1.

Beckman, John, '*The Wonder of a Printed Book*', *Not Man Apart*, October 1974, Vol. 4, No. 14, p. 1.

Brennan, Mathew (Ed.), *People and Their Environment*, Ferguson, New York, 1969.
Grades 1-2-3
Social Studies 7-8-9
Science 7-8-9
Biology
Outdoor Laboratory 1—12

Carson, Rachel, *The Silent Spring*, Crest, 1962.

Ehilich, Paul, *The Population Bomb*, Ballantine, 1968.

Leopard, Aldo, *A Sand County Almanac*, Oxford University Press, 1949.

Meadows, Donella *et al.*, *The Limits to Growth*, Universe Books, 1972.

Quigg, Philip M., 'World Environment Newsletter', *Saturday Review/World*, 488, Madison Ave., New York, NY 10032.

Schimpff, Wayne H., 'The Open Lands Project Environmental Education Program: A Review and Projection', The Open Lands Project, 53 W. Jackson Blvd., Chicago, IL 60604.

Terry, Mark, *Teaching for Survival, A Handbook for Environmental education*, Friends of the Earth/Ballantine, New York, 1971, 213 pp.

The Journal of Environmental Education, Heldref Publ., 4000 Albemarle St. NW, Washington, DC 20016.

Thoreau, Henry David, *Walden*, Mentor, 1854.

Ward, Colin and Fyson, Anthony, *Streetwork: The Exploding School*, Routledge & Kegan Paul, London/Boston, 1973, 139 pp.

WREEC (Western Regional Environmental Education Council), *Resource Guide*, 721 Capitol Mall, Sacramento, Ca 95814.

Additional References

Forest Service, U.S. Dept. of Agriculture, *Teaching Materials for Environmental Education: Investigating Your Environment*, U.S. Govt. Printing Office, Washington, DC. 95 cents. Stock Number 0101-0234.

Stapp, Wm. B. and Cox, Dorothy A. (eds.), *Environmental Education Activities Manual*, Dorothy A. Cox, 30808 LaMar, Farmington Hills, MI 48024 $8.50 per set.

Selected Bibliography on Environmental Study Areas

Bureau of Outdoor Recreation
U.S. Dept. of Interior
Washington, DC 20240
   Education and Outdoor Recreation, 1968, 47 p.

Busch, Phyllis S., *The Urban Environment: A Teacher's Guide K-3*, J. G. Ferguson, Chicago, 1975, 217 pp.

Council for Environmental Education
School of Education
University of Reading
24 London Road
Reading, Berks.
   Advice on the Production of a Resource Guide for Outdoor Studies

Environmental Science Center
U.S. Bureau of Sport Fisheries and Wildlife
Department of Interior
Fort Snelling, MN
National Wildlife Refuges and Environmental Education, 7 p.
   Outdoor Classroom Environmental Education Guide, 1973
      Site Series — 1 Pedestrian Paths
                     2 Roadways
                     3 Succession Models
                     4 Safety, etc.

Educational Facilities Laboratories, Inc.
477 Madison Ave.
New York, NY 10022
   Environmental Education/Facilities Resources

Forest Service
U.S. Dept. of Agriculture
Washington, DC
Teaching Conservation through Outdoor Education Areas, 1970, 22 p.
   Teaching Materials for Environmental Education: Investigating Your Environment, July 1973, 69 p.

Russell, Helen Ross, *Ten-Minute Field Trips: Using the School Grounds for Environmental Studies*, J. G. Ferguson, Chicago, 1973, 173 p.

124

National Audubon Society
Nature Centers Division
1130 Fifth Ave.
New York, NY 10028
  Planning a Nature Center I-E Bulletin No. 2, 1963, 88 p.
  A Nature Center for Your Community, revised, 1969, 40 p.
  Manual of Outdoor Interpretation, 1968, 104 p. Edited by Joseph J. Shomon.
  Trail Planning and Layout, 1965, 1971, 76 p., by Byron L. Ashbaugh and
    Raymond J. Kordish.
  Directory of Nature Centers and related Environmental Education Facilities,
    July 1971, 72 p.

National Education Association
and National Park Service, Dept. of Interior
Washington, DC 20036
  A Guide to Planning and Conducting Environmental Study Area Workshops,
    1972, 50 p.

National Park Service
U.S. Dept. of Interior
Office of Environmental Interpretation
Washington, DC
  National Environmental Study Area: A Guide, 56 p.

S.F.U.
Ostermalmsgatan 80
S-114 50 Stockholm
  Material for a study circle on how to find a good investigation area (in Swedish)

Stapp, Wm., *Integrating Conservation and Outdoor Education into the Curriculum
  K-12*, Burgess, Minneapolis, 1965, 93 p.

Tennessee Valley Authority (TVA)
Knoxville, TN 37902
  Environmental Study Area Inventory and Evaluation Form, September 1971
  Developing Environmental Study Areas prepared by Jonathan Wert, August
    1974.

Town and Country Planning Association
17 Carlton House Terrace
London SW1Y 5AS
  Council for Urban Studies Centres, First Report 1974

Case Study 4.1

Now You Can Easily Locate Those ERIC Abstracts and Reports That You Want in Science Education, Mathematics Education and Environmental Education

ERIC/SMEAC, one of the several Clearinghouses of the National Institute of Education's ERIC System, has as its primary purpose the procurement, abstracting, and announcing through *Research in Education* documents pertaining to science, mathematics, and environmental education; other ERIC Clearinghouses have responsibility in other areas of education. In addition, SMEAC publishes other documents in its areas of concern — directories, compilations, reviews, and the like — in which interest and need has been expressed by practitioners. For example, an annual *Directory of Projects and Programs in Environmental Education* is published, a second *Review of Research Related to Environmental Education* is currently being prepared, two volumes of *100 Activities in Environmental Education* have been published, and a mailing list of environmental educators is maintained.

Among the recent publications of the Educational Resources Information Center for Science, Mathematics, and Environmental Education (ERIC/SMEAC) is *Environmental Education: Abstracts and Index from Research in Education 1966—1972*, a compilation of abstracts published by the ERIC System during those years. Approximately 1,200 abstracts are included, cross-referenced by ERIC descriptors, authors, and institutional authors.

Plans call for updating this effort periodically. A second compilation, containing abstracts of environmental education documents during 1973—1974, is currently being prepared, projected publication date late 1975.

Persons wishing more information concerning ERIC efforts in environmental education are encouraged to write: ERIC/SMEAC, The Ohio State University, 400 Lincoln Tower, 1800 Cannon Drive, Columbus, Ohio 43210.

Who can use ERIC? . . . and How?

School Administrators

To identify new and significant educational developments.

To apply new management tools and practices to the local situation.

To base budget estimates on the latest research data.

Teachers

To obtain the latest information on preservice and inservice training.

To learn about new classroom techniques and materials.

To discover 'how-to-do-it' projects for personal and professional development.

Researchers

To keep up-to-date on research in their field of interest.

To avoid duplication of research efforts.

To obtain full-text documents on research.

Information Specialists

To compile bibliographies and summaries on specific educational topics.

To search ERIC publications for answers to inquiries.

To locate and order documents for local information centers.

Professional Organizations

To assist members in keeping abreast of research in a specific area of education.

To inform members of significant developments or documents in peripheral or related areas of education.

To keep members up-to-date on information systems.

Graduate and Undergraduate Students

To gain access to the latest information for preparing term papers, theses, and dissertations.

To obtain information on career development in education.

To build a personalized, low-cost library on education.

Case Study 4.2

41/Laboratory Activity

(Reproduced with permission from Biological Sciences Curriculum Study, *Biological Science: Patterns and Processes*, revised edn., Holt, Rinehart and Winston, New York, 1970)

Three containers of ice water are used for this experiment. One of you will exercise his hand in the water in container A. He will hold his other hand still in the water in container B. Container C will only have water in it. You will read the temperature of the water in each container once each minute for five minutes. When the experiment is over, you will make a graph showing the temperature readings for the three containers.

Materials (for each team of four)
3 large containers, each capable of holding 1000 ml
3 thermometers
Ice
Stirring rod

Procedure
1. Put 600 ml of water in each container. The water should be 10° C at the start of the experiment. You may have to add ice to the water. Be sure to remove the ice when the temperature gets to 10° C.
2. *First student.* Put your hand under the water in container A. Exercise your fingers by moving them rapidly in the water. Keep this hand moving and keep it under the water for five minutes. Put you other hand under the water in conainer B. Do not move this hand. Keep it as still as you can for five minutes.
3. *Second student.* Hold a thermometer in the water in container A. Read the temperature once each minute for five minutes.
4. *Third student.* Hold a thermometer in the water in container B. Read the temperature once each minute for five minutes. You must also stir the water in this container using the stirring rod.
5. *Fourth student.* Read the temperature in container C once each minute for five minutes. You must also record the temperature readings on the record sheet for every member of the team.
6. Make a line graph of the temperature readings for each of the three containers. You will have three lines on the same graph. Draw your graph below.

TEMPERATURE			
Minutes	Container A (moving hand)	Container B (quiet hand)	Container C (no hand)
1			
2			
3			
4			
5			

Questions

1. Why did you have a container that you did not put your hand in?
2. What happened to the temperature when you held your hand in cold water without moving it?
3. Did the temperature readings change when you exercised your hand in the water? If so, why?

Optional 41/Laboratory Activity
Materials for two students
Thermometer blank
6-inch length of 1—2 inch masking tape
Beaker of ice slush
Beaker of continuously boiling water
6-inch plastic rule

Procedure
Place a strip of masking tape on the thermometer blank so that at least ¾ inch of the bulb area is uncovered and so that the column of red liquid is not covered.

Put the bulb in the ice slush to the edge of the tape and mark the tape at the point where the column of red liquid stops. This is 0° C.

Put the bulb in the boiling water to the edge of the tape and mark the tape at the point where the column of red liquid stops. This is 100° C.

Divide the space between 0° C and 100° C into 10 equal parts. A rule marked in millimeters will help.

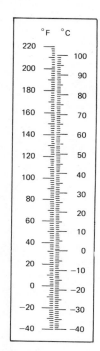

Temperature conversion scale

Divide each of these 10° C divisions in half. Your thermometer is now calibrated in 5° C divisions.

You might calibrate the side opposite the C markings in degrees F. Place 32° F opposite the 0° C, and 212° F opposite the 100° C marking as shown in Fig. 2-2.

You now have 20 equal divisions between 32° F and 212° F. How many degrees will each be worth? Place the proper numbers on your thermometer.

Case Study 4.3

Fishing and Forestry South of the Sahara

Tropical Africa ranks low in the production and consumption of fish. A large variety of fish is available in the extensive coastal and inland waters of Africa. A brief study explains why these fishing resources have not been more fully developed.

In wide areas of the wet-and-dry tropics, the waters of the land seasonally dry up entirely or decrease to mere trickles. This discourages any real dependence upon fish as a year-round food supply. The warm temperatures of much of the area south of the Sahara speed the process of decay. Inefficient transportation handicaps distribution. In the past, lack of any but rather primitive methods of drying, salting, and smoking prohibited wide distribution or lengthy storage.

Many Africans have taboos against eating fish. Pastoral people particularly have this prohibition. For many Africans, fish would be their last choice of food. Yet, there are some coastal and inland peoples who subsist on fish. For example, the lives of the Ovimbundu of Angola and the Tonga of Malawi are regulated by their fishing activities.

Today, African peoples and their governments are taking a new look at fishing potentials. Increases in the population and the growing number of city dwellers have forced reappraisal of traditional food production. Most African governments are keenly aware of the malnutrition which exists among their people.

Fishing is improving along the Atlantic Coast. Although the seas are rough along the shore, and the coast has few natural harbors or favorable launching sites, west coast fishermen have been dauntless in their small boats. In Ghana alone, it is estimated that there are nine thousand fishing boats.

Commercial fishing can be improved by the construction and use of larger boats. Just the availability of outboard motors aids immeasurably. Provision of better nets made from synthetic fibers will increase efficiency. Improved facilities for packing, preserving, canning, and freezing will increase the ease of handling, storing, and selling. The government of Ghana is introducing refrigerated trucks for handling frozen fish. The Nigerian government has improved fishing craft and has established a co-operative fishing community. As in the case of many other African endeavors, the pooling of the talent and resources of many small local producers seems to hold real promise for improving production.

Research by a German expedition in the Gulf of Guinea and the work of Soviet scientists off Ghana have indicated the presence of untapped fish resources in deeper waters. The Food and Agricultural Organization of the United Nations is serving as the agency to coordinate research and to provide advice. The organization has also set up demonstration projects in Nigeria.

Improvements are bound to come where fishing is already established. Ghana, Senegal, Angola, and South-West Africa are the outstanding centers on the Atlantic coast. The presence of large numbers of fish has already drawn commercial fishermen from Western Europe to the coast of Africa. Tuna fishing is one of the major attractions. The Spanish and Portuguese still have bases on the continent, while the French boats fish off the shores of former colonies. Greek and Italian trawlers are present, and factory ships from the USSR and Poland have started working in the Gulf of Guinea. Recently, vessels from the United States and Japan have joined in the activity.

The local fishing fleet at Dakar is served by several small packing plants, but an increasing share of the tuna is frozen. Pilchards, a term for the small fish of the herring family, are available in great quantities. Sardines are canned in large amounts in the Ivory Coast. In Guinea, the West Germans are operating a smoking plant. An ice-making plant in Sierra Leone is a decided improvement for local fishmen.

The potential of fishing can be illustrated in Ghana where, despite the sizable fish trade by African standards, fish must be imported from neighboring countries and from Europe. The demands for fish stimulate a trade which involves many merchants. Prices in the interior of the country often reach levels 200 percent or more above the price paid to the fishermen.

Many of the names of the west coast fish are not familiar to our ears. Others have English names we can recognize, such as sardines, mackerel, mullet, and red snapper. Farther south along the coast of Angola, where the cold Benguela Current flows, anchovy, sole, skate, swordfish, and lobsters are caught.

Case Study 4.4

New Ecology Books for Children

Here are some recently published books for children on various aspects of ecology. This list was compiled with the help of the National Science Teachers Association and Children's Book Council recommendations.

ABOUT GARBAGE AND STUFF by Ann Zane Shanks. Viking. A Photographic essay (printed on recycled paper) on the problems of disposal and recycling of waste.

AIR, THE INVISIBLE OCEAN by Sigmund Kalina. Prentice-Hall. Explores concepts such as 'what air is, how living things use and renew it, and why we must free it from pollution'.

AND THEN THERE WERE NONE by Nina Leen. Holt, Rinehart & Winston. Photographs and descriptions of some of America's endangered species. Includes complete lists of endangered and extinct wildlife, and some organizations currently active in preservation.

BLUE WHALE, VANISHING LEVIATHAN by Joseph J. Cook and William L. Wisner. Dodd, Mead. Traces evolution, development, characteristics, and future of the largest of the whale species. Maintaining marine ecological balance is stressed.

THE CHANGING WORLD OF BIRDS by John M. Anderson. Holt, Rinehart & Winston. Ecological aspects as well as the habits, life cycle, and migration of birds are described by an ornithologist.

CLEAN AIR — SPARKLING WATER: THE FIGHT AGAINST POLLUTION by Dorothy E. Shuttlesworth. Doubleday. Using specific examples and photographs, this book deals with such problems as how to fight pollution of air and water, and how such pollution came about.

THE ENVIRONMENT AND YOU by Matthew J. Brennan. Grosset & Dunlap. Pollution, poison, population, and how the environment works.

ESTUARIES by Laurence Pringle. Macmillan. Ecological information on creatures that live where fresh and salt water meet — birds, mammals, fish, crustaceans, mullusks, and plants.

INTO THE WOODS: EXPLORING THE FOREST ECOSYSTEM by Laurence Pringle. Macmillan. A useful glossary is included in this discussion of a forest and how it helps men.

LAKES by Delia Goetz. Morrow. With emphasis on pollution of lakes, the author describes past and present uses of these natural resources and considers their future.

LITTER — THE UGLY ENEMY: AN ECOLOGY STORY by Dorothy E. Shuttlesworth with Thomas Cervasio. Doubleday. A practical introduction to what has actually been done to cope with litter in 10 U.S. communities.

THE LIVES AND DEATHS OF A MEADOW by Lucille Wood Trost. Putnam's. Details the importance of a balance in nature, and what can be done to restore balance in our surroundings.

THE NEW AMERICAN CONTINENT: OUR CONTINENTAL SHELF by Norman Carlisle. Lippincott. Use, pollution problems, and future of 'the vast submerged terrace' that borders the American continent.

THE NEW WATER BOOK by Melvin Berger. Crowell. Includes experiments easy to perform and understand. There is also a list of several organizations interested in pollution.

SAVE THE EARTH! AN ECOLOGY HANDBOOK FOR KIDS by Betty Miles. Knopf. Full of ideas, experiments, stories, and projects related to conservation of land, air, and water.

SCAVENGERS by Olive L. Earle. Morrow. 'Material not easily found elsewhere about an important aspect of ecology'.

SEYMOUR, A GIBBON: ABOUT APES AND OTHER ANIMALS AND HOW YOU CAN HELP TO KEEP THEM ALIVE by Phyllis Borea. Atheneum. Includes information on how you can work with organizations such as zoos, wildlife refuges, conservation centers, parks, and humane groups.

TRUMPETER: THE STORY OF A SWAN by Jane and Paul Annixter. Holiday House. Story of one of the most endangered species.

WATER, A FIELD TRIP GUIDE by Helen Ross Russell. Little, Brown. Photographs enliven this book about water and its importance.

WATER FOR TODAY AND TOMORROW by R. J. Lefkowitz. Parents' Magazine Press. The fundamental facts of an essential resource.

WHY THINGS CHANGE by Jeanne Bendick. Parents' Magazine Press. 'Words like "evolve", "adapt", "survive", and "extinct" take on genuine meaning . . . in this excellent book'.

WONDERS OF ALLIGATORS AND CROCODILES by Wyatt Blassingame. Dodd, Mead. Describes the range, habitats, habits, and breeding of these reptiles threatened with extinction.

THE WORLD'S ENDANGERED WILDLIFE by George Laycock. Grosset & Dunlap. 'A dispassionate and sincere plea for conservation', this book includes a list of concerned organizations, a bibliography, and index.

Case Study 4.5

Games And Simulations

(Reproduced with permission from Ward, C. and Fyson, A., *Streetwork: The Exploding School*, Routledge and Kegan Paul, London, 1973)

We regard academic gaming and simulation as of the very greatest importance in environmental work, for the emphasis that is laid on pupil involvement and on processes of choice and change in the environment. We devoted a special issue of the *Bulletin of Environmental Education* (No. 13, May 1972) to the theme, and a bibliography and list of relevant games were included, while there was an article by Rex Walford on 'Games and the Environment'. He of course has made a major contribution to the development of games in this country, and his *Games in Geography* (Longmans, 1969) is still a good starting point, while *Simulation in the Classroom* (Penguin, 1972), which he wrote with John Taylor, gives a useful and lucid discussion of the theory of simulations with the benefit of great experience in their use. (The book includes a description of an urban growth model and of Sean Carson's conservation game based on the siting of London's third airport.) His contribution to *Games and Simulations* (BBC, 1972) edited by Chris Longley gave valuable advice on using, adapting and building games. *Simulation Games in Geography* (Macmillan, 1972) edited by R. Dalton, describes games dealing with mining, village settlement, farm growth, service centres, steelworks, and industrial town growth amongst other topics, though some are little more than decision-making exercises rather than simulations of reality.

The best in-depth discussion of gaming methods is to be found in *Educational Aspects of Simulation* (McGraw-Hill, 1971) edited by Pat Tansey. For an attack on the technique read 'Games Models and Reality in the Teaching of Geography in School' by N. Scarfe in *Geography* July 1971. There are also a number of American texts discussing games (see list in *BEE* 13).

For the games themselves, making up your own is probably the most educationally worth-while, especially if the pupils are involved in the process, and it is certainly the cheapest method — copy from a game framework already published to feel your way. *Man in his Environment* (Coca Cola Ltd), *Redevelop your own Town Centre* (Jackdaw), *Streets Ahead* (Liverpool EPA Project) and *The Spring Green Motorway* (Community Service volunteers) are all available cheaply and a number of others are described in the Geographical Association's *Geography in Secondary Schools*. Some, particularly those from America, are very expensive. *Decisions* (Shell) concerns the siting of an oil terminal and comes complete in a plastic brief case for £10. *Portsville* (how a town grows) is part of unit 1 of the American High School Geography Project. But for a mere 50p comes *Tenement*, Shelter's simulation of multi-occupation problems. Cost bears no relationship to the game's likely success.

Those wishing to develop gaming ideas in collaboration with other teachers and to receive a newsletter outlining advances in gaming techniques and forthcoming events, etc., should join the *Society for Academic Gaming and Simulation* (SAGSET). Details from the Secretary, 5 Errington, Moreton-in-the-Marsh, Gloucestershire.

Case Study 4.6

Establishing an Environment Studies Centre:
An Australian Experience (Ian Hore-Lacy)

Field Studies Facilities: Concept and Need
Although educational thinking in the state of Victoria has been moving
in the directions of inquiry-centred method and broadly environmental
themes, little has been done to provide facilities for any specialized
development of these, especially insofar as they are linked together. In
addition, some schools have taken over or built up country camps or
hostels, but these are more often activity-oriented than field-studies
enterprises.

Part of the reason for this lies in the training of teachers themselves,
and there have not been very many teachers convinced of the need to
study natural phenomena in the field, and even less who know how to
go about it.

In addition, where relevant courses are actually run for teachers in
training, or even for university undegraduates, adequate facilities for
intensive fieldwork are often unavailable, making these courses less
effective than they should be in terms of flow-on to professional
situations or opportunities.

In 1970, the Australian Conservation Foundation published a booklet entitled 'Establishing Field Studies Centres in Australia', drawing
upon mainly U.K. Field Studies Council, and also Canadian experience.
This set out some ideas on the matter, and the possibility soon com-
mended itself to a number of people, especially in Victoria. Subsequent
action was due almost entirely to the vision and activity of a relatively
small group of interested academics, teachers, naturalists, and other
citizens.

Phase I. Establishing the Association
Once a group of people had gathered who were prepared to be actively
involved in converting vision to action, and proposition to practice,
they joined themselves into a committee which immediately set about
several tasks:

(a) Drawing in support for the venture from all sections of society,
and propagating information so as to establish such support on a
continuing and increasing basis. The ultimate objective was to promote
environmental education by running first class field studies courses.

(b) Formalizing the constitutional basis of this as an Environment

Studies Association of Victoria, by drawing up Memorandum and Articles of Association for its legal incorporation.

(c) Finding a suitable area in which to select a site for the first centre. This involved months of thorough aerial and ground reconnaisance within a hundred mile (160 km) radius of the main centre of population. Local environmental diversity was the main object of the search, and this was evaluated for one, five, and twenty mile (1, 6, 8, and 32 km) radii from potential sites in each proposed area.

Phase II. Consolidation

The second phase of action involved settling down with a more permanent council and persevering with a number of mundane tasks essential to the consolidation of the whole scheme, including:

(A) Planning and running courses on Coastal Ecology, Alpine Ecology, Urban Studies etc., programmed in weekends at suitable rented sites. These were to show that the Association was a viable, active body capable of running excellent courses even on this sort of basis, with often inadequate facilities.

(b) Approaching state government education authorities with detailed information and proposals to commend the scheme and ensure continued support from that sector.

(c) Working for curriculum reform in the direction of greater environmental education.

(d) Setting up an environmental education resource centre.

(e) Gaining further information about facilities and organizations already existing overseas.

(f) Exploring means of raising the required capital for establishing a centre. The main initial undertaking in this direction was to publish a booklet setting out the proposal for the first centre in some detail. This was entitled 'Project One'.

Phase III. Demonstrating Expertise

By far the most important activity initiated in phase II was the running of day and weekend courses for students and members of the public. Due to the amount of work involved only 18 courses were actually run in 2½ years up to October 1974, but nearly 600 people registered for these and a considerable impact was made. Advertising was mainly through the membership, though also in the press.

One of the main effects of all this activity was that the Association proved that it was competent and determined to fulfil its primary objective: running diverse field studies courses in various environments. As a result of this the state government provided $20,000 in 1973 and again in 1974 towards the cost of a secretariat, headed by a director. There are plans for 17 courses in 1975 alone.

Phase IV. Planning a Field Studies Complex

As phase III progressed, plans continued for the establishment of a permanent centre. The site originally selected lapsed, for reasons beyond the Association's control. However, the state government meanwhile purchased a run-down farm in a very suitable area, and a submission was made asking for it to become the site of the state's first environment studies centre.

Conclusion

This case study has been prepared in the belief that thorough preparation at the levels outlined is the proper basis for wise and fruitful investment of capital and personnel in the immediate future. Guidelines for actually putting up buildings and staffing them are more readily available than those for taking the actual initiative in a frequently discouraging socio-cultural situation.

It must be stressed that the temptation to concentrate on buildings etc. should not be allowed to detract from the primary aim of providing environmental education, in this case by running courses for interested people. Furthermore, it was found necessary to demonstrate the Association's expertise in actually doing the job before any progress could be made in providing expensive facilities.

Case Study 4.7

School Gardens in the Netherlands (Harry Wahls)

History and Conceptual Evolution

The city's Service of School and Children's Gardens, begun in 1919, was originally involved mainly with school gardening projects which were seen merely as a means to an one end only: the happiness and well being of the child. However, after World War II, the purpose of the Service began to broaden as population rapidly grew and increasing industrialization was affecting nature more and more rapidly, as was the increased use of chemical agents. Moreover, between 1948 and 1970, the concept of 'Protection of Nature' began to emerge strongly in close relationship to the new threats developing on one side and ecology on the other.

These changes had consequences for the work of the Service. In the beginning, the accent lay on the individual contribution such as not damaging plants, not killing animals, carefully disposing of wastes. Later attempts were made to help the student to understand that changes of the environment which appear catastrophic are caused by man and therefore he, himself, is responsible for it.

Aftet the Second World War, new teaching methods were also introduced. One of the general teaching principles was:

> Learning should be organized in terms of undertakings that seem real and compelling and valuable to the student, that engage his active purpose, that confront him with significant challenges leading not only to deeper and broader insights, but to more discriminating attitudes and more adequate skills.

Another principle was:

> Successful teaching requires organizing these activities and situations so that the learning will be as meaningful as possible. To give the student insight into actual environmental problems, he must be brought into contact with living nature because that lies at the heart of environmental education.

The Task

The task of the Service for School and Children's Gardens, as a specialized teaching body in this connection, is to offer support to the teachers so they can fill their environmental education task as well as possible. Every school in The Hague receives a program containing various courses concentrated around the environmental area from which a choice can be made. In accordance with the original purpose, these courses are centered only around the living part of the environment.

If teachers take their task seriously, the activities of the Service add to and illustrate what the class covers in the lessons. Consequently, the Service's program limits its lessons to areas which teachers cannot cover themselves either because of lack of specialized knowledge or because of not having access to the materials the Service for School and Children's Gardens can supply.

Children's Farms

In large cities, this kind of educational work should begin as soon as possible. Consequently, the Service begins its activities with three-year-olds. Children's farms play an important role. In the fields at these farms, space is reserved where young children can come directly in contact with small domestic animals. The Service considers that child/animal contact is very important in molding the child. From this contact, an attitude can develop which, in a broader sense, can contribute to environment education. Lessons lasting about one hour are given to pupils of nursery schools and to the lower grades of elementary schools, but the possibility also exists for these students to spend a whole day on the farm. Outside of school hours, parents can visit the farm with their children. Moreover, older students care for the animals after school.

School Garden Work

In The Hague, there are two types of gardening for children:

(a) gardening during school time
(b) gardening after school time

Each forms a practical way of giving biological education. The difference is that after school hours, gardening, under the guidance of experts, falls into the framework of a hobby or leisure activity, while gardening during school hours is part of a course of study. Motivation is reinforced by means of lessons which are given as preparation for the actual garden work.

During the actual gardening period, attention is paid to such matters as soil, indigenous fauna, and food chains. After the gardening sessions, evaluation of the experience takes place in school.

Since 1971, nursery schools have been included in the school garden projects. In special little garden plots, very young students have a chance from about five years of age on, to sow seeds and care for plants as well as caring for small domestic animals.

Demonstration Lessons and Excursions

Demonstration lessons are given in special buildings where students and instructors meet. The purpose of the lessons and the excursions is not to confront students with facts. Instead, by using as much live material as possible, the students are given:

(a) firsthand knowledge of the variety of plants and animals in their own environment; recognition of the interdependence of soil, atmosphere, plants (as producers) and man and animals (as consumers).

(b) ability to identify and explain a biological community in relation to its environment, a concept of the food chain and ecological balance.

During the lessons and excursions, efforts are made to get the students themselves as much as possible actively engaged in the subject.

Evaluation in school is assisted by the mean of working papers which are supplied and which give not only a summary of the lesson but also give assignments. Because of continual diminishing of flora and fauna, it is increasingly difficult, especially near big cities, for pupils to come in contact with living material for biology lessons.

In special gardens, the Service grows wild plants as well as cultivated ones. These plants are supplied to teachers along with background information. Moreover, teachers can borrow many kinds of animals from the Service for their lessons. This includes housing facilities for the animals as well as necessary background information about them.

Nature of the Month

'Nature of the Month' appears six times a year and should be seen as a model for a biology lesson. In addition, the special teacher's editions contain work sheets with many drawings and simple texts, to be used by the students.

Information Centers

There are information centers in every study building where not only teachers, students, but anyone may obtain information about plants and animals. These information centers have simple libraries of their own. Moreover, animals and plants can be borrowed from there for use during school biology lessons.

Nature Trails

The Service has created many nature trails Booklets which are supplied at the nature trails contain descriptions of the flora and fauna as well as continue to direct attention to environmental problems. Purpose of this is primarily to help the hiker learn more about nature, to learn to distinguish as much as possible the different processes that go on in nature. Advantage of the nature trails is that students and adults may take them at any time without needing a guide.

Special trails have been made for schools where students are given assignments to carry out during the field trip. In this way, especially, integration with other school skills such as aesthetics, ethics, language, and economics is strived for. For children between 10 and 14, special puzzle trails have been created. In their free time, children can discover nature while playing.

Visitor Centers

At the visitor centers, information is available about plants and animals which are found in that area. In an exposition area, characteristic plants and animals are present. There are also exhibitions about the planning and research of wise land use and about landscape management as well as about water as a natural resource. These centers are often located right at the entrance of nature trails. A school biologist present there can answer any eventual questions.

These centers should be used more and more as day centers where students can spend the whole day. In the field, practical work can be carried out, while at the center, the technical equipment, library, and other necessary equipment are present, allowing the collected data to be further studied and analyzed.

Landscapes and the Botanical Garden

The Service for School and Children's Gardens has a botanical garden where nearly all of the native plants can be found systematically arranged. Most of the school classes in The Hague visit this garden, but schools outside of the city also make use of it.

Teachers of secondary, high schools and training colleges can get plants from this garden to use in their biology lessons. In order to stimulate use of the garden, people living in The Hague and in adjacent cities may get an annual admission card for a minimal fee. They also receive a publication six times a year which describes plants and flowers, insects, and birds which they find in the garden. In the landscape garden, the most characteristic Dutch landscapes can be found, as they would be found in nature.

Conclusions

In The Hague, many young people are growing up in an environment consisting only of houses, roads and factories with scarcely any contact with nature. The School and Children's Garden Service tries to provide such contacts in order that good environmental behavior may develop.

Case Study 4.8

Mobile Environmental Education Laboratory

Introduction
The foundation of the entire project is a one-half ton, 1972, Ford Econoline van which has been designed and equipped with storage facilities for housing environmental study equipment. (See illustrations on the following pages.) The top side of the unit has been equipped with a large metal storage compartment covered with three aluminum hinged water-tight doors as cover for stored equipment. A roll out canvas canopy which protects students and equipment during periods of inclement weather is attached to the curbside of the storage compartment. Special safety features include extra suspension and the addition of a protective metal screen between the driver and the storage area.

Project Objectives
The primary objective of this project is to demonstrate and verify a new concept in environmental education for the Kingsport City School System by:

   (a) providing in-service training to elementary (including preschool), secondary, and postsecondary education personnel to enable them to participate effectively in environmental education programs;

   (b) developing materials designed to assist the introduction of environmental studies in existing programs and/or strengthen the content of existing environmental programs at all educational levels;

   (c) developing curricula which will provide useful learning experiences leading to an understanding of environmental principles, problems and their causes, and possible solutions to those problems.

In-Service Training
As a part of curriculum development, materials were designed and developed for use in in-service training. These materials are designed for all grade levels and relate to all curriculum areas. The mobile unit and included equipment serve as a basic resource for conducting teacher workshops and in-service training programs on-site at each school or at selected community resource facilities. Before scheduling the use of the unit with a class, the teacher is involved in an in-service program relating to the mobile unit, included equipment, and instructional activities.

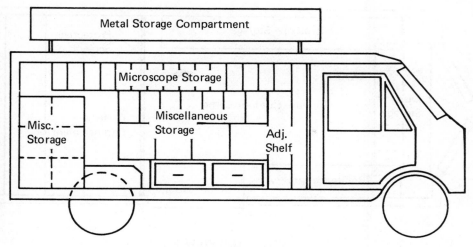

ROADSIDE VIEW

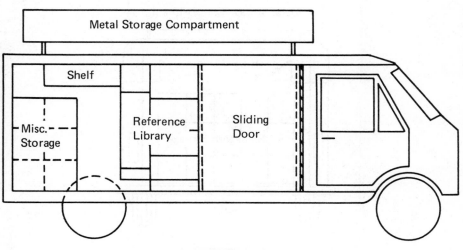

CURBSIDE VIEW

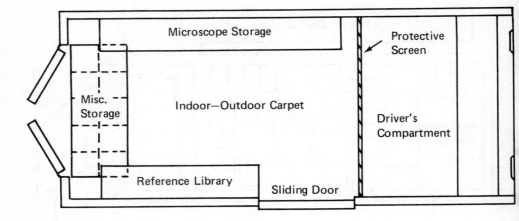

TOP VIEW

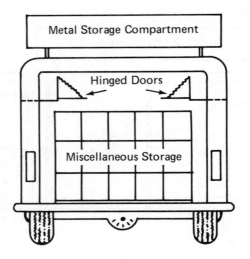

REAR VIEW

Case Study 4.9

Good Planning for Better Learning

(From *Outdoor Classrooms on School Sites* pp. 14–15, U.S. Government Printing Office, Washington, D.C. Stock #0100-1458)

Good planning begins with a look at the available resources and the possibilities for developing learning opportunities. Resource specialists contribute information on soils and plant materials and identify erosion, drainage, and water runoff problems. Teachers and students add their suggestions for making use of the outdoor classroom.

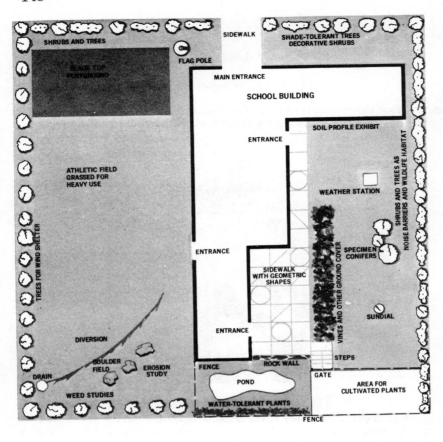

Outdoor classroom for elementary school on a city school site, approximately 500 feet by 500 feet.

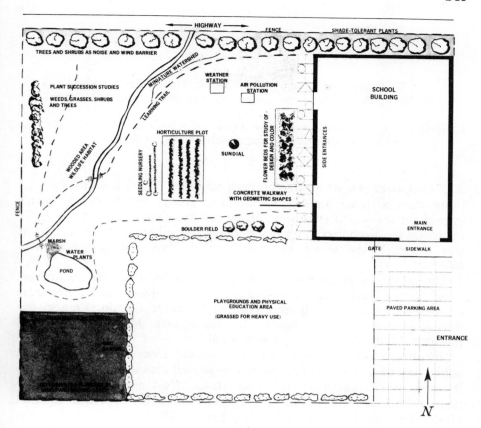

Outdoor classroom for suburban or centralized community school, approximately 16 acres. Pond and water areas are surrounded by chain-link fence built according to local ordinances. Water studies can be made around pool and along creek.

150

A global network of protected natural areas is being established by more than a dozen nations to monitor, study, and report on man's impact on the world environment. Within the next year, some 50 to 60 countries are expected to have designated 'biosphere reserves' as part of this UNESCO-sponsored program, called Man and the Biosphere (MAB).

The biosphere is the thin, life-supporting layer of the earth's surface.

So far the United States has named 20 large, diversified natural areas as reserves; other participating countries include Britain, France, the Soviet Union, Austria, Brazil, the Philippines, Malaysia, Thailand, Indonesia, Poland, Australia, and Senegal.

'Biosphere reserves will be experimental areas where studies are conducted of living, changing plant and animal systems, how they relate to each other, and how man's activities offset and are affected by them', Christian A. Herter Jr., special assistant for environmental affairs for the Secretary of State, told MAB delegates at a recent planning conference in Washington.

Not the only program
'The biosphere reserve programe is only one of the MAB projects, but a very important one', stresses Michel Batisse, UNESCO's director of the Department of Environmental Science and Natural Resources research. 'It is our tool for the whole program, our tool for research on the evolution of ecosystems'.

Other related fields of study include all major types of natural areas — tropical and temperate forests, coastal zones, mountains and tundra, grasslands, island ecosystems, and deserts, as well as urban systems, and the impact of fertilizers, pesticides, man-made structures, and pollution.

'We're trying to find out what we don't know before we make irretrievable mistakes', says Raymond F. Kohn, director of the U.S. MAB committee. Mr. Kohn explains that the committee will be looking at the socioeconomic and cultural effects of what man is doing to the environment as well as gathering purely scientific information.

In selecting the U.S. biosphere reserves, an effort was made to set aside a full, representative range of natural areas from Arctic tundra to deserts. Both pristine and man-modified areas were chosen to allow monitoring comparison. The reserves, consequently, serve several purposes: havens for plant and animal species, protected genetic pools that allow continuing evolution, and scientific workshops to record the rates of change and learn more about methods of speeding environmental recovery.

Many parks included

Most of the U.S.-designated reserves are either national parks or experimental forests managed by the Departments of the Interior and Agriculture. The list includes the Olympic, Great Smoky, and Rocky Mountains, Mt. McKinley, Yellowstone, Glacier, Everglades, and Big Bend national parks, as well as forests, grasslands, and wilderness areas in Colorado, Oregon, Puerto Rico, New Mexico, Alaska, Arizona, and the Virgin Islands.

The largest world reserve eventually may well be in the Amazon region of Brazil, where some 54,000 square miles (an area the size of Florida) is already protected as part of a national environmental plan. Brazilian representatives have indicated that biosphere reserves may soon be established in this area.

'MAB has now turned the corner', assesses Donald R. King, chairman of the U.S. committee, after the week-long Washington meeting.

Three years of planning

After three years of planning with 72 nations taking part, several international cooperative research and educational training programs are being launched. Multinational teams are studying tropical forest problems in Malaysia; Mediterranean countries are planning grassland research projects; Latin-American nations are looking at grazing management problems in the Andes.

Additionally, Venezuela has announced that it is establishing a regional center for tropical forests, the Philippines is interested in establishing a similar center, and France is proposing a center for grasslands study as a base for Mediterranean projects. Organizers predict more than a dozen regional projects will be started within the next year.

'The remarkable thing is that this program is under way — and on an international basis. The reason is, there is something in it for everybody', Mr. King says.

Developing nations, particularly, where environmental studies and conservation efforts are just beginning, are likely to receive a big boost from these scientific exchanges and ongoing technical training programs according to UNESCO officials.

5
Youth Involvement and Community Action

DAVID K. J. WITHRINGTON

Roles

The principle role of out-of-school youth activities is to develop in the individual motivation towards conserving and improving his surroundings. Still, there are important secondary functions, such as accomplishing tasks left undone by the authorities, and giving people a positive freedom to enjoy themselves in their environment. Out-of-school environmental youth activities achieve these objectives by:

1. Imparting practical experience in real-life situations and executing practical conservation tasks;

2. Developing a working knowledge of ecological principles governing the environment in which we live, and identifying our own role in that environmental community;

3. Developing initiative, responsibility, teamwork and real commitment on the part of young people.

The formal education system tends to reinforce the acceptance of the existing values of society. Through the medium of out-of-school environmental activities, young people can appreciate the aesthetic values of human existence and the limited needs for material wealth in a harmonious relationship with the natural environment; moreover, they can derive a real enjoyment from this relationship. A variety of activities can be undertaken, from nature study to urban environmental action; but the emphasis should always be on attaining enjoyment and appreciation, while allowing the maximum responsibility to the young people involved. For the younger child, 6—13 years, methods of initiation include school clubs, museums, field study centres, Cub Scouts, Young Pioneers and the like. For the more mature age-group, 14—25 years, less formalized activities, if possible conceived and arranged by the young people themselves, are more appropriate: camps for study or practical management work; courses for training and instruction of youth leaders; excursions to study an area, either for its own sake or as part of a project; indoor meetings for study, planning or as social occasions; public information — newsletters and bulletins, exhibitions, etc.; environmental action campaigns on local problems or on wider environmental issues. Examples of how youth activities fulfill conservation roles in the U.S.S.R. and Poland are found in Case Study 5.1.

Although out-of-school activities can be self-sufficient in developing a conservation consciousness, we must look at them as supplementary to the environmental education provided at school. Indeed, it would be extremely satisfactory if the school could give the child an overall appreciation of the environmental crisis — the economics of resources, and the ecological balance of the biosphere. Against such a background, extra-mural activities oriented towards environmental action would have a greater chance of success. Quite often actions pursued in good faith may have a negative effect through overlooking the broader implication of the issue at stake. Thus, despite considerable activity in the conservation movement during recent years, environmental deterioration has apparently continued to accelerate.

Activities

The following survey of activities from the programmes of youth organizations active in environmental conservation gives examples, which may be worth following.

Excursions are basic to the programme of local naturalist groups. They may be simply morning of afternoon walks in the neighbourhood, or may be longer whole-day excursions to interesting places farther afield. The main purpose of an excursion is to observe the environment, and it is important in a large group to have at least one person with experience of the area and with knowledge of relevant aspects of natural history. One function of an excursion is to enable the participant to identify different components of the environment and thus learn to build up an ordered picture of the ecosystem. Such an appreciation is helped by the proper tools — for bird-life these would be binoculars and identification book. An aid to the proper enjoyment of the excursion is appropriate clothing and footwear, while safety conditions should also be borne in mind. Surroundings should be respected, especially in terms of litter and noise.

Excursions can have different objectives — to initiate young people in one branch of natural history; to practice ecological field techniques, such as plant transects and surveying; to visit a particular landscape area or nature reserve for aesthetic awareness. to explore new areas of countryside; to take part in a survey project, where the excursion would either consist of a specialist group or split up into specialist groups. Excursion participants gain experience of their environment from the use of public transport to orienteering from a map. They grow to appreciate the interrelationships in their environment — landforms, soil, climate, vegetation, insect and animal life. Above all, excursions combat the increasing alienation of modern man from his natural environment. For town dwellers who may not even know the source of their tap water, it is certainly important to get out into the countryside.

Camps are traditionally the main activity of many youth organizations at a national and international level. These are usually held over public holidays and during long school vacations. European camps are often open to foreign participation. These camps usually take place near areas of natural beauty or ecological importance in order that surveys, observations and practical conservation work may be carried out. For the most part the camps are held under canvas in the youth organizations' own tents, though schools, biological stations, farms and outdoor pursuits centres are used, especially in the winter months.

Camps are an adventure in themselves of which the outstanding feature is camaradie. This sense of togetherness amongst the participants should be furthered by provision of social activities, such as singing, dancing and campfires. The leader derives much useful experience from being responsible for so many people and for the smooth running of the camp. Youth organizations in Britain and Sweden have written down the leader's experience in Camp Manuals for the benefit of future camp leaders. Case Study 5.2 is an account of environmental education camps in The Netherlands.

Practical Conservation Tasks are a successful form of youth activity for environment protection, and form an integral part of the programme of many youth organizations. 'Conservation Corps' have been set up in Britain, U.S.A., Czechoslovakia and the Netherlands. The sort of work done includes clearing of rubbish, construction work, tree planting, ditching, scrub clearance, fencing, reserve maintenance, sand dune reclamation, creation of footpaths and nature trails. Mostly these tasks are undertaken on commission for national parks, local authorities and private landowners. This means that the proper tools are provided. The work may be done on a voluntary basis or a small subsistence may be paid. Apart from their specialized programme, these camps are similar in character to the youth camps described above.

Courses conducted as out-of-school youth activities can range from elementary courses in field study techniques to leader training in administrative, technical and financial methodology. Courses in the practical skills of landscape management and in the basic apsects of ecology are also commonly held. At a regional level courses may take youth leaders from a variety of student organizations, initiate them in the principles of environmental conservation, and demonstrate the opportunities which environmental activities offer for their organizations. The first Eastern Africa Youth Course in Environmental Conservation, held in Nairobi in 1974, with representatives from eight

Participants identify lichens on the Lüneburger Heide during an IYF training course

countries, had as its primary objective the stimulation and development of the conservation youth movement in the region.

On the international level, a successful course has been organized in the Lüneburger Heide, Federal Republic of Germany, since 1955. Originally its programme was a general and practical introduction to conservation, but it has recently been developed into a more specialized training course to provide national conservation youth leaders with experience in the international framework of environmental protection. Representatives of organizations such as I.U.C.N., U.N.E.S.C.O. and W.W.F. (World Wildlife Fund) are invited to explain their function and programmmes, and a critique is given of how governments and international agencies are acting to resolve environmental problems, such as overpopulation and resource depletion. The programme includes practical field biology investigations in different parts of the Heide landscape and a discussion with a city planner of the environmental problems of Hamburg and the work done by officials of the conservation department. Participants are asked to evolve an action campaign on a special topic, such as energy problems and nuclear power. Apart from contributing to insight into the organizational effectiveness of such campaigns, this can provide the basis for an international follow-up action.

In every type of course, it is important to encourage contributions from the participants, whatever the extent of their expertise. This can be done by illustrated lectures to fellow participants, or by mounting an exhibition of the work accomplished during the course for the benefit of the local population and press.

Projects and Surveys give an added value to the customary activities and excursions of a club. Examples of local surveys are analysis of a locality which is changing due to human influence, results can be useful in planning inquiries; observations of changing habitat and fauna over a period of years; plotting of bird and animal migration routes; measurement of pollution levels in the air and in water courses. More large-scale surveys, in which local groups participate, include compilation of atlases of breeding distribution of animal species; observing the comparative phenology of plant and animal species over several countries; conducting an opinion poll of views on environmental problems amongst citizens of different countries; and many environmental action campaigns.

Indoor Meetings are needed for a number of reasons, and it is important that a youth group should have some place to store its equipment as well as the use of a room for social evenings, lectures, exhibitions and general work in preparing publications and results of field surveys. This need should be recognized, and provided for, by the local authorities.

Publications, such as the stencilled bulletin containing news of the forthcoming programme, enable the officers to communicate with the members. Depending on finances, more ambitious printed magazines and yearbooks containing members' articles and photographs are compiled by the organization's editor. The staff may gain considerable knowledge of layout and printing techniques. One of the very successful youth publications on folklore and environment has been *Foxfire*.

Another important type of publication is the report of work carried out in a survey; members will be encouraged in their work if they see the end-product in print. Nowadays, many youth organizations are using their expertise to prepare publications for a wider audience. These may be produced in connection with a particular campaign, giving background information to the public and ideas for practical actions by youth. In the field of general education, *Jeunes et Nature* in France have cooperated with a yoghurt company to produce a popular manual on nature conservation combined with a competition to interest the younger members of the public. In Sweden, the *Sveriges Faltbiologiska Ungdomsforening* have produced a series of project booklets in biology and conservation which are achieving a wide circulation in schools. It is very easy to dismiss some youth publications on the basis of poor quality. However, they are not produced with the object of replacing popular magazines, but for the practical experiences which they offer and the information and ideas which they contain. An extensive list of suggested activities involving students in community affairs is given in Case Study 5.3.

Community in Action

Youth organizations and groups of concerned citizens undertake actions designed to inform the public in the field of environmental issues, or to influence policies which are believed to have an adverse effect on the environment. These environmental actions are proliferating throughout the world, and with an increasingly professional approach are achieving considerable success. That is not to say that major environmental problems are being confronted or alleviated, such as population and food supply, degradation of ecosystems, or artificially created consumption of scarce resources. The relevance of these issues must be forced home to the citizen as examples from his everyday life, so that he will be sufficiently stimulated to review his role as a consumer and polluter, and as a voter, but above all to appreciate the power he has to change society. To quote from a paper on 'Environmental Strategy' by Walter Bos (Netherlands) in 1971:

> Practice teaches that people will not accept such an active attitude when they are just overwhelmed with information. When you come to hear that pollution of the oceans might have serious consequences for the Earth's oxygen supply in the future, you are likely to accept that as an unpleasing fact. But when you read in the local weekly newspaper that a road will be built through the area where you go for recreation at the weekend, or when you notice that there are gradually more dead and less living fishes in your elected fishing pond, you are more likely to join up with other people who are not willing to accept such facts any longer.

There are certain common practical considerations in organizing an environmental action, which by its nature normally involves a group of people coming together to demonstrate. First of all the participants have to be assembled as an effective force, already aware of what they have to do.

Unfortunately, an argument presented calmly and logically has no appeal to the public or to the news media. Thus environmental action groups have to be innovative in order to get publicity. Groups like *Friends of the Earth* have accumulated considerable experience in all these fields. They have been particularly successful in coordinating one-day demonstrations at a local level to publicize national issues, such as the waste of resources by excess packaging and the production of non-returnable bottles. Features such as street theatres will make such demonstrations interesting for passers-by.

In an information campaign, the participants should be fully conver-

Student demonstration in Belgium for milk bottles rather than one-way packages

sant with the issues, therefore research on statistics, etc., will have to be done beforehand; in a specific battle against, for instance, a plan to construct a motorway, the group will probably have to secure equivalent professional advice as the protagonists of the scheme.

Apart from demonstrations, there are several other effective forms of environmental action which can be used: public hearings; collection of signatures; return of polluted or waste materials to responsible authorities; exhibitions; letters to newspapers; token clean-up actions; prosecution of people offending conservation laws; opinion polls; distribution of informative leaflets; boycott of goods; poster campaigns; international camps; blocking roads. The most important aid to the success of environmental actions is the adequate informing of the press and news media because the objects is always to get more people to support your struggle. Other specific examples of environmental action have been a floating conservation exhibition on a barge manned by young people from three nature conservation youth organizations which visited major towns in The Netherlands; poster campaigns and signature collections to prevent the commercial exploitation of a national park in the French Alps; demonstrations in many countries for traffic-free city centres, often showing that bicycles are a healthier form of transport than cars; the exhibition of the stinking corpses of over 5000 oiled sea birds in Belgium, the physical destruction of a dam for hydro-electricity in Iceland; the distribution of leaflets by a Swedish youth organization showing the phosphate and enzyme content of all the leading washing-powders, a campaign taken up also by the national housewives' organization; the maintenance of a league-table of conservation voters in the U.S. Senate and Congress; the selling of organically grown vegetables; and many others.

Structures

Young people pursue environmental activities in a variety of youth organizations. Scouts, Guides and Pioneer movements have been helping young people to appreciate their environment for most of this century. Similar youth organizations for outdoor recreation, such as hiking and youth hostelling, often include in their programme a large element of conservation. Clubs for observation and conservation of wildlife are widespread, either as independent youth organizations or as junior sections of adult societies. Special conservation corps of young volunteers have been formed to undertake tasks in managing and restoring the environment. Young people, especially in developing countries, work in community service projects to improve living conditions, health and agricultural methods. The Wildlife Clubs in East Africa, a popular movement based on secondary schools, are described in Case Study 5.5. Environmental groups are often formed by students of relevant disciplines attached to universities and colleges. There are also organizations which provide young people with the opportunity of scientific research, usually associated with the schools.

Some of the groups listed above have a peripheral interest in environmental conservation, while others have it as their main objective. In the latter, we can distinguish two different organizational structures: first, there are the specialist environmental action organizations like *Friends of the Earth*; second, there are the more traditional self-governing conservation youth organizations. The first of these independent youth organizations, 'Nederlandse Jeugdbond voor Natuurstudie,' was founded in Holland in 1923.

The common features of these self-governing conservation youth organizations are their democratic structure, with statutes and strict age-limits; their background in observing and studying nature; their basic programme of excursions and camps; their educational and absolutely non-commercial activities. Nowadays, a very important part of the programme of these organizations is environmental action. However, the special character of these organizations is that their members develop a commitment to conservation through a close personal contact with, and knowledge of, their environment, a relationship which will give them enjoyment throughout their lives. Case Study 5.6 gives further details on some self-governing youth organizations in Europe.

The new organizations for environmental action, on the other hand, usually gain as members those people who have an intellectual and moral conviction that action to solve the environmental crisis will benefit all mankind. In many countries, the traditional self-governing youth organizations serve both functions, but specialist environmental action groups are being established in increasing numbers. These action groups often have a commercial sideline, such as publishing books on the environment, or adult financial support. This enables them to employ staff and engage professional advice which increases the efficiency of their programme of operations. Thus, while they would not claim to be democratic in structure, these environmental action groups appeal to their members because of their effectiveness in dealing with the issues.

International youth and student organizations are becoming increasingly involved in environmental issues, as was demonstrated at the United Nations Conference on the Human Environment in Stockholm in 1972. Many of these organizations, such as the World Assembly of Youth and the International Student Movement for the United Nations have ongoing environmental programmes. Two international organizations intimately concerned with environmental conservation are described in Case Study 5.7.

All types of independent youth organizations, apart from their considerable service to the community, succeed in developing the initiative of young people. their capacity to assume organizational and leadership respnsibilities, and their commitment to teamwork and to the aims of their organization.

Bibliography

Boz, Walter, 'Environmental Strategy' I.Y.F., Amsterdam, 1972.
Friends of the Earth: Washington (620 C St., S.E., 20003) Jeffrey Knight 202-543-4312, Nairobi, Kenya (Box 24897) Rick Anderson (Karen 2246).
FRIENDS OF THE EARTH, LTD. Richard Sandbrook, *Operations Manager*, 9 Poland St. London WIV3DG, England.
LES AMIS DE LA TERRE, Brice Lalonde, *Coordinator*, 16, Rue de l'Université 75007 Paris, France.
JORDENS VANNER, Ralph Monö, *Director*, Box 9062—10271, Stockholm, Sweden.
FREUNDE DER ERDE, Theda Strempe, *Chairwoman*, Postfach 100221-2 Hamburg 1, Germany.
VRIENDEN VAN DE AARDE, Peter Konijin, *Chairman*, Herengracht 109, Amsterdam, Holland.
PRIJATELJI SVETA, Nenad Prelog, *Director*, 41 000 Zagreb—Adzijina 6, Yugoslavia.
VRIENDE VAN DIE AARDE, Jerry Burdzik, *Director*, Box 11435—Brooklyn, Pretoria, South Africa.
FRIENDS OF THE EARTH, Patricia Cumming, *Director*, 8 Vergemount, Clonskeagh, Dublin 6, Ireland.
FRIENDS OF THE EARTH, Peter Hayes, *Coordinator*, 59 MacArthur Place, Melbourne, Victoria, Australia.
FRIENDS OF THE EARTH, Landsay Jeffs, *Managing Director*, Box 39-065, Auckland West, New Zealand.

162

Wigginton, Eliot, (ed.), *The Foxfire Book*, Anchor Books, Doubleday, New York, 1972, 384 p.

Wigginton, Eliot, (ed.), *Foxfire 2*, Anchor Press, Doubleday, New York, 1973, 410. p.

Additional References

Books

Garner, John W., *In Common Cause*, Revised Edition, W. W. Norton, New York, 1973, 124 pp. pb.

Citizen Action and How It Works. A manual for a citizens' movement intended to reestablish the link of accountability between the citizen and his elected representatives in the U.S.

Ross, Donald K., *A Public Citizen's Action Manual*, Grossman, New York, 1973, 237 pp. Introduction by Ralph Nader, Emphasis upon consumer protection, better health care, equality in taxation, eliminating discrimination in jobs, making government responsive.

Booklets

Building Our American Communities: Chapter Action Booklet 18p.

National FFA (Future Farmers of America) Organization in cooperation with the U.S. Office of Education, Department of Health, Education, and Welfare, Washington, D.C. 20202

Specific programme complete with application blanks.

Citizen Action Can Get Results, Aug. 1972, 8p.
U.S. Environmental Protection Agency
Washington, D.C. 20460
Booklet of case studies.

Community Action for Environmental Quality, 1970, 42p.
The Citizens Advisory Committee on Environmental Quality
1700 Pennsylvania Ave., N.W.
Washington, D.C. 20016
Has section on training younger people. List state agencies and some useful publications.

Do It Yourself Ecology, Fifth Edition, March 1971, 23p.
Environmental Action Inc.
Room 731
1346 Connecticut Ave. N.W.
Washington, D.C. 20036
Hints on cutting down waste. Considers industries an adversary.

Don't Leave It All to the Experts: The Citizen's Role in Environmental Decision Making, Nov. 1972, 20 p.
U.S. Environmental Protection Agency
Washington, D.C. 20460
Pick targets carefully, fight for funds, know your rights.

Environmental Quality and the Citizen: A Teaching Guide for Adult Education Courses Related to the Environment, by Bernard L. Clausen and Ross L. Iverson, 1973, 40 p.
Soil Conservation Society of America
7515 Northeast Ankeny Rd.
Ankeny, Iowa 50021
Ten sessions with behavioural objectives, background information, teaching activities and additional references.

Help! Give Earth a Chance, Revised Edition 1973, 28 p. New York State
Department of Environmental Conservation
50 Wolf Road
Albany, N.Y. 12201
1971 International Award from the American Association for Conservation Information.
A booklet about personal choices. Bibliography.

Man and Resources: Ontario Program Handbook for Study Groups
Ontario Committee for Man and Resources
Box 223
Queen's Park, Toronto
A publicly supported programme involving large numbers of people. See also Case Study 6.4.

Student Ecology Handbook: Guidelines for Environmental Inprovement Action
Free on request from
Environmental Protection Coordinator
Balfour Company
Attleboro, Massachusetts 02703

Article
Allen, Rodney F., 'Suggestions for Community Participation in Environmental Studies,' *The Journal of Geography*, Vol. 73 No. 7, 9 Oct., Dec. 1974, pp. 54—59.
Numerous suggestions for community projects grouped by (1) Environmental Education, (2) Environmental Awareness, (3) Community Environmental Services, and (4) Public Affairs. See Case Study 5.3.

Case Study 5.1

Youth Activity in U.S.S.R. and Poland

U.S.S.R.

The All-Russian Society for the Protection of Nature has over 20 million members in the R.S.F.S.R. (Russia). Other Republics in the U.S.S.R. have similar organizations and their own nature conservation laws. The All-Russian Society has an important part to play in creating and enforcing the nature conservation legislation in the R.S.F.S.R. There are local branches at all factories, collective farms, offices and schools.

Special sections of the All-Russian Society deal with the activities of young people in nature conservation and the education of the general public towards a better understanding of their environment and of the need to conserve natural resources. Every year, hundreds of thousands of schoolchildren participate in environmental actions under the guidance of teachers and voluntary leaders. Amongst other activities, they gather seeds and nuts of valuable kinds of trees as planting material; they plant shelter-belts; they protect forest areas; they erect nesting boxes; they look after animals and birds, especially in winter-time; and they save young fishes from spring floods. To assist the execution of such activities in school vacations, a special 'Day of birds' and a 'Month of the forest' and a 'Month of saving young fish' have been created.

There are now some 3000 'school forests' in the Republic, where schoolchildren carry out nature conservation work under the direction of school authorities. Within the All-Russian Society for the Protection of Nature, a 'Green Patrol' of some 1½ million children takes care of tree planting; a 'Blue Patrol' has recently been established to protect water sources. Children learn about biology and natural history in naturalists' circles, at stations for young naturalists and from enthusiastic teachers in their spare time.

Students also take part in nature conservation activities. Local groups of the All-Russian Society have been founded in about 80% of institutes of higher education, with a membership of over 100,000 students, teachers and technicians. Special student groups ensure the enforcement of hunting laws, members plant trees in urban areas — in the course of 4 years, the local group at the Novosibirsk Agricultural Institute planted a park of 70 sq. ha. Members also deliver yearly about 5000 public lectures and prepare more than 300 radio and T.V. programmes on nature conservation.

National and local newspapers organize 'round-table discussions' with scientific experts and active members of the public. The results are published — often as a special page dedicated to nature conservation. Many exhibitions are staged, notably the permanent Exhibition of Popular Economic Achievements in Moscow where successful anti-pollution devices are displayed. However effective this public propaganda may be, it can only complement the systematic education for environmental conservation within the school system.

(Abridged from: *Nature Conservation in the U.S.S.R.*, by N. A. Gladov, A. A. Inozemtsev and G. N. Ogureyeva, publishing house of Leningrad University, 1972.)

Poland

There is a long tradition of nature protection in Poland centred on the League for Protection of Nature with one million members. Scientific committees have also been very active and, in spring 1972, the Government established the Ministry for Land Economy and Environment Protection. Youth involvement has been steadily increasing and culminated in the formation early in 1972, within the Polish Students' Association, of the Polish Academic Youth Committee on the Human Environment. The following account is adapted from the materials of this Committee.

'Students carry on scientific research along with scientists in some 800 research groups within a variety of disciplines, having some 25,000 student participants. The research panels are organizing a number of summer camps for scientific field work. The results are then submitted for discussion at many seminars and are often used by industry and other responsible authorities.

The so-called multidisciplinary complex research projects are a particularly valuable form of activity. An example of such studies may be provided by summer camps in the Czorsztyn and Ocjow recreational and protected areas. Their objective is to define the complexity of interrelationship between human activities and nature within the reserves and national parks. Students from many branches of technical colleges, universities, medical and agricultural schools, etc. take part in this kind of research. All together about 200 camps are held during the year to carry out research on environment protection. The main direction of the research is a review of industrial areas, reserves, water pollution control, air protection, work on new technologies of the purification processes, population health-care, etc.

Among other forms of scientific activities of students in the field under review, one must mention the annual competition for a student research paper concerning environment protection, a competition for the most active research panel and another for the best diploma of a graduate. Students also carry out their activities to popularize the subject amongst the general public. Environmental issues now play a significant part in the students' press and radio broadcasts. Nature and man become an ever more favourable subject of artistic and creative effort of students — open-air painting and sculpturing sessions and exhibitions are organized. There is also an annual competition for the best poster on the protection of nature, organized jointly with the league for Protection of Nature. A valuable method for the dissemination of knowledge on environmental issues is the organization of student discussion panels — Man and his Environment — where participants from many colleges discuss pertinent questions with scientists, journalists, people of industry and administration.

Tourism is one of the factors influencing students' life. During 1971 there were some 130,000 students taking their vacations in a variety of ways. This is a sufficient number to devastate, if not properly guided, many recreational areas. Therefore, we treat tourism as one of the possible levers to educate people in the principles and practice of nature conservation. To this end, courses for tourist guides and allied personnel are organized each year in collaboration with the Polish Tourist Country Lovers Association.

One of the specific protective forms of student activity is the Nature Protection Guard. Currently there are approximately 1000 students engaged on such duties, and this will be expanded in co-operation with the League for Protection of Nature, the Polish U.N. Students' Association, the Polish Angling Association, the Polish Hunting Association and the Alpine Club.

Large numbers of issues connected with the protection of the human environment go beyond the frontiers of a single country. We fully recognize the need for co-operation of youth from many countries to protect the environment. One possibility to present the achievements of scientific research and to hold discussions with students of other nationalities has been an International Scientific Seminar, 'Man and his Environment', held in Poland in both 1973 and 1974. In 1972 we brought the subject of student involvement in environment protection to the attention of the International Student Movement for the United Nations meeting in Warszawa. We have also organized an exchange with the International Youth Federation for Environmental Studies and Conservation to initiate further cooperation, first of all in the problems of the Baltic Sea.

All the above-mentioned forms of activity are closely interwoven. In many instances there is a need to act jointly with a number of institutions and organizations. These functions of coordination fall on the newly created Polish Academic Youth Committee on the Human Environment'.

Case Study 5.2

Camps of the Institute for Environmental Education — Netherlands

The Instituut voor Natuurbeschermingseducatie was founded in 1960 with the aim of making both young people and adults aware of the necessity of nature conservation and the management of the environment. Its head office is in Amsterdam and there are more than 70 local groups throughout the Netherlands.

One of its activities is the organizing of conservation camps in nature reserves for young people in the 15 to 25 years age-group. This activity was started (more or less modelled after the work of the British Conservation Corps*) in 1962 with three camps and a total number of 125 volunteers. However, some 450 youngsters had asked to be allowed to participate, so the next year seven camps were organized but again there were more applicants than could be admitted. The aim of these camps is twofold: (1) to introduce the volunteers to the problems of nature conservation and the management of the environment and (2) to assist the owner of the reserve (national or regional societies for the conservation of nature, State Forestry Service, etc.) in the practical management, such as timber clearance, scrub cutting, cleaning of ponds and ditches, selective clearance of young trees or plants in order to conserve other, etc. Education forms an integral part of camp life. Talks and lectures on ecology and on the management of nature reserves lead into discussions. Normally the work is done in the morning and afternoon, and the evening is reserved for lectures, film shows and discussions. Each camp starts with a visit to the reserve where the group is going to work and a short lecture on the reason why the work is to be done. For work which demands a certain professional skill, the volunteers are instructed and assisted by the permanent warden of the reserve.

There are still more applicants that can be admitted. The bottleneck in organizing these camps, for which there is now a full-time secretary/organizer, is that for each camp you need some five or six experienced volunteers, who run the camp (the preparatory work having

*The Conservation Corps of the British Trust for Conservation Volunteers was founded in 1959 as a specialist organization for undertaking conservation management work in nature reserves and amenity areas. It operates out of the Zoological Gardens, Regent's Park, London and has three Regional Offices. Some 7000 volunteers in local corps attend tasks in the summer and holiday periods as well as regular weekend work and leader training courses in hedging, ditching and other practical management techniques.

been done by the secretary/organizer). These volunteers are mainly recruited from people who have been on camps in previous years and who have attracted attention as potential staff-members.

Because of the limited number of camps which can be organized, there is a rule that no one is admitted to a camp who has been there in previous years. We regret this very much, because there is no follow-up. Therefore an experiment was started with the organizing of weekend camps, where work could be done all the year round in reserves near a town where volunteers live. In 1971 an analysis was made of some of the backgrounds of the 605 volunteers who came to the camps. As to their ages more than 75% were between 15 and 18 years. Of the 605 boys and girls, 92% were attending secondary schools, teacher training colleges or universities, whereas only 18% were artisans. As a rule, participants of the camps range in age from 15 years to under 26, but one camp a year is reserved for those aged between 20 and 30 years.

Participants have to pay their own travel and insurance, but food and lodging are free. This is paid from a lump sum which the owner of the reserve pays to the Institute and from a yearly grant from the Ministry for Culture, Recreation and Social Welfare.

In each camp there is a volunteer cook who prepares the meals, normally with some volunteer help for peeling potatoes, washing dishes, making sandwiches, etc. Lodging is mainly in the barn of a farm near the reserve, where people sleep on mattresses, bringing their own sleeping-bags. The Institute owns three or four sets of kitchen utensils, big pans etc. and normally in July and August two of three camps are running at the same time. The participants bring their own plates, a mug and cutlery.

After ten years of experience it can be concluded that these conservation camps have proved a rewarding way of bringing young people in contact with nature, the problems of nature conservation and the management of the environment. We regret that owing to the limited availability of camp-staff, participation has as a rule to be confined to once in a lifetime. However, organizing some twenty camps seems to be about the limit of what one full-time secretary/organizer can do. Weekend camps on a smaller scale and organized locally might make it possible to give a follow-up to the education which was started in the camps. Those who are in charge of nature reserves appreciate the assistance which is given by the volunteers and much of the work which is done by them might have to be omitted if it had to be done by paid labour.

Finally the camps seem to be a good outlet for young people who feel the urge to make a personal contribution to the fight against the environmental crisis, while at the same time it arms them with some basic information which, we think, is necessary when one wants to judge whether local or regional authorities are justified in the way they deal with environmental problems. The camps could be especially rewarding for students at teacher training colleges.

(Information supplied by the Institute for Environmental Education, Warmoesstraat 39, Amsterdam, June 1972.)

Case Study 5.3

Suggestions for Community Participation in Environmental Studies
(Rodney F. Allen)

(Reproduced by permission of the National Council for Geographical Education)

Part III: Community Environmental Service

Teaching about the environment and promoting awareness are appropriate, but taken alone — without personal action — they have a hollow ring. The projects in the following list involve students and others in *action*.

1. Paint and place trash cans and litter baskets about the school grounds and, with permission, in parks.

2. Distribute litter bags for cars. Get a local businessman or civic group to underwrite the cost of the bags.

3. Conduct a clean-up campaign in your community. If you want, focus on a specific place like a schoolyard or a park. Get people together to clean it up one Saturday morning and follow-up with a pancake luncheon.

4. Design a park for small children on a small plot or playground. Get permission first, and then be creative.

5. Hold a series of white elephant sales, swap-shops, and exchanges so that people may share their junk! It's a great way to recycle.

6. When something happens to favor environmental quality in your area, develop and conduct a victory celebration (no ticker-tape all over the place!). Victories seem few and far between so get ready and stay ready. Be sure to involve local politicians in the victory celebrations and don't forget the principal and business persons.

7. Conduct a 'Plant a Tree' campaign. Contact the State forest service to secure seedlings, then get them into parks, roadsides, schoolyards, etd. In all cases plan the plant-in with appropriate officials first.

8. Arrange to label trees and other plants in a downtown park to help 'educate' all of us.

9. To supplement #7 above, arrange a booth to distribute seedlings to the public if they promise to plant them. Give out some 'Johnny Appleseed' buttons of your own design and manufacture to each person promising to plant trees. Better, design some 'Freddie Forester' buttons for children and their parents who will plant and care for seedlings.

10. Set up some recycling or can and bottle recycling centers with local companies.

11. Teach a mini-course on auto tune-up everywhere you can during

the next several months. Figure out ways to get as many involved as possible.

12. Hold a contest to accumulate ways to save energy at home and in schools. Once the contest is over and prizes awarded, implement the suggestions!

13. Survey local business and governmental operations and suggest ways to save energy. Figure out what to do if some persons are flagrant in their abuses and will not change. Also check the utility rate structure in your area. Are there good reasons for charging less when a consumer uses more power?

14. Build birdhouses with senior citizens and place them about the community. Also use scraps to construct birdfeeders. Give these away to senior citizens and schoolchildren.

15. Contact the city or county officials and set up a community compost pile. Each person contributes his or his leaves, yard trimmings, etc., and gets back compost. The government official can contribute, too, along with the highway department.

16. If the local government officials aren't turned on to compost, establish a school compost heap. Use it for school beautification projects. Perhaps a way can be found to use waste paper, food wastes, etc., in the school heap.

17. Talk to the faculty and principal to set up procedures to recycle all school paper wastes and metal wastes. Set an example for the community.

18. Use the school grounds to provide community vegetable garden spots. Or get an interested land owner to contribute or rent small plots. Develop the soil and set a model for organic procedures.

19. Contact people on your block and turn them all on to organic procedures. Hold a mini-course. Use your yard as a training ground and a model for recycling and organic gardening.

20. Identify a real sore spot in the community — an environmental sore-spot. Arrange to clean it up, i.e., a pond in a city park, a roadside reststop.

21. Set up a school wildlife management area in conjunction with a landowner or State forest people. Burn it off in fire ecology methods and set a model for others.

22. Find a plot and set up a school herb garden. Give the harvests to community leaders who in environmental battles have stood at Armeggdon. They are our children's children's heroes — add some spice to their lives now.

23. Attend the next rattlesnake round-up in your area and observe. Report your observations to local officials.

24. Work with friends to plant gourds. Once grown and dried, make birdhouses to hang in pine forests.

25. Read Ian McHarg's *Design with Nature* (New York: Natural

Science Press, 1969). Then, redesign your yard using what principles you can. Contact the National Wildlife Federation, Washington, D.C., about their backyard wildlife program.

26. Conduct a public information campaign on what to do in case of an air pollution alert. Muster community media for this task.

27. In cooperation with your State forest service personnel, promote awareness of Arbor Day. Distribute leaflets and arrange for a 'tree sale' with forestry officials. Assign fellow students and friends to specific neighborhoods to get trees planted and cared for in the months following planting. Don't forget to assist senior citizens and children who need help in caring for their trees.

28. Do a three month study of local media (newspaper, radio, TV) on their coverage of environmental matters. Assess the content of the coverage for environmental attitudes and concerns. Report to the publisher or station manager.

29. Develop a nature trail for your school or another school.

30. Develop the organizational structure and objectives for a community-wide organization of citizens to monitor environmental quality and to confront environmental problems. Survey community interest in forming such an organization.

31. Develop an outdoor classroom for your school. Select an area with teachers and school officials. Plant and develop the area, including a place for seating and demonstrations. Inventory the vegetation, physical features, etc. Plan the use of this new facility with teachers.

32. Work with local or county officials to develop an Anti-Litter Campaign and effective local ordinances to control and eliminate littering.

33. Do an air pollution study in your community over several months and report to responsible officials. Use a Ringelmann smoke detection chart on a regular schedule at selected points in the community.

34. Select a stream or pond in your community which is threatened by pollutants. Do a water pollution study over several months, employing ph, dissolved oxygen, and phosphates tests. Report out your findings to the community.

35. Do a litter study in your community. Select fifty foot sections of sidewalks and roadsides randomly in your community. Once a week for several months collect and weigh the litter collected. Report your findings to the community through press releases to newspapers and radio-TV stations.

36. Build, erect and maintain Wood Duck boxes in suitable habitat. Get help and directions from the Game and Fish Commission.

37. Build, erect and maintain a Blue-bird trail. Get help and directions from the Audubon Society or the Game and Fish Commission.

38. Build, erect and maintain a series of Purple Martin houses. Get

help and directions fron the Audubon Society or the Game and Fish Commission.

39. Make up a checklist of the 100 most common species of birds in your neighborhood. Be sure to include the times of the year they are most likely to be found. Distribute the checklist through local birding organizations like the Audubon Society or Wildlife League.

Part IV: Public Affairs

Education, awareness, and personal service are mighty forces in environmental protection. But our society has a political process which reflects social concerns and public demands. It is through this process that the society usually moves on major issues. The following projects involve student in-put for community decisions on environmental issues.

1. Conduct several community-school conferences on alternative sources of energy and/or on the conservation of energy in your community. Then, take some positive action.

2. Survey your community on the possibilities for bike paths — or the improvement of existing bike paths. Develop a plan to encourage the use of the bike paths — for persons of all ages.

3. Survey your community on mass public transit. What facilities exist? Given community needs, what is the schedule like? Who uses the system? Who could be encouraged to use it? Develop and conduct a campaign for better facilities — and more community use of the facilities.

4. Write and distribute position papers on local environmental issues — especially to civic and governmental agencies. Hold dialogue sessions with members of these agencies to elaborate on your mimeographed position papers.

5. Hold a community conference on solid waste disposal and recycling. Present the vast array of alternatives and use small groups to explore each with your community in mind. Present the conference summary to the county or city council.

6. Conduct a community campaign on the need for open space and the acquisition of park lands. Show people what life might look like in your town.

7. Develop and use in the community a slide show on a local issue — i.e., the need for a park, the need to save a local marsh, the need to block a big highway.

8. Hold a community celebration to honor 'Great Environmental Decisions' by government and by individuals in your community. You might plan an awards program, or hold a banquet.

9. Plan and make a video-tape presentation on an environmental problem. Then, use it with civic groups around the city.

10. Do a survey of noise pollution in specific areas of the city (i.e.,

school zones, hospital zones). Report your findings with suggestions for improvements to the appropriate community officials.

11. Conduct a campaign for or against a State bill or local ordinance proposal which will affect the environment in your area. You might even propose an ordinance or bill to the appropriate officials and muster community support.

12. Get copies of Environmental Protection Agency (EPA) pollution regulations — or regulations from State or local agencies. Then survey your community to see how they apply, and to see if they are being violated. You might be especially interested in hazardous waste disposal — toxic, explosive, radioactive, biological, or chemical-industrial wastes.

13. Design, write, mimeograph, and distribute a *Voters' Guide* to a forthcoming election in your community. Survey the candidates and get their position on environmental issues for the guide. Let them re-read their statements before publication. Then, go to print and distribute widely. Don't forget to type in the name and address of your group on the booklet — it's the law!

14. Write up the history of an environmental battle in your area — something like the Jetport, the Cross Florida Barge Canal, Turkey Point Nuclear Power Plants, or land fill operations along the coast. Bind your history and donate copies to local libraries.

15. Using published cartoons on your own, do a *Cartoon Booklet on the Environment* for young children. Print up copies and distribute to schools and to local government officials. Donate copies to the public library and to school libraries.

16. Prepare a photo essay (twenty 8 x 10 prints) on a local environmental problem. Get permission and mount the essay on the walls at city hall or at a bank.

17. Do an *Earth Tool Kit* for your community. Using brightly colored folders, put in mimeographed sheets containing civic and pressure groups concerned about the environment. Household tips on saving energy and preserving nature. Addresses on 'When to Call If . . .' and 'Where to call if . . .'

18. Perform water tests in the local lake, stream, river, water supply over a period of months. Then report to city or county officials what you discovered.

19. Work with the local Tuberculosis and Respiratory Disease Association in public concern programs and in governmental inform-ation efforts dealing with air pollution and air quality legislation.

20. Work up a survey form (questionnaire) and procedures to collect data fron adults in your community on an environmental issue. Report your findings to local and State government officials.

21. Arrange spot announcements on TV or rush in to respond to TV editorials dealing with environmental issues. Conduct letter to the

editor campaigns. Prepare 30 second radio spot announcements — all directed toward a specific local issue involving environmental quality.

22. After reading Ian MacHarg's *Design with Nature*, do a cost-benefit analysis on the channelizing of a stream. Report to the US Department of Agriculture's local representative or to the US Army Corps of Engineers.

23. Prepare a study of the possible uses for a State of National Forest. Rank order these uses given your values. Then, present your findings to the State or National Forest personnel in your area. Send copies to Washington.

24. Visit the sewage treatment facilities in your town (Don't fall into any privies!). Can the job be done better? How? Do some research on treatment and the environmental benefits or proper treatment and uses of sludge. Report to the appropriate officials.

25. Do an energy study of your classroom or school. How is energy being consumed? Is all of that consumption worthwhile? How can the less worthwhile uses be reduced or cut out? Report to the school board — or to the superintendent.

26. Try some more and follow up on #25. Design a classroom of the future or a school of the future, watching how much energy you use. Share you design with school officials, local architects, and the general public.

27. Obtain areal photographs and land use maps of your area. Layout the areas which, in your judgement, should not be 'developed'. State your criteria and arguments; then, present your position to the city or county planning office.

28. Select a governing authority in your area which makes environmental decisions (i.e., rules, ordinances, guidelines). Study the formal decision-making procedures of that authority. Then, prepare a citizens' guide to the informal power structure influences on that decision-making process. Interview persons throughout the community to get their impressions of its decision-making. Who seem to have great influence? Which persons, not officially in the authority, sway the most weight? Why? How?

29. Muster community participation in a letter writing campaign on a national environmental issue. Set up committees to recruit letter writers, to see that the letters are written, and to provide a clearing house for the analysis of the response from politicans and the influence the letters had. Report to the public, via the media, your findings.

30. Locate a burned-over forest area or a site cleared for construction. Do a study of water run-off as it affects streams over several months. Report your findings to local officials.

31. Do a photographic study of public uses of a park of other outdoor recreation area in your community. Collect information on how many people use the facility. Survey the area and design suggest-

ions for improving its use. Report to the public and to responsible officials.

32. Start a campaign to emphasize the plight of endangered species. Get governmental agencies such as Department of Agriculture and Transportation to explain how they consider the special needs of endangered species in their planning.

RODNEY F. ALLEN is Assistant Professor, Science and Human Affairs Program, and Director, Environment Education Project, The Florida State University, Tallahassee.

Case Study 5.4

Analysis of an Action Campaign

The following analysis of a successful environmental action was made by the Sveriges Fältbiologiska Ungdomsforening of their actions in Sweden as part of an international youth campaign against 'Waste of Natural Resources' in 1972.

The action in Sweden was carried out as follows:

(1) A national action guide was written and distributed to local clubs. The whole action was prepared in secret and not released to the press. An 'action week' was chosen in early spring, before people became engaged in general summer activities. The problems connected with waste of natural resources are many, and it was felt that if people were going to listen to the arguments they would have to be shocked.

(2) Local clubs were asked to collect empty non-returnable items, such as beer cans, found out-of-doors, and to prepare parcels and letters of the collected material. These were to be addressed to (a) the Prime Minister, (b) the Head of the National Environment Protection Board and (c) the producer, which is a monopoly in Sweden. They were to be mailed on the same day all over the country, to arrive at the addresses on the Monday. A total of 160,000 empty cans etc. were mailed.

(3) All the parcels and letters were delivered in Stockholm and Malmö causing a chaotic situation in the Post Offices. The participant organizations held press conferences and distributed press releases containing background material on the purpose of the action and making constructive proposals for change in the present national approach to the use of natural resources. The surprise action achieved its purpose — all the press and information media published the aims of the action and the public became interested. The idea behind this form of action was to point out one symptom of a bigger problem. The use of non-returnable cans and bottles is a symptom of a society where the use, or rather waste, of natural resources has no limit.

(4) Every parcel contained a letter to the government, etc. In this way, the organizers forced the government and other recipients to open all the packages and put the letters in files. However, government representatives instructed officials in Post Offices in Stockholm to open the boxes, which is against the law. The organizers had paid a fee to have the post delivered, and the task of the Postal Service is to ensure that material posted reaches it destination. As this was not done, a formal complaint was lodged against the government.

(5) Post Office employees wrote a letter to the biggest newspaper in Sweden giving full support for the action and condemning the government for using them as an instrument in the fight against the organizers.

(6) By Wednesday, the politicians realized that public opinion was in favour of the suggestions made by the organizers; and some politicians presented motions to Parliament. At this time shops and producers started to advertise returnable items.

(7) Local groups started to work on small demonstrations. Five people just walking along the street joined together by a string filled with non-returnable items and signs. The string was 25 metres long — the length of the longest vehicle allowed on Swedish roads. In shops members refused to take away unnecessary packaging, which was peeled off and left in the shop.

(8) Towards the end of the week interest in the action had declined. Most newspapers felt that they had given it sufficient column space. It was then time for a new shock action. On the night of Friday/Saturday, 5000 young people walked along the main roads of Sweden (covering 800 kilometers), picked up litter from ditches and placed it at the side of the road. This was not a 'beautification' campaign, but the opposite. In the morning when people were going on their weekend trips they found themselves driving through an alley of litter. New headlines and an opportunity to ask the public: where do we throw all the valuable natural resources which it takes so much energy to produce?

(9) The action ended formally with big demonstrations all over Sweden — a national demonstration. During the week, many sectors of society had been touched by this action, and representatives and members from all political parties could be found in the demonstrations as well as people from various other citizen organizations.

The results of the action can be summarized:

(1) Several motions to parliament on the question of the waste of natural resources.

(2) New policies for many shop chains.

(3) A new look at the resources question by politicians and public, which exposed the obvious link with aid to developing countries and an equal distribution of natural resources.

(4) A connection between energy production and manufacture of unnecessary goods was presented and accepted by the public. This created stronger actions against the exploitation of rivers in Sweden and against the planned nuclear power programme.

(5) Loss of financial profit for the manufacturer now forced by economic laws to produce more returnable items (bottles and cans as well as other types of packaging).

(6) New community action groups were established as the people realized that this type of action could be successful.

Case Study 5.5

Wildlife Clubs of Kenya

The Wildlife Clubs of Kenya comprise one of the most dynamic youth movements in the whole of the African continent. It is an Association of 225 individual Clubs with a total of about 11,000 members, and is still rapidly growing. Members are from Kenya's secondary schools, teacher training colleges and related institutions. This national organization resulted from the spontaneous interest shown by the students in their country's wildlife. The initial enthusiasm was shown in 1968 at a small seminar held at Kagumo School by a group of students who asked for help in learning more about their country's wildlife. Assistance came from the Ministry of Tourism and Wildlife and several conservation foundations.

Realizing the potential of these Clubs, the Education Section of the National Museum gave valuable assistance. In 1969 the National Association was founded, and its Constitution lists the following objectives:

(a) To spread interest and knowledge about wildlife and the environment among the people of Kenya and East Africa in general;

(b) In this way to make them aware of the great economic, cultural and aesthetic value of natural resources;

(c) To develop a better understanding of the need to conserve natural resources for the benefit of the nation and its people.

Also in 1969, a full-time National Organizer was appointed to coordinate Club activities and the dissemination of information. This person is responsible to a Council consisting of ex-officio and elected members, who confer on matters of policy. The National Organizer handles all correspondence, edits a Newsletter as well as other printed materials, organizes yearly Wildlife Seminars, fund-raising and visits to Wildlife Clubs.

Financial and moral support comes from such bodies as the Elsa Wild Animal Appeal, the National Museum, the African Wildlife Leadership Foundation, U.N.E.S.C.O., the East African Wildlife Society, the Ministry of Tourism and Wildlife, the World Wildlife Fund and the Frankfurt Zoological Society.

The activities of Wildlife Clubs are twofold: those undertaken by individual Clubs, and those done at the national level. Clubs meet regularly after classroom hours. Their activities include discussions on conservation and related topics, and on the use of natural resources.

They also go on field trips, construct their own museums and bird feeding-tables, and invite outside speakers to visit their Clubs. Recently some Clubs have done magnificent work by visiting primary schools where they teach the children elementary principles of sound conservation.

At the national level, each Club can send one delegate to the annual Wildlife Seminar organized by the National Headquaters. The Seminars are held in National Parks or Reserves for one week. During this time the delegates engage in such activities as game viewing, bird watching, attending lectures and film shows. They also have time to discuss different aspects of conservation and Wildlife Club activities. Each delegate reports to the others on his or her own Club's activities during the past year. In 1973 a National Art Competition was organized where more than 200 entrants illustrated Wild Animal Folk Tales collected by members.

In 1970, with some assistance from U.N.E.S.C.O., a series of Wildlife Club Radio Programmes was launched on Voice of Kenya Radio. During the school year, a different Club presents one programme per week on a topic of its own choosing. The programmes are taped by Club members themselves and edited by the National Organizer.

In response to serious Elephant poaching in 1973, Wildlife Club members staged a two-hour peaceful 'anti-poaching demonstration' in Nairobi to express their concern over reckless killing of the country's natural heritage. They presented a petition signed by 7300 members and friends to the Minister of Tourism and Wildlife — urging more action against poaching.

The success of the Wildlife Clubs is an indication of the response by Kenyan youth to some of the pressing problems facing their country and their desire to reach a compromise with modern technology.

(From the Kenyan National Report to the Eastern Africa Youth Course in Environmental Conservation, March 1974.)

Wildlife Clubs of Zambia

There is a rapidly growing movement of Wildlife Clubs in secondary schools and colleges in Zambia, as well as more than 120 Chongololo Clubs in primary schools. These Clubs are sponsored by the Wildlife Conservation Society of Zambia. Considerable assistance has been given by the Education/Information team of the UNDP/FAO/GRZ Luangwa Valley Project: the following extract from their booklet 'How to start a Wildlife Club' gives suggestions for Club activities.

'Remember your Club's objectives when planning activities, but also remember to enjoy yourselves! Below are some examples of activities, but do not forget that these are samples — maybe you will have some bettter ideas yourselves. If so — please tell us!

Local field trips: into the countryside around you — observe, record and study the wildlife in your immediate area.

Career opportunities: make inquiries about wildlife and related career opportunities and the necessary qualifications. Try to arrange visits to/by wildlife career men.

Correspondence: with other wildlife clubs/organizations to exchange ideas, information and results of club activities.

Government: learn the Government's role in wildlife conservation, the responsibilities of the Ministry of Lands and Natural Resources, the Department of Wildlife, Fisheries and National Parks, and the Game Scouts in the Parks and the officers in local government. Learn about the laws on hunting, poaching, pollution, etc.

Guest lecturers: invite speakers to your club or school from the Ministries, Game Wardens, agricultural, veterinary and wildlife officers, members of the Wildlife Conservation Society of Zambia.

Field trips: day or weekend visits to a National Park, local hiking/camping trips (each to study something specific, such as birds, small mammals or plants).

Debates: study and discuss principles of wildlife conservation such as pollution, game-cropping, evolution, etc.

Wildlife international: learn what other nations are doing in wildlife conservation — compare Zambia's efforts with other African nations.

Competitions: quizzes, crosswords, essays within your own club or with other nearby clubs.

Artistic work: wood carvings, sculpture, drawings, paintings, photos, poems and essays can be used for display or sold to raise funds.

Wildlife collections: insects, birds, snakes, reptiles, plants and bones can be kept. Aquariums, reptile pits, fishponds and bird baths can be built.

Local history: speak to the village elders about what the local wildlife was like years ago, to compare with today.

Special Projects

These projects are important in that they provide your club with long-term activities which can be worked on all the year round and will improve your club. They are also important as ways of interesting non-members — students, primary school children and local people — in wildlife. Because of their large scale, as far as work and thought needed are concerned, these activities should be organized and carried out by a group of especially keen students under the guidance of a committee chairman.

Club library: prepare a bookshelf to hold club books and periodicals; include correspondence with other clubs and organizations, research you have collected, and records of all your own club activities and projects; prepare a notice board where recent wildlife-related news, illustrations and notices can be posted and read by all.

Club museum: in order to better preserve, store and exhibit club collections, projects and artistic work, a museum to house these might be a valuable project.

Club newsletter: this can contain items about activities or projects or interesting essays, and might also be used to educate other people such as primary school children, etc.

Wildlife exhibit: organize a Wildlife Day or Week where displays, demonstrations, film/slide shows, lectures by members or invited speakers could be presented and also artistic work and posters could be displayed.

Case Study 5.6

There is a great tradition in North-West and Mid-Europe of independent youth organizations for nature study and environmental conservation, mostly on a national basis. All of these organizations are linked internationally through the International Youth Federation for Environmental Studies and Conservation (I.Y.F.). In recent years, increasing attention has been given to environmental education and environmental actions. The accounts which follow amplify these aspects of youth involvement in environmental issues.

Sweden

'*Sveriges Fältbiologiska Ungdomsforening* — S.F.U.': this is an independent *Swedish Association of Young Field Biologists* founded in 1947 under the auspices of the Swedish Association for the Conservation of Nature. We now have about 7500 members, most of them between 15 and 20 years old. The members are organized in 170 local clubs, divided into 8 districts, covering most of the country. The executive board is elected by an annual congress, and it meets in Stockholm where we have a small office staffed by a consultant and a secretary. Some members of the board are responsible for working groups on field biology, camps and courses, and environmental actions.

For many years we have been holding each spring a phenological investigation in cooperation with Finland, Denmark and Norway. In Sweden, the local clubs have a wide range of activities, including excursions and lectures on environmental problems and on aspects of field biology such as ornithology, botany and limnology. They also do practical landscape management, cleaning of shore lines and roadsides, and local actions and demonstrations.Each year some 30 camps, some of them international, are organized; these include expeditions to other countries such as France, Tunisia, East Africa and Iceland. In addition, some 20 training courses are organized and government support is given to special education camps for young children.

During recent years we have conducted various campaigns, usually with publicity in newpapers and on T.V. and radio. Themes have been, for instance, the negative aspects of modern forestry practice, with large clear-cut areas often mistreated with fertilizer and pesticides; the waste of natural resources exemplified by non-returnable bottles and cans for beer and soft-drinks; endangered animals and plants, featuring a fund-raising effort to save the Cranes; air-pollution in towns caused by cars standing with their motors running; the destruction of National Parks by roads and power stations.

S.F.U. has two different regular publications: the *Field Biologist* which goes to all the members, and a contact-bulletin for the leaders of local clubs, containing more practical information. Other publications are produced on special subjects such as Energy and Nuclear Power, biological study material for members and for schools, including an introduction to ecological principles for 7 to 12 year olds which has recieved support from the Swedish government.

S.F.U. takes turns to host the Nordic Conference of I.Y.F. member organizations in the Scandinavian countries and plays its part in regional activities, In 1972, S.F.U. assisted and coordinated the I.Y.F. input to the U.N. Stockholm Conference on the Human Environment, and later on hosted the I.Y.F's. 17th General Assembly attended by youth from 16 countries.

(Information supplied by Sveriges Fältbiologiska Ungdomsforening.)

Norway

'*Natur of Ungdom* — N.U.': in 1974, N.U. had about 50 local groups with 1400 members out of a national population of 3.8 million. Our groups are very spread out, including the most northerly I.Y.F. group in the world in Kirkenes near the Soviet border. It is hoped that the recent establishment of a full-time secretary and a permanent office in Oslo will improve communications. Our publication *Skog og Mark* comes out four times a year and is sent to members and others in Norway working with environmental problems. In addition, an internal newsletter is sent each month to leaders of local groups. Our finances are guaranteed by the Ministry of Environment.

In 1974 we concentrated on the following activities. For World Population Year we cooperated with our adult Norwegian Association for the Conservation of Nature to make a pamphlet. The topic has also been discussed with the other organizations in the I.Y.F. Nordic Region. We are working on some special population studies with the Norwegian Development Programme. Our local groups have been very active on the theme of 'Endangered Animals and Plants', where we have been working with the Norwegian Scout Association. A special issue of our magazine has been produced on this theme, and N.U. has joined in the campaign to protect birds of prey. We have also put pressure on the Norwegian government to vote for the 10-year moratorium on the killing of whales. This year we are making a series of small field-biology booklets which we hope can be a field-biology workbook. We have also participated in the Nordic phenology investigations. We sense a growing interest for field biology among our members.

We have undertaken an action on 'garbage'. This came at the same time as a government report on recycling garbage, and we hope that public opinion will now be in favour of recycling Norway's litter and garbage. The Ministry of Environment has made a plan for protection of wetlands and bird reserves, including some wetlands investigated by our local groups. Although nominally protected, the continuing technical and industrial activity still threatens many of these wetlands. We have protested about the building of a road between Kiruna in Sweden and Narvik, through the Abisko National Park, where an I.B.P. project is running. We also object about the road because there is already a railway between the two towns, and because the native Lapps feel that the road will have detrimental effects on their culture.

Norway has the highest per-capita energy consumption in the world, and we think that it is now time to stop. We suspect that the oil in the North Sea will be extracted too quickly, we propose that only 1% should be taken out each year, so that it will last 100 years. We have participated in an action against nuclear power-stations in Norway; they are not necessary and their safety remains to be proven, therefore Parliament should forbid their construction.

N.U. builds its work on ecological principles, and we try to get members interested in eco-philosophy through courses and articles in *Skog og Mark*. Most of the members of our executive board have studied eco-philosophy at the University of Oslo, one of very few which teaches this subject, and we have an ideology committee working on ecological education among the members.

Austria

'*Osterreichische Naturschutzjugend* — O.N.J.': was founded in 1952 and now has more than 10,000 members between the ages of 10 and 25 years in 50 local groups throughout Austria. One of our main aims is to bring young people into contact with nature. To reach this, more than 70 youth camps are organized each year; some of these are international camps open to I.Y.F. members. During these camps we try to inform young people about environmental problems, we invite experts from the government and the Osterreichische Naturschutzbund to give lectures. We try to demonstrate ways to become active at a local level — practical conservation tasks, protest letters, actions, etc. Scientific observations are also carried out during the camps as all camp-sites are located in areas we want to have protected.

An activity which also helps local groups financially is that of landscape cleaning actions for local authorities. However, we are not intending to act merely as cheap labour, so newspapers are informed and rubbish is collected and often brought to the central square of a village where the young people make a demonstration demanding that both private persons and the authorities take more care of a clean countryside.

Our older members are able to undertake more complex work: one student group projected a plan for the first National Park and organized a campaign for its establishment, with demonstrations, letters to newspapers, delegations to the government and concerned institutions. Other activities include youth leader training courses, and special courses for teachers in cooperation with the Ministry of Education. Nature trails are constructed as well as study centres where camps take place. O.N.J. owns three houses in interesting parts of Austria that were built by the labour and handicraft of its members. At the moment, a new house is being built at the Neusiedlersee, which is Austria's most famous area for birds. In order to give older people and tourists the possibility to come in contact with nature, we set up 'Nature Parks', where we build the paths and make nature trails; here the people can find recreation and learn something about ecological systems at the same time. It is not difficult to get money for these projects from tourist institutions and local authorities.

Besides this we organize meetings for young people during the year where we not only speak about nature and environmental problems, but also have parties with dancing and discussion about other problems. It is always important to remain non-political, as many parents are afraid of sending their children to the political groups. Nevertheless, our members are sometimes forced to become active in policy too — whatever political party they prefer.

We organize an Austrian Conservation Competition in cooperation with other youth organizations — Scouts and political groups — where the whole youth of Austria is invited to do environmental work. Prizes have been secured from industry, private institutions and the government. Similar competitions were organized at a local level, mostly in collaboration with school authorities. A special law initiated 8 years ago by O.N.J. allows us to recruit members in school groups — a privilege not granted to other organizations. We do a lot of public work in organzing 'conservation weeks', when young people give lectures in school classes and the public about the necessity of conservation. We organize a poster competition on the I.Y.F. Year Theme 'Endangered Animals and Plants'.

We publish a magazine *Gletscherfloh* which is distributed to all O.N.J. members, and also a special education series for our youth leaders issued five times a year. Our new development plan includes sone rather professional advertising, which has already resulted in the establishment of some new groups. It is our aim to double the amount of members within the next five years.

(Information from Osterreichische Naturschutzjugend, 1972 and 1974.)

Belgium

'*Belgische Jeugdbond voor Natuurstudie* — B.J.N.': in 1974, 20 camps were planned for the members by the General Board. Five of these were work-camps to execute management measures in nature reserves. During ordinary camps, the environment is examined in search of all possible organisms, especially birds and plants. Specialized camps can concentrate on inventories or a specific branch of nature study, or on training of specialized cadre-people.

The General Board also takes care of publication of two periodicals. The first *Filoe* contains articles on nature protection and more general articles. The second *Euglena* (a joint publication with Natuur 2000 and Wielewaal Jongeren) contains popular scientific articles and inventories. Working Groups stimulate natural history activities — e.g. birds, plants, mammals and beach; each year they plan some small-scale research and specialized camps. A conservation working group gathers document-ation, while two secretaries follow all environmental matters to take action when necessary — these actions are taken up by all the B.N.J. sections.

In fact, the greatest part of the activities takes place in the 14 local sections of B.J.N. which make an excursion each week to a nearby natural area, have indoor meetings and film evenings, undertake protest actions, and often organize their own weekend camps. The sections lead an autonomous existence; their work is not controlled by the General Board, but by the internal statutes of the organization. At the annual congress of B.J.N., the work of the General Board is submitted for approval; each function is discussed separately and the lines of conduct for the next year are stipulated. In this way the members can determine democratically the working of B.J.N., and the General Board sees to the execution of the planned course of action.

B.J.N. has been working on the I.Y.F. Year Theme 'Endangered Animals and Plants'. Most of the campaign has been concentrated on the problems of industrial hunting of whales. A translation into Dutch has been made of the 'Project Jonah' booklet, which has been distrib-uted in schools in 10,000 copies. A sticker has been produced, and we have received more than 25 kilograms of children's drawings, which have been sent to Russia and Japan. All our sections have been asked to visit some animal traders; we got a list of these from someone in the government service. Although we got little information, we can mention one trader where you could buy lions (25,000 B.F.), pumas (80,000 B.F.), leopards or vultures. We have continued to work against bird catching in Belgium, but with less priority since the catch is now legally limited to 120,000 birds.

Together with Natuur 200 (another I.Y.F. member) and the Flemish section of the Young Friends of Animals and Nature, we realized a big programme during the spring called 'Live by Recycling'. Propaganda has been distributed through the whole of Flanders, but the action has mainly taken place in Antwerp. We made an exhibition about recycling paper, metals and glass, including a slide series. There has also been an action in the streets with pamphlets, sandwich men, street theatre (the folkloristic figures Teun the egg-seller and Lijn the milk-woman discussing in dialect on the topic). During two actions we reclaimed about 10 tons of wastepaper. In 1974 we were also joint hosts with Natuur 2000 to the 19th General Assembly of I.Y.F.

(Information from the Belgische Jeugdbond voor Natuurstudie.)

Case Study 5.7

International Youth Organizations and The Environment

International Youth Federation for Environmental Studies and Conservation — I.Y.F.

I.Y.F. is a federation of national and regional youth organizations concerned with the study and conservation of the environment, with an emphasis on nature study, founded in 1956 in Salzburg and enjoying the sponsorship of I.U.C.N. As the only international youth organization with this background, I.Y.F. has the responsibility to spread an appreciation of environmental conservation among young people thoughout the world. I.Y.F. comprises some 70,000 young people under the age of 28 in 27 member organizations chiefly in Europe, but also in Asia and Africa. Its programme is run on an entirely voluntary basis by a team of officers elected by member organizations at an annual General Assembly.

In order to keep contacts with active environmental groups and young environmentalists throughout the world, I.Y.F. distributes its International Bulletin to some 100 countries and operates a system of Regional Coordinators. One of the most encouraging results of this international work has been the first Eastern Africa Youth Course on Environmental Conservation attended by 8 countries in Nairobi, 1974. Youth cooperation on environmental problems was elevated to the world level in 1971 by the International Youth Conference on the Human Environment attended by 75 countries in Canada and coorganized by I.Y.F.

The backbone of the Federation's activities are the annual summer camps — usually some 30 in number — where young people from several countries come together to study the natural environment or to undertake conservation work. An annual training course has been organized on the Lüneburger Heide since 1955; nowadays it aims to introduce youth leaders to field biology techniques and the international framework for environmental conservation. Conferences and seminars are regularly organized on special topics, ranging from 'Youth Strategy in Environmental Conservation' to 'Youth and National Parks'. The I.Y.F. Landscape Planning Working Group has assembled young professional planners at a symposium in Yugoslavia, 1974, on 'Environmental Planning and European Integration' and another is planned for 1975 in Sweden on 'Planning Methodologies for Future Growth Alternatives'.

International projects are another basic activity of I.Y.F. and members' attention is concentrated on a specific Year Theme for which action guides are distributed — 1974 'Endangered Plants and Animals', 1975 'Wetlands'. Besides this, two or three other projects are running each year, which may be of particular interest to certain regions, e.g. a Red Area Book to study endangered habitats in Europe, Bird Phenology Investigation, Oiled Birds survey (North Sea Coasts), Environmental Actions against Waste of Natural Resources, Energy and Environment, and Detergents and Environment.

An I.Y.F. Working Group on Education has been established to develop a series of Education Packs for use in schools and youth organizations, and to organize educational seminars including the annual I.Y.F. training course. Publications include an international bulletin, *Taraxacum*, Yearbooks, conference and project reports, and an ·educational series with early titles on *Methods in Field Biology study*, *Introduction to Ecology*, and *The Social and Political Implications of Environmental Conservation*. Bulletins and posters, etc. are also produced at a regional level.

I.Y.F. has regular consultations with the U.N., U.N.E.S.C.O., Council of Europe, World Wildlife Fund, I.U.C.N. and other international organizations. It is fighting for the recognition of the root-causes of the environmental crisis, and also for greater assistance for the efforts of young people in combating this crisis. I.Y.F. itself has suffered from a severe shortage of funds, and has been seeking for some time to establish a permanent bureau to improve its services to young conservationists around the world.

Boy Scouts Bureau

In dealing with the Boy Scout movement, we should not overlook the very similar activities undertaken across the world by Girl Guides, Girl Scouts, Pathfinders and Pioneers. The following account is based on a leaflet on 'Scouting and the Environment' issued in 1972, but is updated to take account of recent special attention given to environmental conservation by the Boy Scouts World Bureau:

Begun in England in 1907, the Scout movement today has over 15 million members in 150 countries, islands and territories. Within international pronciples, each national Scout association has considerable autonomy and great flexibility to adapt its Scout training and programme to its own country's development, social, cultural and environmental needs. As a form of 'complementary education', from its inception Scouting has taught young people about 'the outdoors' through required and optional tests, badges and activities appropriate for their skill and learning levels. Most Scouts gain a number of badges which are connected with nature and require special training. These include: agricultural, bird study, botany, camping, cotton farming, fishing, foresting, geology, landscape architecture, reptile study, oceanography, soil and water conservation, weather and wildlife management. The most important of these badges is the 'Conservation of Natural Resources' merit badge which was gained by 168,554 American Scouts in the first three years after its inception in 1967.

The young Cub Scout is introduced to the marvels of nature in many ways. He plants seeds on blotting paper to see how the roots, stem and leaves grow. He learns about animals, what they eat and what they need to live. He begins to be aware of the interrelationships between living and natural resources. He may take part in a larger project such as 'One Cub, One Tree' in France where 35,000 Cubs are planting 'youth forests of 35,000 trees. The Boy Scout programme usually involves considerable outdoor activity as the Scout develops his abilities in self-reliance and teamwork. His tests and camping teach him to enjoy and not destroy the natural environment. His activities may vary from building and improving camping and natural areas to sophisticated pollution experiments and surveys.

Concern leads to action. Scouts join in massive projects such as building extensive wilderness trails in Canada and New Zealand, planting 3 million trees in the Philippines, a nation-wide anti-litter drive in the United States, and village hygiene in Guatemala. Individual groups develop and carry out their own projects such as reclaiming forest for agriculture in West Africa, reconstructing Roman ruins in England and France, using an island as an ecological library in Sweden, and clearing streams and building wells all over the world.

In order to give an added impetus to this activity, the World Bureau has cooperated with the World Wildlife Fund to evolve a four-point conservation programme. First, the World Bureau has published five booklets — *Clean Water, No Litter, Precious Soil, Pure Air* and *Free Wildlife* — as source books for practical conservation projects by Scouts. Second, the Scouts are joining in W.W.F.'s 'Operation Tiger' to secure nature reserves for saving the Tiger from extinction. Third, it is intended to convert Scout Training Centres — there are more than 100 in the world — into models of conservation practice. Fourth, a World Conservation Badge has been launched with a set of overall guidelines which can be adapted to local conditions. Further on a 'Pilot International Seminar on Environment Education Methodology in the Scouting Programme' has been convened by the World Bureau in Sweden.

Scouting's broad experience in environmental education for all ages from 7 upward, for urban and rural youth, for any geography or climate, is being exchanged among all potential users of proven ideas and projects. Based upon the remarkable response of young people to environmental education, Scouting sees the opportunity, for the first time in man's history, of training a generation of citizens and decision-makers determined to avoid the ecologically disastrous decisions of the past.

6
*Evaluation**

MICHAEL MALDAGUE

Variables

The assessment of the quality of environmental education needs to take varying elements into account if it is to achieve a high level of reliability. If it is true that the performance of students is a function of the quality of teaching, including the value of the textbooks and the capabilities of the instructor, then the general improvement of these performances cannot be realized without a constant effort to perfect the basic tools of evaluation.

The verification of school instruction is a continuing function of applied pedagogy. The precise results of evaluation can reveal deficiencies where methods in use lack objectivity and may have regrettable effects on their recipients. Without rejecting traditional ways, the field of environmental education offers the alternative of building on more varied, more complete, and less artificial techniques for determining standards and values at different stages of development.

This chapter will examine the different ways of evaluating environmental education. Rather than being exclusive, the different methods are indeed complementary if one gives the term *evaluation* a general meaning which 'implies the idea of judgements and basic decisions based on the synthesis and analysis of diverse data' (Planchard, 1968). To go further, it is necessary to measure the deep effect of this education on the level of reasoning, on behaviour and on perception.

The most extensive empirical study ever carried out in comparative education was done by the International Association for Evaluation of International Achievement. Involving 19 countries and over 250,000 students, it was an attempt at multi-national analysis of differences between schools, students and educational systems. Vol. I: *Science Education in 19 countries* examines the factors accounting for between-country and within-country differences and shows how these relate to the socio-economic, cultural and educational environment of the student (Comber and Keeves, 1973). Relatively little research takes place on such a global level, but informed educators should be generally

*Translated from French by the editor.

aware of such efforts. Some of the procedures used in international and national assessments are applicable to, and may be derived from, evaluations at the local and regional levels.

Writing on national assessment in the United States, Jean Fair (1974) points out,

> Efforts to gather evidence soon confront the basic questions: what should young people be learning, what should they achieve, and to what extent are they doing so? (p. 398)

As applied to environmental education by Dean Bennett (1973), the three basic evaluation questions become:

1. What kinds of environmental education learning experiences can you evaluate?
2. What outcomes of environmental education learning experiences can you look for?
3. How can you determine the extent to which these outcomes have been achieved? (Bennett, 1973, p. iii)

The response to question one, as provided by Dean Bennett, is given in Case Study 6.1. Of particular interest in this case study are the figures which illustrate the process as a student moves through three modes of learning experiences. This process can undoubtedly be applied to a wide variety of topics at different grade levels. The role of evaluation in problem identification is here especially significant, as noted in the example where students evaluate their community to see conditions which need correcting. However, the essential concern of this chapter is the problem of evaluating students' understandings, skills and attitudes.

Evaluation of Knowledge

In the primary school, oral questioning frequently goes back and forth. This form of test always has a role to play. It is nevertheless difficult to use as a means for broadly categorizing environmental understandings and skills since it is highly individualistic and subjective, relying mainly on the teacher's judgement.

In the secondary school, regular tests are generally anticipated by the students. Such tests also respond to the need of the teacher to establish a relationship between given information and its application to a new or unknown situation. Teacher-made tests attempt to reinforce the understandings and skills acquired in the preceding instruction. Objective testing cannot be accomplished without a precise instrument which furnishes evaluations less subject to the personal equation. Such instruments take time and skill to construct. The scientific working out of a test should assure the following fundamental qualities (Planchard,

1968):

1. *Validity*, the capacity of a test truly to measure what it purports to measure;

2. *Reliability*, the stability with which a test measures variables at determined intervals; a test should not give results more variable in one application than another;

3. *Age standards*, the difficulty of a test ought to correspond to a given age if it concerns itself with testing intelligence, where, within a determined range, it denotes a special aptitude;

4. *Standardization*, a consequence of sampling. If norms are truly points of legitimate comparison, it is necessary that the conditions of application of correction and of interpretation be minutely fixed and scrupulously respected. It is for this reason that each test carries with it instructions to which the tester must conform if he wants to be a able to report the findings according to established norms.

In the ordinary examination, the selection of items to be tested is generally made by the teacher as he desires. Test writers, by contrast, consult all the available school texts, interrogate competent specialists, and inform themselves on the ultimate use of ideas in order to determine what is more important and what is less so. This permits the validating of each part of the test. One should note, however, the risk of introducing a source of error by relying too heavily on the frequency of an idea in the textbooks for its absolute importance. The biases which may result from this come from the specific interests that authors may have, and such biases may carry over to other ideas and distort them out of proportion.

A means of achieving a balanced and rational selection of test items is presented in Case Study 6.2 by the Commission on Undergraduate Education in the Biological Sciences of the American Institute of Biological Sciences. Although the example given applies to college biology, the same process could be used for other subject matter at lower grade levels. The items illustrating the means of testing various kinds of knowledge are especially noteworthy. It will be noted that the emphasis throughout is on cognition.

The development of knowledge and skills acquired in the course of a given programme can be appraised by the method of pre-tests and post-tests. By this method, one can respond to the question: Does the programme permit the stated objectives to be attained? Testing the pupils before they have entered into a programme and retesting them afterwards is a means of evaluating intervening changes as a result of the programme. Pre-tests and post-tests should be objective and equivalent. That is, they should be parallel, but need not be identical. It is possible to administer the same test before and after the learning experience if more than a month elapses between tests. The results of the tests permit evaluation of the choice of materials, the validity of the assumptions concerning the students, the attainment of the objectives, and perhaps the general context in which the programme has been carried out.

Evaluation of Skills

Ideally, all real instruction calls for effective participation on the part of the student. Numerous practical tests can be envisaged for judging environmental education skills. We do not mean by this the current practical work such as exists in biology laboratory experiences, in observations on the land, dissecting animals, preparing a collection, etc. The practical tests considered here aim essentially to measure the reactions of students in the face of complex problems, such as are present in the real environment where a number of factors impinge. Methods for such inquiry include interviews, organized discussions, analysis of situations, compiling a global inventory of resources, workshops for the study of problems, lively and informal gatherings, and assembling dossiers on environmental problems. Activities for the occasion allow students, singly or in groups, to give free run to their imagination, to their creativity, and put to the test their spirit of initiative for analysing a problem and seeking its solution.

Maloney and Ward (1973) point out that

> ... most persons have a relatively high degree of verbal commitment and affect, with lower levels of actual commitment and knowledge. In colloquial terms, most people say they are willing to do a great deal to help curb pollution problems and are fairly emotional about it, but, in fact, they actually do fairly little and know even less. (p. 585)

Practical tests permit not only the judging of general understanding but also the degree of interest and the students' capacity to intervene in a concrete situation and to take a number of interrelationships into simultaneous consideration.

It is particularly appropriate in environmental education to introduce an element of reality in the classroom, as this stimulates personal involvement. From the situation proposed as an object of study a true problem should arise from which the students, motivated, go searching for information, make observations, and do research with a view to finding a solution. When they approach the limits of their provisional responses, it is necessary to give them a chance to put their hypotheses to the test, finally to establish the validity of their findings. It is important to ensure that the work appropriate to the criteria is carried on enthusiastically.

The skills which students develop from practical work can be determined by an evaluation in the form of a questionnaire, a written composition, or an oral interrogation. For example, a test can judge the attention which students manifest during a study trip, or the interest which the trip itself has elicited. If the test shows that the majority of the students in a group do not feel that the trip was profitable, the way the activity was organized may be at fault. In certain cases, an audio-visual presentation constitutes only a passive registering of sounds and images. Evaluation provides a control of the activity itself and feedback provides an opportunity for any necessary modifications.

Appraising Changes in Attitude

According to the law of creativity, each child sees himself as an individual different from all others. The goal of education is not to achieve an acceptable mean, or to level the differences; on the contrary, diversity constitutes a richness to be encouraged.

Oral examinations have qualities which other tests do not have and which make a commendable and complementary way to judge the progress of students. More than other tests, they allow the teacher to make an assessment of certain human values residing in the candidate, and of changes in attitude which have been progressively established within students as a result of the development of their knowledge concerning the environment. Of course, a great deal of subjectivity intervenes, and, to this end, the oral exam is undoubtedly more arbitrary than other forms of interrogation. The intervention of the students themselves constitutes a factor for variability. Oral exams may work to the advantage of the mixed-up student who has the ability to mask his ignorance. On the other hand, the written exam favours the student who is highly literate.

An attitude in confronting an environmental problem results from two groups of factors: (i) an inner predisposition which may be more or less influenced by one's surroundings, (ii) the extent of knowledge and skills which can be applied to the problem. This is interestingly illustrated in Case Study 6.3 from Japan. It can be supposed that the progressive development of environmental understanding, if effected in a coordinated fashion, will influence the creation of certain attitudes on the part of the students.

Changes in attitude can be measured by comparing them at the beginning and end of a determined period of time. At the beginning of the period in which one supposes that a change of attitude will occur, the pupils are given a questionnaire which is constructed not to test their knowledge, but rather to judge their reactions to certain situations.

Case Study 6.4 gives examples of how environmental attitudes can be surveyed. By simply placing a check mark, the respondent can indicate if he agrees, disagrees or is undecided about the statements given. Some bias in the phrasing of environmental statements seems inevitable, but this can be rejected by the respondent. However, it must be noted that decisions are made on the basis of semantic differentials. Students may also, with the aim of satisfying the teacher, give answers which do not correspond to their real feelings. As with pre- and post-tests of knowledge, by comparing initial and final tests it should be possible to make a judgement on changes of attitude produced within the students.

Another method of evaluating changes in attitude of a group is through observation of discussions. Such discussions can be prompted by assigning short reports on concrete problems occurring in the environment throughout the period of a designated programme. It is important that the reports be as spontaneous as possible so that the evaluation gives preference to attitudes rather than knowledge. From the discussions following the reports, the teacher can note the evolutions of thought, the development of understanding, the changes of attitudes, and the augmenting of an objective spirit and a degree of maturity.

Horizontal and Vertical Evaluation

The problem remains of finding a way of making a global evaluation of a collection of specific understandings resulting from teaching a series of units. For example, take the case of a school where environmental education has been integrated into different prescribed courses of study, such as language, mathematics, geography, history, science, etc. Here is the place to proceed beyond the discipline under consideration to an evaluation that is particularly associated with the environmental concepts integrated into each of the subjects.

Such an evaluation can be made by probing with a widely ranging questionnaire. The probe should analyse the level of environmental understandings and not the context in which they have been applied. This type of evaluation presupposes integration and coordination necessitating the close collaboration of teachers. It thus leads to standardized forms of evaluation because of (i) the dispersion of concepts related to the environment among several subjects; and (ii) the intervention of several teachers in the presentation of these ideas. Universal standardized tests permit objective scoring and transcend the subject variables.

In the foregoing we have examined the problem of evaluating environmental understandings horizontally across a particular level of studies. Now we shall examine vertical evaluation which aims at measuring progress from one stage to another. Here evaluation constitutes a means of attaining the objectives which were defined at the outset.

Once the overall objectives are established, the level of complexity to be obtained must be determined at each level, as well as at the end of the different stages, i.e. primary, middle and secondary. This establishes coherent and progressive programmes as a function of objectives. The means of evaluation eventually takes the form of a battery of tests of school achievement, standardized and ordered. The advantages of an integrated evaluation lie in the fact that this involves a coordinated effort in instruction and requires extraordinary consideration of the objectives to be attained. Also, thanks to a progressive complexitity, the multiple interrelationships and dynamics among the different factors of the environment are brought out.

The preparation of standardized tests is a complex task requiring the collaboration of highly qualified persons in the disciplines involved, of teaching consultants, and of specialists in the techniques of evaluation. From specialized work of national and international research groups it should be possible to proceed to testing environmental education at national levels. Such testing interposes a certain factor of stimulation.

Case Study 6.5 gives an example of what can be done in the way of a national effort. In November 1973, the Canadian Council of Resource and Environmental Ministers sponsored a Man and Resources Conference aimed at providing a national forum through which Canadians could participate in shaping guidelines and policies for future resource management. In preparation for the conference, an opinion survey was conducted among 1600 family heads in Ontario. Attitudes were recorded on ownership of natural resources, implications of urban expansion, recreation, environmental quality, resource—use conflict, and communication. The results of this survey could be useful in teaching situations, and similar surveys could be conducted among students and teachers on attitudes concerning environmental education concepts.

Inevitability

Evaluation is always with us. Students evaluate their teacher at the first meeting. In daily life, whenever a value judgement is made, the process of evaluation is being exercised. While much evaluation is done in an informal way, this chapter has been primarily concerned with formal evaluation.

As in curriculum design, either a structured or a non-structured approach can be used. The structured approach is high programmed with pre-set objectives. The non-structured approach is more experiential following the accumulation process. The structured approach tends to be statistical whereas the non-structured approach is more humanistic. The two positions represent the extremes of a continuum and a balanced position would occur somewhere in between. In general, however, the formal means of evaluation using a structured approach have not been extensively developed for environmental education, hence the emphasis in this chapter. Nevertheless, the value of human intuition in the evaluation process cannot be discounted.

The variable factors entering into human choices have only been hinted at. Because tests and questionnaires are so often used for grading purposes, their utility as a learning experience is frequently diminished. Since anything can be evaluated, the methods used in evaluating environmental education are not greatly different from those used for standard subjects in the curriculum. It is mainly the objectives which differ, and ultimately environmental education aims at a change in behaviour, possibly a change in lifestyle, and certainly it requires the internalization of an environmental ethic.

Evaluation eventually determines the extent to which environmental education is incorporated into the curriculum. Psychologically we tend to repeat those activities which are satisfying, which meet our needs. Often this judgement is made on a 'gut feeling', but there are those who need to be convinced by a standard of measurement based on hard, objective data.

Bibliography

Bennett, Dean B., *Guidelines for Evaluating Student Outcomes in Environmental Education*, Maine Environmental Education Project, Yarmouth, Maine, 1973, 48 pp. + appendices.

Comber, L. C. and Keeves, John P., *Vol. I: Science Education in 19 Countries*, International Studies in Evaluation, Halsted Press, Division of John Wiley & Sons, Inc., New York, 1973, 403 pp.

Fair, Jean, What is National Assessment and What Does it Say to Us?, *Social Education*, Vol. 38, No. 5, May 1974, pp. 398–403.

Maloney, Michael P. and Ward, Michael P., Ecology: Let's Hear from the People; An Objective Scale for the Measurement of Ecological Attitudes and Knowledge, *American Psychologist*, Vol. 38, No. 7, July 1973, pp. 583–586.

Planchard, E., *La Pédagogie Scolaire Contemporaine*, Casterman, 1968, 368 pp.

Additional References

Bowman, Mary Lynne Cox, 'Assessing College Students' Attitudes Toward Environmental Issues', *The Journal of Environmental Education*, Vol. 6, No. 2, Winter 1974, pp. 1–5.

Morrison, Douglas A., Moeller, George H. and Benjamin, John C., 'Measuring Environmental Attitudes of Elementary School Students'. A paper presented at The Children, Nature, and the Urban Environment Symposium, The George Washington University, Washington, DC, May 19–23, 1975.

Case Study 6.1

Guidelines for Evaluating Student Outcomes in Environmental Education (Maine Environmental Education Project, Yarmouth, Maine, 1973)

1. What kinds of environmental education learning experiences can you evaluate?

Within recent years there has been an increased recognition of the need for environmental planning and decision-making responsibility on the part of all citizens. This, coupled with the current emphasis on the reappraisal of American education and on curriculum reform, has given impetus to the establishment of education programs which relate to man and his environment.

The Goals of Environmental Education

It is clear today that environmental education, as it is called, is directed towards the development of attitudes and behavioural skills in the area of environmental decision-making and problem solving. Accordingly, the Maine Environmental Education Project defines environmental education as a process aimed at producing a citizenry that is *knowledge-able* concerning the total environment and the role of man, *able* to participate in activities for maintaining and improving the quality of the environment while meeting human needs, and *motivated* to do so.

Derived from this goal and definition are the following subgoals:

1. (*Affective Subgoal*). To help individuals acquire strong feelings fundamental to developing a concern for the environment and a motivation to participate in activities for maintaining and improving the quality of the total environment.

2. (*Cognitive Subgoal*). To help individuals acquire basic understanding of the total natural and man-made environment, their relationship with this environment, and common environmental problems.

3. (*Behavioural-Skill Subgoal*). To help individuals develop the necessary thinking and behavioral skills for the prevention of environmental degradation, the correction of environmental abuses, and the alteration and use of natural resources to enhance the function and quality of the environment to meet ecological, including human, needs.

Environmental Education as a Process

Environmental education is viewed as a *process* in which the student participates in three levels of learning experiences:

(1) discovery and inquiry,
(2) evaluation and problem identification, and
(3) problem solving.

Problem identification and problem solving as used here involve not only the recognition, prevention, and resolution of environmental problems but the activities in which students alter and create components in their environment to enhance its function and quality. Students may either act directly on the environment or communicate a concern to others to encourage their participation.

The environmental education learning process emphasizes first-hand experience focusing on the total environment of the community and immediate surroundings of the student, for example, the school site or neighborhood. The three phases of the process also include classroom experiences.

Discovery — Inquiry	Evaluation — Problem Identification	Problem Solving
Classroom activities — Learn about the characteristics, interrelationships, changes, and uses of trees through lessons, books and publications, resource people, films and other instructional aids.	Group or independent development of criteria to assess: 1) how well trees meet ecological needs, e.g., hold soil, prevent erosion, provide homes for wildlife, etc., and 2) how well trees meet human needs, e.g., physical needs, shade, etc.; psychological needs, aesthetics, etc.; social needs, gathering places, etc. Evaluate how well trees meet these needs in a real or hypothetical situation to identify environmental improvement opportunities.	Select a hypothetical problem, e.g., landscape a small park with trees. 1. Investigate the problem — needs, kinds of trees, etc. 2. Develop alternative solutions, plans for different plantings in a variety of locations. 3. Choose a solution after considering effects of each. 4. Develop plan of action — list steps and items needed. 5. Present plan for evaluation by others.
On-site activities— Investigate the trees on the school site and map and describe the kinds present on the site, their locations, sizes, condition, environmental effects, etc.	Develop evaluative criteria as above and assess extent present trees on the school site meet criteria. Identify: 1) existing conditions which need to be corrected — diseased trees, storm damaged trees, etc., 2) conditions which could be enhanced by planting trees, and 3) conditions threatening trees which should be prevented.	Select a tree problem to resolve on the school site; for example, white pine blister rust, etc. 1. Investigate causes, effects. 2. Develop alternative solutions. 3. Choose a solution. 4. Develop a plan of action. 5. Carry out plan. 6. Evaluate results.

Figure 1. The process of environmental education
Natural environment example: *Trees* (plants)

The process may be carried out by students participating in studies relating to the components of the total natural and man-made environment and related social, political and economic aspects. Figure One suggests how the environmental education process may relate to the study of a natural component of the environment. Figure Two is an outline for the study of walkways and pathways as examples of a man-made environmental component. It should be stressed that it is not particularly important which of the many environmental components is studied nor that all the components be studied. Rather, it is the process and associated cognitive, affective and skill outcomes which should be emphasized and which will carry over with the student.

Discovery — Inquiry	Evaluation — Problem Identification	Problem Solving
Classroom activities — Learn about the kinds, locations, functions, and characteristics of walkways and pathways through lessons, books and publications, resource people, films, and other instructional aids	Individual and group development of criteria to assess: 1) effects of walkways and pathways on the natural eco-system — altering drainage patterns, changing microclimate, removing vegetation, etc., and 2) how well walkways and pathways meet human needs: physical — safety, etc., psychological — aesthetics, etc., and social — bringing people together, etc. Evaluate walkways and pathways in a real or hypothetical landscape design plan.	Select a hypothetical problem, e.g., develop a plan for a new pathway. 1. Investigate the problem — needs, kinds of pathways, etc. 2. Develop alternative solutions — routes, kinds of pathways, etc. 3. Choose a solution after considering effects of each. 4. Develop plan of carrying out solution. 5. Present plan for evaluation by others.
On-site activities— Investigate walkways and pathways on the school site or in the community. Map and describe the kinds, locations, characteristics, conditions, and human and environmental effects.	Apply evaluative criteria as suggested above to walkways and pathways being assessed on site. Identify: 1) existing conditions which need to be corrected — erosion, potholes, rerouting, etc., 2) conditions which should be prevented — footwear erosion from overuse, encroachment of vegetation, etc., and 3) conditions which would be enhanced by creating new pathways, signs, etc.	Select a walkway or pathway problem to help resolve on the school site or in the community. 1. Investigate causes and effects. 2. Develop alternative solutions. 3. Choose a solution. 4. Develop a plan of action. 5. Carry out plan. 6. Evaluate results

Figure 2. The process of environmental education
Man-made environment example: *Walkways and pathways* (transportation—circulation areas)

Case Study 6.2

Testing and Evaluation in the Biological Sciences (Publication No. 20. Commission on Undergraduate Education in the Biological Sciences, November 1967)

(Reproduced by permission of the American Institute of Biological Sciences)

Section 5. Categorization and Coding of Test Items

As suggested in the previous chapter, categorization of test items can help the instructor to see (1) how well the items reflect the goals of a course as well as the material covered in the lecture and laboratory, and (2) which items can best be used to construct achievement examinations that are meaningful and representative.

The remainder of this publication consists of test items that have been categorized and coded according to the criteria in the three-dimensional grid shown in Figure 3. The grid is divided into three categories: *Content (x-axis)*, *Organizational Levels, (y-axis)*, and *Behavioral Objectives (z-axis)*. Each category has subdivisions (e.g., x-1. *Energetics and Metabolism*; y-1. *Molecular*; z-1. *Knowledge*) and each item is coded according to its characteristics as they pertain to these subdivisions. For example, an item dealing with evolution (x-7) at the population level (y-4) devoted to analyzing (z-4) a research paper on industrial melanism in moths is coded 7-4-4 to indicate its categorization on the x-, y- and z-axes of the grid.

The intellectual abilities and skills included under behavioral objectives (z-axis) are of a hierarchical character. When an item relates to several of these subdivisions it is assigned to the highest one. For example, an item that requires him to utilize knowledge and to demonstrate comprehension. Such an item will be assigned to the highest subdivision (i.e., z-4, analysis).

The z-axis category may not be as familiar to biologists generally as the categories represented on the x- and y-axes. The following amplifications and examples are therefore offered.*

Behavioral Objective: z-1. Knowledge
Knowledge as defined here involves recall. The knowledge objectives emphasize most the psychological processes of remembering. To use an

*The organizational outline used in the Behavioral Objectives category, and the descriptive excerpts which follow, have been adapted with permission from the *Taxonomy of Educational Objectives*, B. S. Bloom, et al.

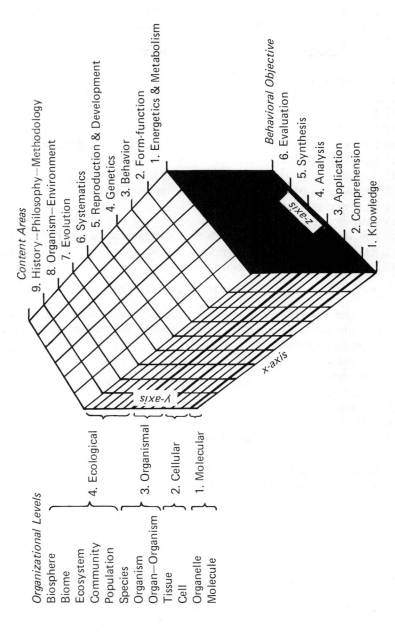

Figure 3.   Three-dimensional grid to serve as a guide in the creation and categorization of test items.

analogy, if one thinks of the mind as a file, the problem in a knowledge test situation is that of finding in the problem or task the appropriate signals, cues and clues which will most effectively bring out whatever knowledge, relevant to the situation, is filed or stored in the mental files.

z-1.00 Knowledge
   1.10 Knowledge of specifics
   1.11 Knowledge of terminology
   1.12 Knowledge of specific facts
   1.20 Knowledge of ways and means of dealing with specifics
   1.21 Knowledge of conventions
   1.22 Knowledge of trends and sequences
   1.23 Knowledge of classifications and categories
   1.24 Knowledge of criteria
   1.25 Knowledge of methodology
   1.30 Knowledge of the universals and abstractions in a field
   1.31 Knowledge of principles and generalizations
   1.32 Knowledge of theories and structures

The following nine examples are test items that measure knowledge:

13.16. The viewpoint that the human body is directed by a vital force not amenable to scientific investigation is vitalism. This directing force is commonly called
   (a) typhlosole.
   (b) entelechy.
   (c) chiasma.
   (d) stroma.
   (e) nous.
(B) 9-3-1 (1.11 — Knowledge of terminology)

1317. Charles Darwin published a book on changes in soils which concerned especially the influence of
   (a) trace elements.
   (b) grass roots.
   (c) burrowing insects.
   (d) moles.
   (e) earthworms.
(E) 9-4-1 (1.12 — Knowledge of specific facts)

946. The scientific name of the American elm is *Ulmas americans*, L. Which of the following is correct concerning the way this name is written?
   (a) The L. means that this particular name is from the Latin language.

(b) The L. means that the Swedish botanist, Linnaeus, gave this tree its scientific name.

(c) The L. actually has nothing to do with assigning this name to this tree.

(d) The name is not written properly — the first letter in *americana* ought to be capitalized.

(e) The words *Ulmus* and *americana* are underlined to give them emphasis.

(B) 6-3-1 (1.21 — Knowledge of conventions)

9. The "first step" in photosynthesis is the
   (a) formation of ATP.
   (b) ionization of water.
   (c) excitement of an electron of chlorophyll *a* by a photon of light.
   (d) attachment of CO_2 to a 5-carbon sugar.
   (e) joining of two 3-carbon compounds to form glucose.

(C) 1-1-1 (1.22 — Knowledge of trends and sequences)

1033. On the phylogenetic "tree" of animal life, which of the following is assumed to be more primitive than a dinosaur but more complex than a shark?
   (a) Crayfish
   (b) Starfish
   (c) Amphioxus
   (d) Salamander
   (e) None of the foregoing

(D) 7-3-1 (1.23 — Knowledge of classification and categories)

1312. Gametes are reproductive cells produced by individual organisms. There are two kinds of gametes: one kind, the sperm, is produced by the male; the other kind, the egg, is produced by the female. The sperm and the egg unite to form a new organism. This union is called fertilization. The new cell formed by the union of gametes is called a zygote.

In the context of the foregoing passage on sexual reproduction, which one of the following is a *primitive* term?
   (a) Gametes
   (b) Cells
   (c) Fertilization
   (d) Zygote
   (e) None of these

(B) 9-2-1 (1.24 — Knowledge of criteria)

1313. Which of the following developments was most instrumental in enabling us to determine the function of mitochondria?

(a) Techniques of cell disruption and ultracentrifugation
(b) Techniques of culturing bacteria
(c) Techniques of plastic imbedding and ultrathin sectioning
(d) The electron microscope
(e) The phase microscope
(A) 9-1-1 (1.25 — Knowledge of methodology)

1314. In 1838, Schwann, on the basis of his own observations as well as the observations of others, advanced the tentative conclusion that all living things are composed of cells. This statement, when first made in 1838, was
(a) an assumption.
(b) an observation.
(c) a generalization.
(d) an analogy.
(e) a law.
(C) 9-2-1 (1.31 — Knowledge of principles and generalizations)

13.15. Which of the following was *most* influential upon Darwin's formulation of the theory of natural selection?
(a) DeVries' concept of mutations
(b) Lamarck's ideas of inheritance of acquired characteristics
(c) Malthus' essay on population
(d) Mendel's genetic studies on peas
(e) Wallace's paper on survival
(C) 9-3-1 (1.32 — Knowledge of theories and structures)

Behavioural Objectives: z-2. Comprehension
Comprehension represents the basic level of understanding. It refers to a type of understanding or apprehension such that the individual knows what is being communicated and can make use of the material or idea being communicated without necessarily relating it to other material or seeing its fullest implications.

z-2. 00 Comprehension — ability to make use of materials or ideas.

2. 10 Translation — ability to deal with an idea when expressed in different phraseology from that in which it was originally encountered.

2. 20 Interpretation — ability to deal with materials or ideas that have been reordered, rearranged or organized into a different format, such as graphs, tables of data, charts, diagrams, and the like, depicting data that were originally in descriptive paragraph format.

2. 30 Extrapolation — the extension of trends or tendencies beyond the given data to determine implications, consequencies, corollaries, effects, etc., which are in accordance with the conditions described in the original communication. Skill in predicting continuation of trends.

The following three examples are test items that measure comprehension:

829. Which of the following best illustrates feedback in development?

(a) As tissue X develops it secretes something that inhibits the development of tissue Y.

(b) As tissue X develops it secretes something that induces tissue Y to develop.

(c) Tissue X secretes RNA which changes the development of tissue Y.

(d) As tissue X develops it secretes something which slows down growth of tissue X.

(e) Rates of development in tissue X and tissue Y are controlled by the pituitary.

(D) 5-2-2 (2.10 — Translation)

169. Consider the following graph.

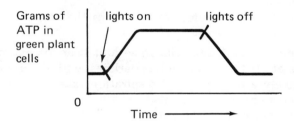

The above graph of research data indicates that

(a) ATP is produced by green cells only when there is light present.

(b) most of the ATP of green cells comes from photosynthetic activity.

(c) chlorophyll is essential for photosynthesis.

(d) water is the source of the oxygen by-product of photosynthesis.

(e) promotion of ATP production is vital to the world's economy.

(B) 1-1-2 (2.20 — Interpretation)

124. Consider the following reaction:

$$
\begin{matrix}
CH=O \\
| \\
CHOH \\
| \\
CH_2OPO_3H_2
\end{matrix}
\ + \ H_3PO_4 \ + \ NAD \longrightarrow
\begin{matrix}
\overset{\displaystyle O}{\overset{\|}{C}} - OPO_3H_2 \\
| \\
CHOH \\
| \\
CH_2OPO_3H_2
\end{matrix}
\ + \ NADH_2
$$

In this reaction, what has occurred?
   (a) An important coenzyme has been oxidized.
   (b) A three-carbon compound has been reduced.
   (c) A high energy phosphate bond has been formed.
   (d) More than one of the above.
   (e) None of the first three above.
(C) 1-1-2 (2.30 — Extrapolation)

Behavioral Objective: z-3. Application
Application involves the use of abstractions in particular and concrete situations. The abstractions may be in the form of general ideas, rules or procedures, or generalized methods. The abstractions may also be technical principles, ideas, and theories which must be remembered and applied. Examples are: applications of the scientific terms or concepts used in one paper to the phenomena discussed in another: the ability to predict the probable effect of a change in a factor on a biological situation previously at equilibrium.

z-3. 00 Application
The following three examples are test items that measure application:

215. Equal masses of paramecia, mice and bean plants are placed in respirometers at $20°C$. in continuous darkness with O_2 in excess. Which is the most likely arrangement of respiration rates — *slowest to fastest*?
   (a) Paramecia, mice, bean plants
   (b) Mice, paramecia, bean plants
   (c) Mice, bean plants, paramecia
   (d) Bean plants, mice, paramecia
   (e) Bean plants, paramecia, mice
(D) 1-4-3 (3.00 — Application)

1231. A biologist was experimenting with a protozoan, and noticed that the animal's contractile vacuole stopped contracting although the other parts of the organism seemed to be in good health and normal activity. Which of the following experiments was the one which might have produced this result?
   (a) Cooling the medium from $20°C$ to $10°C$
   (b) Changing the pH of the medium from 7.0 to 6.5
   (c) Moving the protozoan from a Syracuse dish to a ten-gallon aquarium
   (d) Transferring the protozoan from a lighted environment to a dark environment
   (e) Transferring the protozoan from pond water to sea water.
(E) 8-2-3 (3.00 — Application)

857. Year after year, men cruising timber or hunting deer in the Blue Mountains of eastern Oregon had come back with the same story. Near the little hamlet of Kamela, they had often heard a faraway tinkling, a ghostly bell ringing. No one was ever able to track down the strange sound. It would fade away in the sighs of the wind through the big pines. Skeptics accused the men of hearing things. Last week, slashing a right-of-way for a power line from Bonneville Dam, lumberjacks brought down a ponderosa pine. Tied by a shriveled leather thong, high in the treetop was the answer to the mystery of Kamela: a bronze cattle bell, inscribed with the date 1878. . . . The people of Kamela guessed that a pioneer had tied it to a sapling that grew into a towering pine. (*TIME* Magazine.)

Which of the following is the best appraisal of the concluding sentence in this report?

(a) Logical — because a tree elongates from the ground up.

(b) Logical — because this particular tree could have attained great height since 1878.

(c) Illogical — because no one knows with certainty when the bell was tied to the sapling.

(d) Illogical — because elongation occurs only in the region of meristematic cells.

(e) There is no basis for appraising the concluding sentence of the report.

(D) 5-3-3 (3.00 — Application)

Behavioral Objective: z-4. Analysis
Analysis involves the breakdown of a scientific report into its constituent elements or parts, such that the relative hierarchy of ideas is made clear and/or the relations between the ideas expressed are made explicit. Such analyses are intended to clarify the communication, to indicate how the communication is organized and the way in which it manages to convey its effects, as well as its basis and arrangement.

s-4.00 Analysis — Dissection of a scientific paper, abstract or problem solving procedure.

4.10 Analysis of elements. The ability to recognize unstated assumptions. Skill indistinguishing facts from hypotheses.

4.20 Analysis of relationships. Interaction and interplay of ideas. Ability to check the consistency of hypotheses with given information and assumptions. Skill in comprehending interrelationships among ideas.

4.30 Analysis of organizational principles. What holds this report together? Ability to recognize the relevance and significance of this report to the larger context of the scientific discipline. How the

212

deductions or inferences of this report relate to the postulates or premises of a broader theory, e.g., heredity or evolution.

The following three examples are test items that measure analysis:

Items 881—883 are based upon the following experiment performed to determine the origin of germinal cells which become gametes.

Endoderm cells in 10 three-day old chick embryos were marked with a vital stain (i.e., one which does not kill the cells). One embyro was killed and preserved immediately and every six hours thereafter for 30 hours a different embryo was sectioned and made into slides which were examined microscopically. The location of the stained cells was recorded. No stained cells appeared within the gonads. It was concluded that endoderm cells do not become germinal cells.

881. What must be assumed if the results of this experiment are to be considered valid?
    (a) Endoderm cells usually form the gonads.
    (b) Ectoderm cells become gametes.
    (c) Gonads are comprised of cells from various parts of the embryo.
    (d) The presence of stained cells indicates that they actively move.
    (e) The vital stain does not affect the cells' functions.
(E) 5-3-4 (4.10 — Analysis of elements)

882. How is the conclusion related to the experimental results? It is probably
    (a) valid but is not supported by the results.
    (b) valid and is supported by the results.
    (c) not valid but is supported by the results.
    (d) not valid and is not supported by the results.
    (e) not valid but is unrelated to the results.
(B) 5-3-4 (4.20 — Analysis of relationships)

883. Which theory was the experiment most likely designed to investigate?
    (a) Darwin's theory of pangenosis
    (b) Embryonic induction theory
    (c) Theory of epigenesis
    (d) Theory of inheritance of acquired characteristics
    (e) Weismann's germ plasm theory
(E) 5-3-4 (4.30 — Analysis of organization principles)

Behavioral Objective: z-5. Synthesis
Synthesis involves the putting together of elements and parts so as to form a whole. This involves the process of working with pieces, parts,

elements, etc., and arranging and combining them in such a way as to constitute a pattern or structure not clearly there before.

z-5.00 Synthesis — Putting together parts or elements so as to product a new pattern or structure.

5.10 Production of a unique communication or experiment, reflecting excellent organization or ideas.

5.20 Production of a plan, or proposed set of operations. Ability to propose ways of testing hypotheses, of designing experiments to solve specific problems.

5.30 Derivation of a set of abstract relations. The development of a set of abstract relations either to classify or explain particular data or phenomena, or the deduction of propositions and relations from a set of basic propositions or symbolic representations. Ability to formulate appropriate hypotheses based upon an analysis of factors involved, and to modify such hypotheses in the light of new factors and considerations. Ability to make generalizations.

The following three examples are test items that measure synthesis:

439. A new ultramicroscopic ($<0.1\ \mu$ long) cell organelle is reported by an electron microscopist. Another biologist challenges the report and claims the organelle is an artifact formed by the deposit of the chemical compounds used in the preparation of the cells. Which experimental procedure would provide the best test of this hypothesis?

(a) Analyze the cells chemically to see if they contain the chemical compound in question.

(b) Look at living cells with a phase contrast microscope.

(c) See if any other report of the organelle exists in previous literature.

(d) Use different electron microscopic preparation procedures on similar cells and see if the organelle is present.

(e) Use the same procedure as the electron microscopist used on many different cells to see if they have the organelle.

(D) 2-2-5 (5.20 — Production of a proposed set of operations)

1143. Charles Darwin's presentation of the theory of evolution by natural selection may be expressed in a set of propositions:

1. Organisms of the same species compete with each other for the necessities of existence.

2. As environments change, selective factors will be different.

3. More offspring are produced than the ecologic niche can support.

4. The best adapted forms tend to survive and reproduce in greater numbers than the less well adapted.

5. Members of any species vary widely, some being well adapted, others poorly adapted, to their environments.

214

6. Adaptive characteristics are passed from generation to generation by heredity.

7. Mutations produce new characteristics (post-Darwinian).

8. New species are produced when new selective factors preserve different characteristics.

The best sequencing of these propositions in a logical construction of the natural selection theory is:

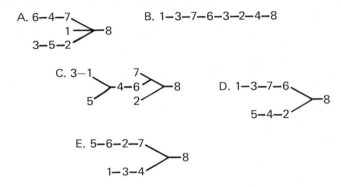

A. 6–4–7
1 8
3–5–2

B. 1–3–7–6–3–2–4–8

C. 3–1
5 4–6 7 8
2

D. 1–3–7–6
5–4–2 8

E. 5–6–2–7
1–3–4 8

(c) 7-3-5 (5.30 — Derivation of a set of abstract relations)

Many aspects of synthesis can better be examined by the use of the open-ended essay questions, of which the following is an example:

566. Propose a procedure to determine what the mechanisms are for "playing possum" in opossums.

3-3-5 (5.10 — Production of a unique communication or experiment)

Behavioral Objective: z-6. Evaluation

Evaluation involves quantitative and qualitative judgments about the value of material and methods for given purposes, the extent to which material and methods satisfy criteria, or the use of a standard of appraisal. The criteria may be those determined by the student or those which are given to him.

z;6.00 Evaluation — making judgments in relation to criteria.

6.10 Judgments in terms of internal evidence such as logical accuracy, consistency, and other internal criteria. Ability to indicate fallacies in logic in a statement or sequence of statements offered as support of a proposition or hypothesis.

6.20 Judgments in terms of external criteria such as comparison of major theories, generalizations and facts that relate to certain phenomena. Using external standards to compare a procedure or product with another of recognized excellence in the field.

The following three examples are test items that measure evaluation:

902. The biologist Dr. Fritz Went found that if coleoptile tips were removed and placed on agar for one hour the agar would produce a bending when placed on one side of freshly-cut coleoptile stumps. Of what significance is this experiment?

(a) It is the basis for quantitative determination of small amounts of growth-promoting substances.

(b) It made possible the isolation and exact identification of auxin.

(c) It is the basis for the experimental support for the hypothesis that IAA is auxin.

(d) It demonstrated polar movement of auxins.

(e) It made possible the discovery that roots respond differently than do shoots to different quantities of IAA.

(A) 5-1-6 (6.10 — Judgment in terms of internal evidence)

Items 1154 and 1152 are concerned with the following:
A biology test included the question: "Show that communities, as well as species, evolve." A student wrote an answer which included the following:

"The essence of evolution is permanent change. When a species evolves, its characteristics change. These characteristics are outwardly phenotypic changes, but behind every phenotypic change is a genotypic change, also called a mutation. Environmental changes are responsible for species changes.

"When a community evolves, its characteristics change. These characteristics are kinds of plants and animals, their relative numbers, and their interrelations. When the kinds of organisms and their numbers and interrelations change, these are environmental changes in the sense of the previous paragraph, and bring about species changes. So, communities evolve not only in the sense of changing their faunal and floral composition but also in changing their species characteristics."

1154. The second sentence of the second paragraph is

(a) an acceptable statement for his purposes.

(b) unacceptable because the kinds of organisms it contains are not characteristics of a community.

(c), unacceptable because the interrelations of different species are not characteristics of a community.

(d) unacceptable because relative numbers are not characteristics of a community.

(e) unacceptable because there are other characteristics of a community which are not mentioned by the student.

(A) 7-4-6 (6.10 — Judgment in terms of internal evidence)

1152. The student's statement about evolution is

(a) adequate for the use he makes of it.

(b) inadequate because not all evolutionary changes are permanent.

(c) inadequate because some phenotypic changes occur without corresponding genotypic changes.

(d) inadequate because not all genotypic changes are mutations.

(e) inadequate because it does not state the mechanism of evolution.

(A) 7-3-6 (6.20 — Judgments in terms of external criteria.

Case Study 6.3

Case Study from Japan. The Flow of Materials and Energy in Japan
(Takahisa Hanya)

(From *Environmental Accomplishments to Date: A Reason for Hope* International
Symposium II, July 1974 Expo '74, Gonzaga University, Spokane, WA. Edited by
George M. Dalen I and Clyde R. Tipton, Jr. Battelle Memorial Institute, 505 King
Ave., Columbus, OH 43201)

Takahisa Hanya is a Professor of Chemistry of Tokyo Metropolitan
University, Japan. His fields of specialty include the geochemistry of the
hydrosphere, the chemistry of natural waters, water pollution and the
relationship between man and nature. With regard to these interests,
Hanya has coined the term 'sociological geochemistry' and has written a
book by the same title on this subject. Dr. Hanya is also a member of
the Nature Conservation Council of the Japan Environmental
Protection Agency and serves on the Council of Water Pollution
Prevention of the Tokyo Metropolitan Government.

Mr. H. Takayama of the Institute of Child Research in Tokyo
conducted a survey on the living consciousness among 400 school
children aged 10 to 11 years (200 male, 200 female), fifth grade pupils
in the Tokyo Prefecture. It was carried out in March, 1974.

Of the many questions, there was a question, 'Do you think that
mankind will perish during your lifetime?' Half of the children, who are
to bear the burden of the next generation on their shoulders, feel
darkly about the future of mankind.

Fifth Grade Pupils	YES	NO	NO ANSWER
TOTAL	47.8	51.8	0.5
Male	55.0	44.0	1.0
Female	40.5	59.5	

Figure 1. Distribution of Answers to 'Do you think that mankind will perish during
your lifetime?'

There were questions, in addition, about the causes of man's possible
extinction: (1) Outbreak of a nuclear war, (2) Coming of a glacial age,
(3) Air and water pollution, (4) Invasion of the men from outer space,
(5) Food shortage, (6) Drain of natural resources, and (7) Spread of an
incurable disease.

Of these suggested causes of man's extinction, air and water pollution was given the biggest weight by both male and female pupils.
Particularly, 33.5 percent of girls regarded it as the most likely cause.

As for boys, 21.0 percent believed that pollution was the danger — roughly equivalent to the number of pupils (20.5 percent) who considered the coming of a glacial age as a cause. This shows the deep impact of the danger of environmental pollution upon the minds of young generations.

The second cause of the doom of mankind was the coming of a glacial age as cited by 20.5 percent of male, while 17.5 percent of female attached importance to the drying up of resources necessary for living. The third cause was the drain of resources, selected by male, and the coming of a glacial age, chosen by female.

Male respondents thought that the attack from the outer space men constituted the fourth cause, while female respondents chose food shortage. The fifth went to food shortage, by boys, and the attack from outer space, feared by girls. Nuclear war was considered the sixth by both male and female, and the seventh was an incurable disease, selected by both boys and girls.

No one knows how seriously the grade school pupils answered the questionnaire. There is a possibility that being aware of the type of answers interviewers may have expected, they replied as their curiosity moved them. Also, they may have been influenced by what are currently in vogue in Japan — science fiction, prophecy, occultism, doomsday theories propagated by mass communication.

At any rate, one thing is certain: we adults have not provided the next generation with an outlook on environmental problems supported by solid scientific logic. This absence may have affected our children's susceptibility to the trend of the age in such a way that they gave these answers.

Whatever the reason, the fact that these children, full of imagination for the future, offered such replies is hardly comforting.

Case Study 6.4

Environmental Thrust Series — Population

Population

(Reed S. Roberts, Utah State University)

Introduction

You have probably heard it said that we are experiencing a population explosion and if we don't do something about it, the problem will engulf us with disastrous results. In fact, you may have read that we have already passed the point of no return. In contrast to the above, you have heard it said that the population growth is leveling off and within a few years will not be a problem. And, you may have heard it said that population growth is not a problem, and we need not be concerned about overpopulation either now or in the future.

You have probably heard the statement that if all of the food produced in the world were equally distributed, there would be enough for everyone. You have also heard it said that if we wanted to we could double or triple food production just by utilizing modern farming techniques on a world-wide basis. What you probably haven't heard, although it has been said, is the statement that if all of the food produced in the world were distributed equally, we'd all be suffering from malnutrition, especially from a lack of protein. It is now estimated that over 10,000 people die from malnutrition and starvation every day. How soon can we expect that rate to increase to 20 or 30 thousands a day?

Eco-living Discussion Questions

Well, regardless of what you have heard or read, what do you believe? Considering the above, how would you respond to the following statements?

Key to Symbols: A — Agree; D — Disagree; U — Undecided

Part A — World-Wide Overview	A	D	U
1. The population explosion is critical. We are rapidly approaching the point of no return.	___	___	___
2. World population growth is starting to level off and by 1975 will become stabilized.	___	___	___
3. Population growth is simply not a serious problem.	___	___	___

Part B — America	A	D	U
1. Population growth may be a problem in other places such as the Orient, but not here in America.	___	___	___
2. Population growth is a problem in the big American cities, but not here in Utah.	___	___	___

Part C — Utah	A	D	U
1. The rapid increase in population in Utah is cause for serious concern.	___	___	___
2. The increase in population in Utah is not a problem. We can support thousands of additional families.	___	___	___
3. The increase in population in Utah is only a problem in Weber, Davis, Salt Lake, and Utah counties. It is no problem in the rural areas of Utah.	___	___	___
4. Due to overcrowding in the major Wasatch front counties, we have witnessed a deterioration in the quality of life in these areas, such as more crime and more congestion.	___	___	___

Part D — If you feel that population growth in Utah is a problem, then answer the following questions. If not, then please go on to Part E.	A	D	U
1. We should actively discourage people from moving into Utah.	___	___	___
2. We should encourage family planning to slow down the rate of population increase.	___	___	___
3. Birth control information should be made available to all citizens 16 years of age and over.	___	___	___
4. We should remove tax exemptions for all dependents except the parents, two children, and non-children dependents such as the old and/or disabled.	___	___	___

Part E — If you feel that the population growth in Utah is not a problem, then please the following.

1. How many people do you think we could accommodate in the state of Utah before the quality of life would be adversely affected: (Consider total population.)

a. 1,500,000   b. 2,000,000   c. 2,500,000   d. 3,000,000
e. 5,000,000   f. Over 5,000,000

2. If 500,000 people should move into Utah within the next seven years, where would they live?

a. along the lake fronts   b. In the mountains   c. In the deserts
d. In new cities yet to be built   e. In our present cities
f. In all of the above listed places.

3. How many more people could your county accommodate; that is, with a "nice" place to live, before the quality of life in your country would begin to deteriorate?

a. 25,000   b. 50,000   c. 100,000   d. 200,000   e. over 200,000

NOTES AND COMMENTS:

Recycling

Community wastes, such as garbage and rubbish, are literally piling up and it is becoming more and more of a challenge to know what to do with them.

One proposed solution which is not new is that we recycle as many of the items as we can. Similar to this is the proposal that we use containers which can be reused, such as glass pop bottles.

Eco-living Discussion Questions

For each of the following statements, indicate your reactions.
Key to Symbols: A — Agree; D — Disagree; U — Undecided

Part A	A	D	U
1. All metal trash from homes and businesses should be put in separate containers, collected, and recycled.	___	___	___
2. Old newspapers should be saved, collected, and recycled even if such a collection would cost each subscriber $1 a month more for his paper.	___	___	___
3. Everyone who turns an old car in for recycling should have to pay a fee of $10 to help cover the costs.	___	___	___
4. Garbage should be composted and used as fertilizer.	___	___	___

Part B	A	D	U
1. Reuseable glass milk bottles should be used in place of cardboard containers . . . even if it means the milk will cost the consumer more.	___	___	___
2. Soft drinks and beer should be made available in reuseable bottles only.	___	___	___

Part C	A	D	U
1. We should reuse plastic knives, forks, and spoons.	___	___	___
2. We should use carbon paper several times before discarding it. It is very wasteful to use carbon paper only once.	___	___	___

Part D	A	D	U
1. We don't have the technology at present to recycle many of the items now being discarded.	___	___	___
2. Nearly all of the above items, if recycled, would hurt some existing business or industry and possibly result in an increase in unemployment.	___	___	___
3. Recycling could bring about many new profitable industries and create thousands of new jobs.	___	___	___

Case Study 6.5

Response: An Opinion Survey on the Use, Ownership and Management of Natural Resources (Ministry of Natural Resources, Ontario, 1973)

Ownership of Natural Resources / Propriété des richesses naturelles	Questions / Questions	Response percentages / Pourcentage des réponses	
Issues investigated in this Section: What controls should be placed on the ownership of Ontario's natural resources? What should be the extent of these controls? In this section of the survey respondents were asked to rank the intensity of their opinions on a five point scale. The percentage "agreeing" with each statement includes those who recorded a 1 or 2 as their response, a 3 was "neutral" while a 4 or 5 was interpreted as a "disagree" response. / *Questions abordées dans cette section:* Quelle réglementation devrait-on exercer sur la propriété des richesses naturelles de l'Ontario? A quoi devrait-on limiter une telle réglementation? Dans cette section du sondage, on avait demandé aux personnes interrogées d'indiquer la force de leur opinion selon une échelle de 1 à 5. Celui qui était d'accord avec le commentaire donné le faisait savoir au moyen d'un 1 ou d'un 2. Un 3 représentant une réponse "neutre", tandis qu'un 4 ou un 5 indiquait que la personne interrogée n'était pas d'accord avec le commentaire en question.	1. A fisherman should be allowed to go through privately owned lands to fish in public waters / 1. On devrait permettre à un pêcheur de traverser des terres privées pour aller pêcher dans eaux publiques	Agree/D'accord	30
		Neutral/Neutres	7
		Disagree/Pas d'accord	62
		No opinion/Sans opinion	1
	2. A hunter should not be allowed to hunt on privately owned land. / 2. Un chasseur ne devrait pas avoir le droit de chasser sur des terres privées.	Agree/D'accord	78
		Neutral/Neutres	5
		Disagree/Pas d'accord	17
		No opinion/Sans opinion	0
	3. The wildlife found on private lands is the property of the owner of those lands. / 3. Le gibier trouvé sur une propriété privée appartient au propriétaire.	Agree/D'accord	27
		Neutral/Neutres	8
		Disagree/Pas d'accord	64
		No opinion/Sans opinion	1
	4. If privately owned land especially suitable for natural resource management is about to be sold, the Ontario Government need *not* be given the first opportunity to buy or lease it at market prices. / 4. Si une propriété privée convenant particulièrement à une forme de gestion des richesses naturelles doit être vendue, on ne doit *pas* donner au gouvernement de l'Ontario la priorité dans l'offre d'achat ou de location au prix en cours.	Agree/D'accord	31
		Neutral/Neutres	10
		Disagree/Pas d'accord	58
		No opinion/Sans opinion	1
	5. The Ontario Government should exercise control over the ownership of private lands by non-Canadians. / 5. Le gouvernement de l'Ontario doit exercer son contrôle sur les propriétés privées appartenant à des non-Canadiens.	Agree/D'accord	74
		Neutral/Neutres	5
		Disagree/Pas d'accord	19
		No opinion/Sans opinion	2

Response percentages/ Pourcentage de réponses		Questions	Questions
Agree/D'accord	53	6. The Ontario Government should *not* have the right to expropriate privately owned land for recreational purposes.	6. Le gouvernement de l'Ontario ne devrait *pas* avoir le droit d'exproprier des particuliers dont la propriété doit servir à des plans récréatifs.
Neutral/Neutres	12		
Disagree/Pas d'accord	33		
No opinion/Sans opinion	2		
Agree/D'accord	19	7. The use of our present supplies of non-renewable natural resources such as natural gas, oil, minerals, etc., need *not* be limited to any extent.	7. Il n'est pas du tout nécessaire de limiter l'usage de nos richesses naturelles non renouvelables telles que le gaz naturel, le pétrole, les minéraux, etc.
Neutral/Neutres	12		
Disagree/Pas d'accord	65		
No opinion/Sans opinion	4		
Agree/D'accord	64	8. Current surplus water should *not* be sold to other countries but should be kept for Canadian use.	8. On ne devrait *pas* vendre les surplus d'eau aux autres pays, mais plutôt les conserver pour l'usage des Canadiens.
Neutral/Neutres	9		
Disagree/Pas d'accord	25		
No opinion/Sans opinion	2		
Agree/D'accord	60	9. Non-Canadian individuals or corporations should be allowed to develop natural resources in Ontario so long as they obey Government regulations.	9. Toute personne ou société non canadienne devrait pouvoir exploiter les richesses naturelles de l'Ontario, du moment qu'elle respecte les règlements du gouvernement.
Neutral/Neutres	9		
Disagree/Pas d'accord	29		
No opinion/Sans opinion	2		

Implications of Urban Expansion

Conséquences de l'étalement urbain

Issue investigated in this Section:
When urban expansion interferes with the present use of land, what should the policy of the government be in regards to alternative uses?

Question abordée dans cette section:
Lorsque l'expansion des agglomérations urbaines nuit à l'utilisation actuelle du terrain, que devrait être la ligne de conduite du gouvernement quant aux autres possibilités d'utilisation?

Response percentages/ Pourcentage des réponses		Questions	Questions
Yes/Oui	65	1. Do you feel the Ontario Government should develop potential recreational areas on land close to urban areas that could be used for, say, residential or industrial developments?	1. Estimez-vous que le gouvernement de l'Ontario devrait projeter d'aménager des secteurs récréatifs à proximité de secteurs urbains qui pourraient servir, par exemple, à la construction de projets résidentiels ou industriels?
No/Non	31		
No opinion/Sans opinion	4		

2. Should farming be continued on land close to urban areas that could be used for, say, residential or industrial development?

2. Devrait-on poursuive l'exploitation agricole sur des terres proches de secteurs urbains qui pourraient servir, par exemple, à la construction de projets résidentiels ou industriels?

Yes/Oui	69
No/Non	27
No opinion/Sans opinion	4

3. Should the production of forest products be continued on land close to urban areas that could be used for, say, residential or industrial development?

3. Devrait-on poursuivre la culture de produits forestiers sur des terrains proches de secteurs urbains qui pourraient servir, par exemple, à la construction de projets résidentiels ou industriels?

Yes/Oui	51
No/No	41
No opinion/Sans opinion	8

4. Should existing recreational areas be kept on land close to urban areas that could be used, say, for residential or industrial development?

4. Devrait-on conserver les secteurs récréatifs existants situés à proximité de secteurs urbains qui pourraient servir, par exemple, à la construction de projets résidentiels ou industriels?

Yes/Oui	89
No/Non	9
No opinion/Sans opinion	2

5. Are you in favour of the Ontario Government restricting development by private enterprise where necessary to *control* urban growth in order to meet Government objectives in regional planning

5. Étes-vous en faveur de la restriction par la gouvernement de l'Ontario, de projets de développement d'entreprises privées, lorsque nécessaire, afin de *réglementer* l'étalement des agglomérations urbaines, pour suivre les plans régionaux du gouvernement?

Yes/Oui	71
No/Non	20
No opinion/Sans opinion	9

7
Teacher Education

JAMES W. CLEARY

Alternative Futures

Throughout the world, environmental education is part of the process by which deterioration of the environment can be retarded. Presumably there is a positive correlation between environmental education and enhancement of the quality of life. Vaughan (1972) believes that the problem of environmental deterioration must be attacked on three fronts: (i) engineering, (ii) enforcement and (iii) education. Referring to education, Budowski (1972) points out, 'The results at this stage have been far from encouraging, when viewed on the world scale'. He attributes this lack of results to emotionalism, non-scientific approaches and lack of inter-disciplinary communication, as well as the absence of a common language regarding basic objectives and methodologies. The United States' situation is this regard is documented in Case Study 7.1.

If the problems cited above are representative of the state of environmental education at the international level, they are also true of the state of teacher training in the field of environmental education. For instance, a lack of specific training objectives could lead to inability to evaluate teaching outcomes. Another divisive and counterproductive element in teacher preparation is what can be labelled a 'value disconuity' between the way a teacher is educated and the content of the education itself. As an example, if a training teacher is being taught ways to help students make good use of time and at the same time is himself being subjected to long and dull lectures, meaningless assignments and lock-step course requirements, then there exists a destructive double message in values which is a value discontinuity.

Methodological ambiguity, emotionalism and a uni-disciplinary approach are indeed factors which impede the development of competent environmental education teachers both intra- and internationally. This in turn contributes to an ineffective environmental preservation effort. To the extent that these problems exist in other countries, then to that extent there is an international environmental teacher-training problem.

This chapter will focus on an attempt to outline the prospects for better teacher training; on the problems that can be expected; and on a model with which to analyse the present state of teacher training in different countries.

Before discussing these prospects, a word about how this section is organized. First, an event, trend, issue or concern arising outside the teacher-training area will be cited. The implications for teacher-training will then be discussed. The final result should be one alternative future, or image, of a forward looking teacher-training programme. This alternative future should not be seen as a forecast or a blueprint. It is but a stimulus with which the reader can carry out a similar process in order to develop for himself, the most desirable alternative future for his country's particular standards, concerns and priorities.

Prospect 1 — Imaging the Future

We are now developing systematic conceptual tools with which to image the future of mankind. The Delphi Technique and the Monte Carlo method for projecting the effect of sequential decisions are two such tools (Henchley and Yates, 1974). Mathematical models have been generated to project the effect of current governmental policies in the area of land use and natural resource use as these are related to population growth. One example is the *Limits to Growth* study sponsored by the Club of Rome (Meadows, 1972).

Our capacity to image the future, even at a fairly gross level, should enable us to project the teacher-training model which will most closely relate to the needs of that future. For instance, let us project a future in which mankind's population growth will level off. This will reduce the need for traditionally inflexible classroom-oriented school buildings. Schools could then depend less on fixed classroom space for environmental education and more on multi-purpose learning centres for children and adults. (See Case Study 7.2.) Teachers will therefore be needed who can operate effectively in that setting. The concomitant teacher-training model would therefore have a field-based dimension.

If we image a future in which there will be a large prison population made up of humans who destroy man's human and physical environment, we might also want to place an environmental educator in every prison, based on our projections of the high cost of failing to reeducate this particular population in environmental preservation. (A future of this sort is imaged in Burgess' *A Clockwork Orange*.) The reader is invited to develop some implications for teacher training using other variables such as famine, inflation, new technological innovations, etc. and to draw his own conclusions.

Prospect 2 — The Application of Behavioural Science Concepts and Research to Environmental Education

Behavioural scientists in the United States are currently focusing on such national human problems as school drop-outs, worker morale, drug use, cigarette smoking, alcholism and poverty. Some are trying to understand why employees steal money, goods or time from employers. Another topic of great interest is the accountability of government agencies, large corporations and school systems for both the quality and quantity of output.

Research in the general area of how to persuade an individual to inhibit a harmful behaviour or habit, or to adopt a 'good' habit, is providing some insights which can be applied to environmental preservation. Specifically, this research should eventually delineate the conditions under which individuals are willing to care for the environment. 'Perceived freedom' is a construct under investigation which will enable us to understand how people develop the commitment to the environment which causes them not to leave litter, even when the law enforcement agencies are not around (McCauly and Berkowitz, 1970).

Still another construct being studied is altruism and helping behaviour. Helping behaviour relates very directly to environmental preservation. As a result of this study, we will begin to understand better the relationship between freedom to 'help' the environment and the amount of help given. Investigators have found that the amount of help given relates directly to the freedom from being forced to help. What we are saying here is that we cannot mandate environmental preservation unless we are willing to have a monitor for every person who could potentially hurt the environment.

Accountability for each other's welfare has distinct implications for preservation of the human and physical environment. Social scientists have demonstrated that the probability of bystander intervention into emergency situations was inversely related to group size. Individuals in a large group felt that someone else would take the responsibility and therefore remained inactive.

Investigators have studied the moral aspects of accountability and have identified responses which illustrate a lack of acceptance of accountability such as (i) a transformation of relevant norms (a denial that certain norms apply to a given situation); and (ii) a denial of consequences for a given act (the new highway will not threaten our wildlife).

Behavioural scientists have studied the effect of involvement in decision-making and feelings of job satisfaction. By doing research in industrial settings they showed the positive effects on productivity when employees participated in decision-making. Therefore, the involevement of persons in planning environmental preservation will have great implications for individual willingness to carry out the plan.

The assumption one makes about the learner will also have great implications for the learner's willingness to cooperate in environmental conservation (McGregor, 1960). Theory X assumptions (the learner is lazy, he is not to be trusted, he needs to be told what to do and just how to do it) cause a negative response. This takes place because self-esteem is lowered. Theory Y assumptions (the learner can be trusted, he can be a partner in the enterprise, he is not lazy, etc.), because they enhance self-esteem, should increase the probability that the learner will be a more willing agent of environmental preservation. This construct has much to say to us about the differential effect of our X vs Y approach to the learner, be he teacher or pupil, and his ability to accept our environmental priorities.

The humanistic psychologist's conceptualization of human-need structure should also help us to realize that unless basic needs for survival are met, the individual will not be able to focus his attention on the environment (except as a 'taker', using it primarily as a means to stay alive). If one studies the environmental preservation groups in the United States, it can be observed that they are usually persons who have these basic needs for security and self-esteem met at fairly high levels. The reduction of poverty therefore will be a necessary antecendent to eventual productive environmental conservation efforts.

The diversity of ecosystems, in which form follows function and diversity constributes equally as much as sameness to survival, should help us to realize the requirements of a truly human environment, one that is capable of sustaining different humans in differing socio-cultural as well as physical environments.

If we are to produce effective environmental educators, **we must apply the above behavioural science concepts to training programme design.** We must encourage a deep commitment by involving teachers in all aspects of training-programme design and implementation. We must develop a climate in which perceived freedom, within the range of freedom allowable to an individual in a society, is high; where accountability is encouraged rather than demanded; where help is elicited rather than forced; where the learner (in this case the training teacher) sees himself as valuable in his own right (a theory Y approach), as well as being an instrument of environmental preservation. We must attempt to develop teacher-training environments in which the teacher's basic needs for security and for self-esteem are met. In this way we will increase the probability that they in turn will convey the basic acceptance of their students which, as behavioural scientists are pointing out, is necessary to evoke the requisite environmental preservation behaviours in these students. They will 'teach as taught'.

In the present context, this implies that the successful environmental education teacher-training programme must produce teachers who are models for children. They must be willing to conserve pencils and time, to turn out lights in empty classrooms, to recycle reusable classroom materials, to contribute to the community's conservation efforts by voting, etc. To attempt to train teachers outside the value system we are trying to inculcate in students will set up a most destructive value discontinuity. As we develop and implement new curricula models based on value development in the learner, this possible value discontinuity will become painfully obvious. The contribution of the behavioural scientists mentioned above to future-oriented teacher-education programmes should provide some potent guidelines for development of effective environmental educators.

Prospect 3 — Technological Sophistication

Nowhere has there been a more dramatic technological breakthrough than in communications technology. Cable T.V. (the linking of T.V. stations and homes by underground cables), video cassettes, satellites, etc. have enabled us instantaneously to link widely separated geographic areas. We can show the effects of an environmental disaster, such as an earthquake, soon after it happens. A method for transmitting hour-long T.V. programmes in minutes has been perfected. Printing presses programmed by computer can now print newspapers in several languages simulataneously, again in widely separated locations.

Laser technology is being applied to delicate eye operations. Different strains of corn and rice can be developed for different climates and soil conditions in a fairly short period of time. Microwave ovens can cook meat in minutes. Artificial meats are being made from soybeans to have the same colour, texture and taste as meat. The list of technological innovations is practically endless.

It is almost obscene to permit teacher education to be insulated from this technological revolution. Yet this is what will happen unless we make a deliberate attempt to realize and apply the available technological expertise in such areas as communication, computer technology and systems analysis and design. For instance, training programmes, in the form of mini-courses, would be transmitted in a short period of time to other countries via satellite. Already teachers engaged in practicums and internships 100 miles from their campus have had courses taught over closed circuit T.V.

Instructional technology has been developed to the point where a given concept can be analysed, where learner behaviours (performance objectives) can be specified, and the appropriate media connected with it. This forns a self-contained, learner-controlled, package called a *module* or 'learning activity package'. These modules are portable, and can be designed to accomodate a fairly wide range of learner characteristics. A module on solid-waste disposal for primary children and their teachers has been adapted to videotape and produced by the Great Plains Television Library in cooperation with the National Council for Geographic Education (Boehm). Possibly modules developed for teacher training could be exchanged from one country to another.

Computers are now being used to analyse learner characteristics, and to relate these characteristics to a wide variety of learning resources.

These resources can be sorted, stored and retrieved by hand or by computer. Teacher characteristics and teacher-training materials (simulations, games, case studies, etc.) can also be dealt with via computer. This should result in more precise, individualized training programmes for teachers as well as for their students.

Teacher behaviour, both verbal and non-verbal, can now be analysed via a dozen or more instruments (Simon and Boyer, 1967). Such variables as teacher style (direct — non-direct) and teacher reinforcement preferences can also be charted fairly precisely. Micro-teaching, along with the above behaviour analysis instruments, will now permit the clinical analysis of teaching behaviours as they relate to pupil growth.

Evaluation of teacher effectiveness will be more possible with the development of heuristic, fairly simple assessment devices. Teacher-trainers will be more capable of researching the effectiveness of their programmes. Competency-based education utilizing pre-defined behavioural objectives should also provide a technology with which to assess the output, (the effectiveness) of teacher-training programmes (Gage, 1973).

In summary, man should be more able to control his learning environment because of this technological teaching revolution. Consequently he should be better able to control his living environment. But we must recognize the potential contribution of these educationally relevant technological developments and apply them internationally.

Problems to Overcome

It would be naive to suppose that by imaging the future, or by applying behavioural science concepts and technological innovations to teacher training, we will also be able to overcome all present-day problems. Different national political systems, different stages of industrial and agricultural development, and different levels of educational programme sophistication, all of these factors will play a major role in the type of teacher training which is carried out in a country. We still have to overcome the barriers imposed by poverty, lack of readiness to share, and lack of resources by committing ourselves to career-long training of all educators as the first line of attack on environmental destruction. Paraphrasing Jacques Cousteau, through teacher and administrator training we will have to transform man from a destroyer of the environment into a defender of the environment.

Problems such as these can only be overcome if we muster an international attack on the problems mentioned above. Yet perhaps we are not as far apart as we appear to be. A recent visitor to China observed that the Chinese behaved as did the early Christians, who in their time were in a similar survival-oriented situation. A saying of Chairman Mao, 'Wei Run Min Fu Wu', ('Serve the people' or 'For otherness rather than for the self',) is much like, 'Love Your Neighbour as Yourself'. We see that this ethic is applied in two different political contexts. Can we not conclude that core of the environment is perhaps not a politically bound ethic? It is a biosphere ethic. A corollary of this is that teacher-training methods are perhaps also apolitical and, therefore, can be studied in the context of what they achieve, no matter what the political context. The last section of this chapter will attempt to describe a model by which this study of international teaching training for environmental education can be undertaken.

A Model for Studying the Characteristics of Environmental Education Teacher-Training Programmes

A model is useful if it enables the user to perceive, examine, analyse, (pointing up similarities and differences) and synthesize current teacher-training programmes in environmental education on the international level. In effect the model should be able to:

1. Identify a wide range of the variables which affect teacher education in the area of environmental education.

2. Focus on the process by which teacher competencies in this area are developed in different nations at the pre-service and in-service levels.

3. Assess the effectiveness of the training both in terms of teacher competence, and eventually in terms of pupil competencies.

4. Relate the teacher-training-for-competency variables to the isomorphic competencies required by supervisors and administrators, teacher-trainers and parents, (to recognize the role interdependency of the total training enterprise).

5. Point up the relationship (and perhaps superordinate quality) of environmental education and environmental education teacher training to all other training, be it educational or industrial, at both pre-service and in-service levels, and over the life-span of the individual.

6. Describe and differentiate the pre-service and in-service aspects of teacher training; also show how those levels are articulated into a logical sequence of competencies of ever-increasing complexity.

7. Integrate and differentiate the environmental concepts utilized in environmental education (some of which are described in Chapter 1, e.g., Taxonomic List of Concepts, etc.).

The above considerations were used to design the model of Figure 7.1.

The table below this model shows how it can be used as a macro-level and micro-level structure for studying teacher-training programmes. Descriptors which can be used to treat a main heading such as 'context' are included. Thus, characteristics of each teacher education programme can be identified and then compared to other programmes. After the reader has become familiar with them, he can read Case Study

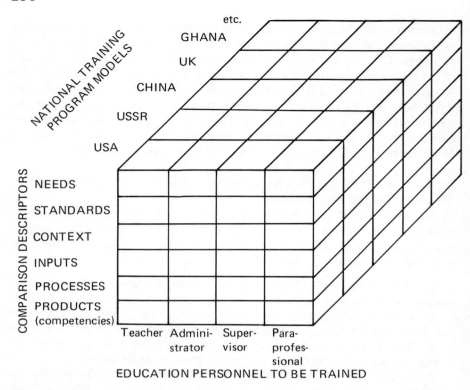

Figure 7.1 A Model for the Study of the Characteristics of International Environmental Education Teacher Training Programmes

Expansion of the model for studying the characteristics of international teacher-training programmes

Main descriptors	Sub-category descriptors
Needs	Needs assessment of teachers, administrators, etc. (for training)
Standards	Statements of values — what is most valuable in terms of how training should be carried out, or what should be the criteria for acceptability of behaviour
Context	Political system/Stage of development of educational technology/Goals/Incentives/Curric. model (content)/General assumpt. (Assumpt. about the learners)/Image of future/Interface with other training programmes concept (administration, supervision, etc./Problems of the country
Processes (training activities)	Courses, conferences, institutes, field experiences, media, models, methods, etc.
Products (output)	I. Teacher competencies (skills) II. Pupil competencies (skills) III. Positive changes in environment

7.3 by Zverev. In this way, practice in using the model as an analytical tool can be obtained. The reader will notice that descriptor appear as headings in the case study. This indicates that the author of the case study is discussing content which appears to relate to a given descriptor. The reader is then invited to apply the model independently with the remaining case studies.

Bibliography

Boehm, Richard O., *The Magic Birthday Party* (based on the PEEP module, Solid-Waste Disposal), Great Plains National Instructional Television Library, University of Nebraska, Lincoln, NB 68508

Budowski, G., 'Environmental Conservation for Development and the Relevant Role of Education', International Workshop on Environmental Studies In Higher Education and Teacher Training, Univ. Of Western Ontario, London, Canada, 1972.

Gage, Nathaniel Lees, *Second Handbook of Research on Teaching*, A project of the American Education Research Association, Edited by Robert M. Travers, Rand McNally, Chicago, 1973, 1400 p.

Henchley, J. P. and Yates, J. R., *Futurism in Education Methodologies*, McCutchan, Berkeley, 1974.

McCauley, J. and Berkowitz, L. (eds.), *Altruism and Helping Behavior: social psychological studies of sone antecedents and consequences*, Academic Press, New York, 1970, 200 p.

McGregor, Douglas, *The Human Side of Enterprise*, McGraw-Hill, New York, 1960, 246 p.

Meadows, Donella et al., *The Limits to Growth*, Universe Books, New York, 1972.

Simon, Anita and Boyer, E. Gil (eds.), *Mirrors for Behavior: An Anthology of Classroom Observations and Instruments*, Research for Better Schools Inc., Philadelphia, 1967, 14 v. + suppl.

Vaughan, A. T., 'A Proposal to Foster a Program of Internationsl Environmental Education', Inormal Paper, International Workshop on Environmental Studies in Higher Education and Teacher Training, Univ. of Western Ontario, London, Canada, 1972.

Additional References

Honikon, B. (ed.), 'Perception, Gaming and Delphi: Experimental Approach to Environmental Education' in AP 70: *Proceedings of the Architectural Psychology Conference at Kingston Polytechnic*, Kingston Polytechnic, 1971, p. 35—40.

Swan, James A. and Stapp, Wm. B. (eds.), *Environmental Education*, John Wiley and Sons, New York, 1974.

Case Study 7.1

Professional Development in Environmental Education

(Reproduced by permission of Professional Educators Publications, Inc., from R. Thomas Tanner, *Ecology, Environment, and Education*, pp. 86—87.)

In 1968, one researcher did a survey of environmental studies in various departments and schools in twenty-four American universities. One of his several conclusions was that perhaps the most serious shortcoming observed in the entire study 'was the absence of any vigorous EE program in the Departments of Schools of Education. . . . Overall a very modest and uncoordinated teacher training effort in the area of EE was the rule at every institution studied in the inventory.'[8]

In a more recent study — limited to environmental science — another researcher found that only 19 percent of the universities in his sample offered a course in methods of teaching environmental science. The survey was done in 1970; it was repeated in 1972, with identical results.[9]

The slowness of schools of education to offer preservice programs of courses in EE is not hard to understand. The environment has been a widely popular issue for only a few years, and it is not clear whether it will remain such. State requirements for certification of teachers cannot be changed that quickly, which is perhaps just as well, lest programs be in constant flux and confusion in response to current social issues. Also, EE is just one concern among many which compete for the attention of college deans, legislators, state boards of education, and others who determine certification requirements. Finally, such policymakers are not yet sure what the nature of such changes should be. Leaders agree that EE should be K-12 multidisciplinary, which might suggest at least one EE course for *all* undergraduates. But EE is still perceived by many in education as an intermediate-grade, one-week, outdoor school experience, which would suggest, at most, a course for those preparing to be elementary teachers at the intermediate grade levels. So, for a time being at least, most teacher education projects in EE will continue to aim at experienced teachers, and will often be initiated outside the schools of education.

[8] Spencer W. Havlick, 'A Glimpse and Analysis of Environmental Education Opportunities in American Higher Education', *Journal of Environmental Education*, 1 (1) (Autumn 1969) p. 24.
[9] John H. Trent, 'Are Teacher Education Colleges Increasing their Environmental Education Involvement?' (Paper presented at the Area Convention of the National Science Teachers Association, San Diego, Dec. 2, 1972.)

Case Study 7.2

The Cross Cultural Learner Centre

The Cross Cultural Centre is a place which brings people and ideas of different cultures together. This is done in an effort to correct the misconceptions which we have about each other's culture as well as our own, and provide information on the changing state of global community relationships.

Using human and technological resources to facilitate cross cultural learnings and communication, the Centre attempts to present an interrelated picture of the world's social, economic and political conditions. The presented information shows people of different cultures that the illusions of racial and intellectual supertiority or inferiority they may hold, are invariably the products of ignorance, naievety and misinformation. In this approach, culture is seen as a product of perceptions, processes used and manner in which humans adapt to their own particular conditions of existence.

Resource Materials

The Centre's resource materials consist of films, videotapes, slide-tape shows, cassette recordings, books, magazines, and data files containing relevant printed material. A unique layout encourages the search for information in a manner conducive to the understanding of the relationships that exist between different disciplines. Users have the opportunity to obtain as total and comprehensive a picture as possible rather than general fragmentary aspects of a topic, at the same time being made aware of and analysing their own attitudes and values.

The information in the Centre deals with North American Native Peoples, Eastern, Western, Central and Southern Africa, Latin America, the Caribbean, parts of Asia and the Canadian Mainstream. There is also information on general development concepts and cross cultural relations.

Resource People

The Centre's most important resources are its people. They come from a wide variety of cultural backgrounds with varying interests and perceptions which prove valuable in obtaining unique perspectives both in content and manner of information gathering while in the Centre.

The people are members of steering committees each representing a different culture. They help to either select or produce the resource materials they consider most useful for an accurate understanding of their particular area.

On a global basis people are very fundamental to the Centre's existence. Besides linking the Centre with its important international contacts, this network provides vital feedback and information on important current trends. This allows the Centre to extend its horizons, enabling it to exist in a more planetary context.

Using the Centre Library

Following short simple instructions on machine function, users are encouraged to flow along at their own pace. People can pick suitable material by selection from catalogues or by going at random through the shelves. One especially unique aspect of information retrieval is the computer. A keyboard terminal connected to the University computer is located at the Centre, giving the user access to printout lists of information sources pertaining to specifically requested topics. These lists are obtained by entering the appropriate keyword on the terminal's typewriter. The printouts can be used as a guide to selecting material.

Mini-Mobile

The Centre's outreach is facilitated by a mini-mobile which travels to areas in and around South Western Ontario making available Centre resources to people who would otherwise be unable to make it down to the Centre. Interested groups can arrange for the mobile to come to their area with a specific programme or to stimulate interest in general about aspects of the world on which the Centre has information.

Orientation Workshop

The Centre also provides orientation programmes designed for individuals or groups visiting Asia, Africa or Latin America; workshops to stimulate and support community based development education programmes and increasing understanding of development and world problems.

Why the C.C.L.C.

Canada is experiencing involvement with the world's new and renascent reactions and its people both within and without its borders. Canada and Non-Western nations with highly developed cultures dating back thousands of years have much to offer each other. As the world's peoples strive to satisfy their needs and aspirations and secure a place of dignity and respect in the intellectual community, the manifestations of their actions may not always be presented in a comprehensive manner. It is mandatory that some place should exist that serves to clarify the issues of this process. This place is the Cross Cultural Centre. Knowledge is understanding. Drop by sometime.

Case Study 7.3

Environmental Education in Teacher Training in the U.S.S.R. (Ivan D. Zverev)

Standards
The training of teachers requires them to master special sciences, as well as psychology and pedagogy. Teacher education should develop valuable moral qualities, lofty ideals of faithfulness and devotion to the Motherland, and aspirations for service for the benefit of the people.

Process (Courses)
Courses on conservation of nature are compulsory in pre-service teacher training at faculties of natural sciences, chemistry and geography. They are taught according to a syllabus endorsed by the Ministry of Education during the third or the fourth year of pre-service training. These courses are optional for students at other faculties. Case Study 7.4 gives further details on the course content.

Process (Courses)
A number of teacher training institutes include the problems of nature conservation in their special courses. It is especially important to provide integration between the nature conservation course and other compulsory subjects (especially ecology, botony, zoology, physical geography, etc.). The social aspect of conservation is thus connected with the scientific ecological apsects.

Process (Field Experiences)
Compulsory practical field work in nature conservation is of particular value and importance. Scientific research work of the students in the field varies, depending of local conditions, capacities of the respective teacher training institute and student's interests. It may include expeditions into distant areas of the country, for example, to the flood-lands of the Ob river (Tomsk Teacher Training Institute), to Kandalaksha Reserve and Bieloviezha virgin forest (Leningrad Teacher Training Institute), ecological and botanical investigations of meadows and pastures (Tula Teacher Training Institute). Scientific and educational issues related to school instruction are recommended for inclusion in research plans. The introduction of environmental conservation work within the activities of Student Scientific Societies is strongly encouraged. Scientific conferences with consequent publication of papers presented by students are held. Investigations on fish

conservation and management in the North-West lakes and on use of polymers for the purpose of soil aggregation carried out by students of the Leningrad Teacher Training Institute brought interesting results.

Students work out course and diploma theses on conservation topics. Sometimes the problems of nature conservation are included in a more general topic of a diploma thesis — anti-pollution measures in the papers on chemical technology (Astrakhan) for example.

Process
Scientific topic-oriented seminars on nature conservation in some areas of Siberia, Caspian Sea, Lake Baikal are held in the Kaluga Teacher Training Institute. The students of that institution have worked out a project of contra-erosion measures and they have also been engaged in the study of complex utilization of natural resources leading to recommendations to local organizations in charge of exploitation and management.

Product (Pupil Competencies)
Citizen action is an integral component of environmental conservation training of future teachers. Various forms of student action favourably develop their creative activities emerging from the experience of teacher-training institutes. Most important is the student involvement in growing and planting of bushes and trees in gardens, parks and boulevards of the cities.

Product (Pupil Competencies)
Groups of students become members of local sections of the Republic's Society for Conservation of Nature. They conduct important work in dissemination of conservation awareness among the local population as part of their involvement in the Society. Students willingly take part as guards controlling poaching and participate very actively in youth work and recreation camps. The entire voluntary involvement is carried out according to the principle — 'Save the Nature of the Motherland', which means, in the first place, the natural environment of the local area. Thus the results of student involvement serve the benefit of protection and improvement of the local environment.

Process (Field Experiences)
Practical and experimental activities of the student teachers are of special importance to the process of developing attitudes to guide pupils. Students test themselves as teachers. Usually they organize environmental conservation teaching activities in experimental and sponsored schools in which they practice teaching. Within these activities the teacher students organize 'Days of birds', and 'Days of forests', guide groups of Young Pioneers in assisting local fishing and

hunting inspectors, organize exhibitions of wildlife photographs, establish contacts with the Stations of Young Naturalists, form 'green' and 'blue' youngsters' patrols, work in school forest nurseries, guide experimental and practical work of pupils, hold discussions with students and parents, deliver lectures for young people in People's Universities, organize film-shows for children and conduct other forms of work.

Product (Teacher Competencies)

The success in teacher training in environmental conservation and education depends a good deal on a proper integration of all forms of their educational activities. It is particularly important to provide future teachers with the special knowledge and skills necessary for an effective and successful execution of their mission.

Case Study 7.4

Environmental Conservation Curriculum for Teachers Training Colleges In the U.S.S.R. (Vladimir Galushin)

Environmental education in teachers' training colleges (pedagogical institutes) of the U.S.S.R. has been existence for at least 10—12 years. Enthusiasm of pioneers of environmental education in these colleges was founded on the sound idea: to awaken a sense of care for the environment in the rising generation, first of all through properly educated school teachers.

At Moscow State Pedagogical Institute, for instance, a compulsory course on nature conservancy has been included into the curriculum of the Biology-Chemistry Department in 1968. From experience in teaching this course, Professor A. V. Mikheev and Dr. V. M. Galushin worked out a syllabus on 'Nature conservancy' for students who would be teachers of biology, biology and chemistry as well as biology and geography. In 1970 it was approved by the U.S.S.R. Ministry of Education as the first State Syllabus on Nature Conservancy for Pedagogical Institutes.

Since the academic year 1970—71, the compusory discipline 'Nature Conservancy' has been included in the curricula of all the 200 pedagogical institutes in the Soviet Union. For students specializing in 'Biology' (duration — 4 years) and 'Biology and Chemistry' (duration — 5 years), the course is taught in the second term of the 4th year and is allocated about 30 lecture hours (50 minutes each), i.e. 3 hours per week. The course of Nature Conservancy is fortunately preceded by the newly introduced course of General Biology with 50 lecture hours.

The syllabus on nature conservancy is based on the concept of the biosphere as an entity, on the concept of human environment as a whole. The global scope of the problem has been emphasized from the beginning of the course.

Another thesis emphsized is the real character of the basic contradiction forming the very essence of the problem of environmental conservation, namely, it is an actual contradiction between the interests of the present and future generations. The need for a careful consideration and comprehensive study of all the aspects of specific manifestations of this main contradiction is underlined before resolving it in favour of 'today' or 'tomorrow'. Some attention to the history of nature conservation in the Soviet Union and other countries is given so that the students may not form the wrong impressions that no one before ourselves has ever been concerned with these problems.

The major part of the syllabus deals with the present state of various natural resources and measures to protect them. Due to rapid changes of situation this part of the syllabus represents only a general scheme for constructing the corresponding sections of the course. To select necessary illustrations the lecturer should use not only textbooks and guides but also new books, magazines and other publications. In order to form optimistic and active approaches among students, selection of not only negative but mostly positive examples of successful actions in cleaning and maintaining good quality environments is specially emphasized.

The syllabus is wound up with an important section, namely, 'nature conservancy and school' which offers the teacher ways for involving youth in the process of nature conservancy and maintenance of environments.

The main content of the syllabus is as follows.

1.	Introduction (general aspects of environmental conservation)	2 hours
2.	Short history of nature conservancy	3 hours
3.	Air conservancy	1 hour
4.	Water conservancy	2 hours
5.	Soil conservancy	4 hours
6.	Plant conservancy	6 hours
7.	Wildlife conservancy	6 hours
8.	Conservancy of natural landscapes	2 hours
9.	International efforts in nature conservancy	1 hour
10.	System of nature conservancy	2 hours
11.	Nature conservancy and school	3 hours

Total — 32 hours

The 200 pedagogical institutes all over the U.S.S.R. will graduate tens of thousands of school teachers annually who will have a special training in environmental education. It gives hope that millions of their pupils will enter life having developed the sense of care and responsibility for maintaining a high quality of human environment.

Case Study 7.5

Higher Education Programmes in Environmental Education in Great Britain
(R. A. Eden)

Syllabus Content

Exponents of the 'holistic' school regard the environment as being the natural medium for child education. They believe that the teacher's task is to provide opportunity for discovery and exploration unhampered by projections of adult ideas, either in the form of subjects with a common objective 'local' or by excessive structuring of the process of exploration.

The widely differing syllabuses of Colleges of Education Environmental Studies courses reflect the variety of thinking behind the courses. The main devision of thought would appear to be between those who:

(a) Expect students should master the methods and sources for individual and group enquiries and the specific facts emerging from their own locality, and

(b) those who expect students to master general knowledge from the different contributing disciplines. The latter tend to be more highly structured courses and place less emphasis on individual and group enquiry.

It is difficult to make a comprehensive and detailed comparative study of syllabuses since many are unstructured and open-ended in their approach.

Analysis of an unstructured syllabus does provide some information about the approach and nature of the course, the standard and quantity of work expected from the students, the techniques and skills to be mastered.

Thus:

1. Subjects studied include, Geography, history, science, architecture and religious studies.

2. Practical skills are developed at all stages of the work designed to encourage initiative, individual interests and a desire to try out new ideas. Tape recordings, films and model-making can take the place of visual presentation on paper. Emphasis is placed on direct observation in the field and on visual presentation.

Domestic, street and urban environments are examined from a wide range of view points, historical, locational, scientific, aesthetic and others. The rural environments of farm, soil and natural habitats are further studied.

3. Written work is kept to a minimum and students are encouraged to collect information by visiting archives, offices, libraries and museums.

4. Knowledge of facts and relationships revealed by field and library study may be tested by oral examination. Students are expected to study each other's work and to discuss common problems.

5. Later in the course time may be given to a close study of an arbitrary area of land from the viewpoint of conservation, development or redevelopment and amenity in all its aspects.

6. Students also compile a study of a parish or similar area of land. Emphasis in assessment here is placed on the degree to which historical, geographical, scientific and other aspects have been integrated and related one to another. Students therefore must avoid the danger of a mere compilation of correlated facts.

7. Lectures introduce themes for assessed study. They also consider the place of Environmental Education in schools, aspects of rural and urban studies, techniques of map making, equipment, course planning and the availability of reference material. An analysis of more structured courses in five colleges of education is given in the following table (see Table 1).

TABLE 1   Table to show the range of syllabus content of five colleges of education with structured courses in environmental studies

| Major aspects of the course | Sub-divisions | Colleges of Education | | | | |
		A	B	C	D	E
Aesthetic	artistic		X			
	literary		X			
	musical		X			
Ecological	habitats and ecosystems	X	X	X	X	X
	conservation	X		X	X	X
	pollution	X			X	
	biological control		X		X	X
	soils	X			X	X
	tillage, drainage, etc.	X			X	X
	food supply			X	X	X
	disease			X	X	X
	heredity and selection			X	X	X
Economic	structure of economy		X			
	distribution of wealth		X			
	trade					X
	populations (human)			X	X	X
Geographical	land forms and structure	X	X			X
	maps	X				
	climatology	X			X	X
	land use	X	X		X	X

Table 1 (continued)

Major aspects of the course	Sub-divisions	Colleges of Education				
		A	B	C	D	E
Geological	lithology				X	X
	evolution of land forms	X			X	X
Historical	growth of settlements					X
	urban growth	X	X		X	X
	communications	X			X	X
	history of science			X		
Political	party politics		X			
	freedom and authority		X			
	nationalism and international		X			
	local government	X				X
Pre-history	pre-man			X	X	
	early man	X			X	
Religious and Philosophical	free will and responsibility		X			
	truth		X			
	God		X			
	Christianity		X			
Sociological	home and family		X			X
	social change	X	X		X	
	work and leisure	X	X		X	X
	social services	X			X	
	control over life and death			X		
Technological	industrial change	X			X	
	energy		X	X		
	industrial processes		X	X	X	
	radioactivity		X	X		
	space research			X		
	new materials			X		
	natural resources	X			X	X

Case Study 7.6

Natural and Man-made Communities: A New Approach to Teacher Training in Environmental Education (Joan Rosner, Hy Rosner)

(From *The New Era*, ISSN 0028 5048, Vol. 56, No. 1, Jan./Feb. 1975, pp. 26—29)

In the summer of 1965, we spent two consectutive weeks in highly rewarding group experiences; the first, at a teacher training session at one of the National Audubon Society's Ecology Camps; the second, at a Family Camp conducted by the American Friends Service Committee. We were impressed by the potential for combining the high-lights of both programs, and establishing a Teacher Training Workshop/Family Ecology Camp — thereby achieving the 'best of both worlds'.

Rationale

There were several facets in the philosophy and rationale underlying the design of our Workshops. Basic was that a course in ecology and communities should be conducted in the field, and should be a living experience. Involving teachers in such a program means taking them away from their homes for several days. We felt that such a course could be combined effectively with a vacation experience for teachers and their families. People usually learn best when they are happy and relaxed, when their minds are at ease.

Another aspect of our workshop program is that, in order to be repeatable, it should be financially self-supporting. Members of staff, drawn from college and high school faculties, as well as from the neighbourhood, are paid modestly for their contributions. Costs for the participants are kept to the minimum and usually regarded as an inexpensive form of family vacation and as a way of earning Board of Education in-service, or graduate school, credit.

A third fundamental notion on which our planning was based is that concepts of biological and human ecology can be learned equally well in urban or rural settings, and can then be transferred to other environments. The basic principles of succession, diversity, adaptation, interrelationship, and interdependence apply equally well in a mountain forest, or in the woodlands of a city park, in a pastoral meadow, in a city school yard, or a vacant lot. Locating our Workshop in a vacation setting adds to our participants' comfort and enjoyment. It does not detract from the course's relevance to the environment in which these teachers work during the year.

One final aspect of the original rationale has repeatedly been proven correct during the past seven years. We felt that the Workshops should be directed at concentrations of teachers and supervisors from a school district. We believed this increased the potential for carry-over into the classroom. An isolated teacher who has a stimulating summer experience can have difficulty in conveying its impact to her unititiated colleagues. With this in mind, the first Workshop was conducted in 1968 for fifty teachers and supervisors, as well as their families, from New York City's School District 30 in Queens.

The experimental program worked extremely well, it was repeated the following year for District 30, and another session was added for School District 25. Here, the direct involvement of the President of the School Board as co-director of the program, and of the Community Superintendent, who participated with his family, helped pave the way for substantial classroom, school, and district follow-up during the ensuing school year. Since 1969, one session has been conducted every summer for each of the two pioneer districts. Many teachers from other parts of the city also have been welcome participants.

Getting the Most Out of Twenty-Four Hours

The parameters of environmental education have broadened and deepened significantly in the seven years of the Workshop's existence. Our curriculum modifications have kept up with, or have anticipated, current trends in the field, but the goals and organizational pattern of the course remained relatively unchanged. We have always felt that learning from real life, rather than sitting in the classroom, is as essential an aspect of teacher training as it is of the education of children. At the summer Workshops, all parts of the programs, from the most overt to the most subtle, become living experiences. Pond food webs, woodland plant succession, diversity in a meadow are all observed directly. Human interactions and interdependencies are learned through shared responsibilities in a family-style dining room, and through closely inter-related activities during a week of intensive community living. Methods for investigating the environmental history and problems of a neighborhood or town are identified by studying a local community.

The curriculum includes total involvement for a total day, minus a few hours for sleep. The daily program is sandwiched between optional bird watching at 7 am and optional sky study at 11 pm. It starts with three hours of field work during the morning; early afternoons are spent investigating human communities or taking trips to neighboring bogs, waterfalls, or forests. Late afternoons are given over to recreation — swimming, volley ball, sunbathing. The post-supper periods start a 'new ball game'. During the early evening, an open classroom atmosphere pervades the campus as small, 'do your own thing' groups settle in for arts and crafts, twilight singing, technique workshops, fossil hunting, or quiet walks. When it gets too dark outside for these activities, the large group reconvenes for a formal evening program of films, lectures, seminars, or environmental games, Snacks, folk- and square-dancing, and campfires round out a full, happy, and productive day. The enthusiasm of staff and participants is interactive, and leads to a situation in which fatigue is an unaccepted and unrecognized condition. As verbalized by most of the participants, 'We can rest next week'.

The family aspect of the Workshop is its most exciting feature. Spouse and children are integral parts of the group, often becoming more involved (if possible) than the person taking the course. The only time in which children are separated is during the morning field study period. They enjoy the same field experiences as their parents, and are taught by the same instructors. Their sessions, however, are shortened to two hours, and are followed by a pre-lunch swim. During the remainder of the day, children and adults follow their own interests in a totally integrated group atmosphere.

The reaction of the children to the Workshop has been one of the most rewarding parts of the entire experience. Many of them admit quite openly that they accompanied their parents with real misgivings, if not downright resistance. They expected, at best, to be able to tolerate the week. To their surprise, they were excited by the highly motivating subject matter and the hands-on discovery approach out instructional staff uses in all classrooms, indoors or out, with all students, children or adults. Watching our young people has been a dramatic reminder, to all educators present, that environmental education is an excellent 'turn on' agent, and that children, properly motivated and instructed, love to learn.

Putting it all Together

The various components and activities of the Workshop are fascinating. Each has its individual, intrinsic value. But the course would not achieve its full potential if these different factors were not woven together into some cohesive 'master plan' for the session.

The Workshop's fundamental goal is to effect change in the participants, both as professionals and as members of their community.

A key to establishing such a curriculum was discovered during the first summer, and its effectiveness has been reaffirmed each succeeding year. We try to provide every participant with an enriching and satisfying experience; to keep alive a sense of wonder, and the joy of living in and with the natural world. The awareness that comes from taking a new look at one's surroundings leads quickly to deepened understanding and appreciation, and to a sense of man's role as only one part of the total environment, not its master. In many cases, concern is the next step, followed by action both in the classroom and the community.

More subtle, but parallel, is an intangible metamorphosis which takes place in the human community formed by the participants. Although the human relations aspect of the Workshop seems more accidental and incidental, less planned than the basic curriculum, development of human relations is an important goal, and it plays a major role in making the total experience a memorable one for all involved.

To stimulate and back up the affective and attitudinal changes in teachers taking the course, the curriculum has been planned to include a balanced combination of content, skills, techniques, and resources.

The subject matter of the course of study stems from the conviction that environmental education is multi-disciplinary and interdisciplinary, and that the environment is composed of abiotic, biotic, and cultural components. 'Communities' is a unifying theme, and the communities experienced are not only those in pond, lake, stream, bog, field, forest, but in neighbouring town — as well as in the community the participants themselves have established for the five-day period. The concepts of similarity and variety, adaptations, change, succession, niches, inter-relationships and interdependence, are explored in each of these communities. Earth history and abiotic factors are seen as the base on which natural and man-made communities are built. And, the inter-actions among the three factors, abiotic, biotic, and cultural, are identified and studied.

During the past few years, attention has been directed toward the human community and its interactive role with the natural com-munities on which it impinges. The Workshop in 1973 focused on the neighbouring town of Corning, New York, which had been devastated by the 1972 Hurricane Agnes flood. The area was studied from its geological formation by Ice Age glaciers to its current state of developments and organization. Local experts and average citizens were interviewed for opinions about the causes of the disaster and plans to avoid its repetition. We conducted these investigations for the purpose of understanding Corning's environmental problems and to establish a basis for conducting classroom and community studies back in New York City.

Re-entry

Having mastered these concepts, our students reach the end of the session eager to re-enter their home and professional communities and to share their insights and missionary concerns with classes, colleagues, and friends. They want to know how they can communicate and build upon the exciting glow of this experience when they get back to the sidewalks of New York. Our final evening program is structured to meet this need to implement this newly-developed potential for responsible social action.

Each year, as a starter, the group decides upon a significant environmental issue on which to focus during the fall term. One year, hundreds of Workshop 'alumni' conducted a 'teach-in' to pressure for the preservation of the world-famous Jamaica Bay Wildlife Refuge, endangered at that time by threatened expansion of Kennedy International Airport. Two years ago, concern for vandalized and neglected New York City parks led to the formation of an organization, ESP Educators Serve Parks, which works in cooperation with New York City Park Department to preserve and restore these much-needed green and open urban spaces. One of ESP's most dramatic achievements was the establishment of an environmental education center in a Queens park and the assignment of a Park Warden, first in New York City, to this center.

To meet the clamor for 'refresher courses', Saturday reunions are scheduled several times a year in city parks and other open spaces. For five years, spring weekend reunions were conducted to reinforce learnings and to satisfy a desire shared by most of the alumni to meet and discuss classroom accomplishments and problems. For, after all, the classroom is what the Workshop is all about.

The most spectacular classroom outgrowths of the course were two school camping experiences attributable to the initiative and resourcefulness of two teachers, both Workshop alumni. School camping, an established activity in many school systems, had never been tried in District 25. The pioneering determination of these two teachers and the success of their camping experiences have resulted in an all-district pilot school camping program planned for the spring of 1975. We chalked this up as another victory for the Workshop.

Several graduates started Ecology clubs in their schools. One junior high school club won a Presidential award for its community efforts. The same club presented testimony at Hearings to prevent wetland encroachment and spent several days of hard work on a reforestation project in a city park.

Environmental learnings are woven into all subject areas in many classes where teachers awakened to biological and human ecology, have helped their students understand that the web of life is all-embracing, and that each man is inextricably linked to, and dependent upon, the natural world, the human beings around him, and the nations which share, with him, Planet Earth.

Appendix A

BIBLIOGRAPHY

American Association for the Advancement of Science
Commission on Science Education
1515 Massachusetts Ave. NW
Washington, DC 20005
Science for Society: A Bibliography, Second Edition, 1971, 76p. John A. Moore, Chm.

BEE Bulletin of Environmental Education
17 Carlton House Terrace
London SW1Y 5AS
Delta — The Directory of Environmental Literature and Teaching Aids

CCM Information Corporation
866 Third Ave.
New York, NY 10022
International Development and the Human Environment: An Annotated Bibliography, M. Taghi Farvar, Project Director, 1972.

Conservation Education Association
Interstate Printers and Publishers, Inc.
Danville, IL 61832
Environmental Conservation Education, A Selected Annotated Bibliography, 1974.

The Conservation Society
12 London St.
Chertsey, Surrey KT16 8AA
Guide to Resources in Environmental Education Lists and annotates available teaching materials — courses, books, audio-visual, charts, games, study kits, periodicals, and television programmes. Prepared by P. S. Berry, annually.

Council of Europe
European Committee for the Conservation of Nature and Natural Resources, Sub-Committee on Information and Training
Survey of teaching materials and aids for environmental education, Strasbourg 17 April 1974 43p.

Crowell, Fred A., 'Tracking the Environmental Information Explosion', *The Journal of Environmental Education*, Vol. 6 No. 1, Fall 1974, pp. 23—28.

Education Associates, Inc.
Worthington, Ohio
Environmental Education: A Bibliography of Abstracts from Research in Education (RIE) 1966—1972, Compiled by Robert E. Roth *et al.*, 1973

Environmental Information Center, Inc.
124 East 39th St.
New York, NY 10016
Environment Information ACCESS A three-step information service providing abstracts, indexes, and a retrieval system.

EPA Socio-economic Environmental Studies Series
U.S. Government Printing Office
Washington, D.C. 20402
> *Environment: A Bibliography of Social Science and Related Literature* Nearly 5000 unannotated items. Available from the U.S. Government Printing Office, for $7.45 (Socio-economic Environmental Studies Series EPA-600/5-74-011), or from the National Technical Information Service (accession No. PB-237 948/AS) for $10 45 (microfiche $2.25). compiled by Denton E. Morrison, Kenneth E. Hornback, and W. Keith Warner,

Group for Environmental Education, Inc.
1214 Arch St.
Philadelphia, PA 19107
> *Yellow Pages of Learning Resources*, 1972, 94p. A guide to the people and places and processes in any town or city offering a boundless curriculum in the urban environment.

International Clearinghouse on Science and
    Mathematics Curricular Developments
University of Maryland
College, Park, MD 20742
> *Working International Bibliography on Trends in Environmental Education —*
> *1975*

Massachusetts Audubon Society
Prepared for the U.S. Office of Education
Dept. of Health, Education, and Welfare
Washington, DC
> *Environmental Education Bibliography*
> > For Pre-School — Grade 3
> > For Grades 4—6
> > For Grades 7—9

Microfiche Publications
305 E. 46th St.
New York, NY 10017
> *Envirofiche*
> A complete environmental library on microfiche, including the full text of more than 5,000 titles per year, gathered from more than 3,500 periodicals.

Ministere de L'Education Nationale
Grand-Duche de Luxembourg
Service Central des Imprimes de l'Etat
19, rue de Hollerich
Luxembourg
> *Guide pratique pour l'etude et la protection de l'environnement*, Courrier de L'Education Nationale No A2/74 Mars 1974, 56 p. Compiled by Jeunes et Environnement

National Association for Environmental Education
5940 S.W. 73 St.
Miami, FL 33143
> 'An Annotated List of Outstanding Books on the Environment Published in 1971—1972', *Newsletter* Vol. 1 No. 9, April—May 1973

National Education Association Publications
The Academic Bldg.
Saw Mill Road
West Haven, CT 06516
Environmental Education: An annotated bibliography of selected materials and services available

The Ohio State University Libraries
Columbus, Ohio
Natural Resources Bibliography, Irene B. Hoadley, compl. 1970, 242p.

Tennessee Valley Authority
Environmental Education Section
Department of Personnel

Knoxville, TN 37902
A Bibliography of Documents in the TVA Environmental Education Resource Materials Center 16p.

Superintendent of Documents
Government Printing Office
Washington, DC 20402
Ecology Price Lists of Government Publications PL 88/1st Edition/February 1972, free

UNIPUB, INC./R.R. Bowker Co.
New York & London
Man and the Environment: A Bibliography of Selected Publications of the United Nations System 1946—1971 Harry N. M. Winton, ed., 1972, 305p.

U.S. Environmental Protection Agency
Washington, DC 20460
An Environmental Bibliography, February 1974

Appendix B

LIST OF CASE STUDIES WITH CONTACT ADDRESSES

Chapter 1

Case Study 1.1   Financial Assistance for Environmental Education Projects
Office of Education
U.S. Dept. of Health, Education and Welfare
Washington, D.C. 20202

Case Study 1.2   Recommendation 96 Report of the United Nations Conference
on the Human Environment
United Nations Environment Program (UNEP)
Nairobi, Kenya

Case Study 1.3   Common Environmental Terms: A Glossary
Office of Public Affairs
U.S. Environmental Protection Agency
Washington, D.C. 20460

Case Study 1.4   Taxonomic List of Concepts for Environmental Management
Education, Technical Report No. 126 Center for Cognitive
Learning, The University of Wisconsin, Madison, WI 53706
Dr. Robert Roth
Eric Information Analysis Center
400 Lincoln Tower
1800 Cannon Drive
Columbus, OH 43210

Chapter 2

Case Study 2.1   On the Introduction of the Principles of Nature Conservation into
Education
Chef en Centre european d'Information pour la Conservation de
la Nature
Conseil de l'Europe
67 Strasbourg, France

Case Study 2.2   Three Approaches to School Environmental Education as
Consecutive Stages of Its Implementation
Dr. Vladimir M. Galushin
Lecturer at the Moscow V. I. Lenin
Pedagogical Institute
Kibalchicha Street, 6
Moscow, I-243, U.S.S.R.

S. Doraiswami
Department of Science Education
N.C.E.R.T.
Aurobindo Marg
New Delhi — 16, India

258

260

Index

264